Born up a Close

memoirs of a Brigton Boy

HUGH SAVAGE
(1918 – 1996)

edited, annotated and with an introduction by
James Kelman

ARGYLL✣PUBLISHING

© executors of the estate of Hugh Savage 2006
© introduction James Kelman

First Published by
Argyll Publishing
Glendaruel
Argyll PA22 3AE
Scotland
www.argyllpublishing.com

The rights of the authors have been asserted by
them in accordance with the Copyright, Designs
and Patents Act 1988.

**British Library Cataloguing-in-Publication Data.
A catalogue record for this book is available from
the British Library.**

ISBN 1 902831 97 7 hardback
ISBN 1 902831 46 2 paperback

Printing & Binding Bell & Bain Ltd, Glasgow

Contents

REMINISCENCE
SCOTT SAVAGE

My first recollections of my dad's meetings were at 33 Montieth Row in the Calton which looked right over the People's Palace, the best playground any boy could have in Glasgow in the late 1940s and 50s.

I remember Hughie coming home after work on his Andy McNeil bike. McNeil was a famous bike builder based in Govan. Hughie cycled from the Calton to Lesmahagow every day, to the Blackburn prefab housing site. I also remember the cycle bag stacked with scrap, with old bits of lead and copper pipes which he brought back every week and kept and saved up until our Fair Holidays. It must have been a 50 mile trip every day.

On Sunday mornings we went round Calton delivering the *Daily Worker*, going up and down closes. It took all morning. After our tea on Sunday evenings Hughie would get his steps/soapbox; it was a nice brown colour. We would walk round to London Road and catch the tramcar and get off at Argyle Street then walk up to Drury Street next to the Horseshoe Bar where he met Harry McShane and Les Forster – it always seemed a lovely summer night – and the meetings got underway.

In the 1950s around Calton lots of guys joined the Merchant Navy. So they were home for a few weeks waiting on their next trip. One was John Doran who helped Hughie with his slogans – white-washing the streets. One night they were round near Tobago Street Police Station hoping nobody would appear. So as they nearly finished painting the words on the pavement, they got as far as:

A penny for the building workers
a shilling for the police and soldier

when a big police inspector appeared. 'Oh! What's going on here?' Wee John looks up, quick as a flash, 'but we haven't finished yet officer,' and he adds in:

5

to which they richly deserve.

The big polis laughed and tells them to get on their way.

Once Hughie was doing a meeting outside John Brown's at Clydebank. He got a fair wee crowd and across the road was the 'Sally Ann', the Salvation Army, and their poor wee guy had nobody listening. After a few weeks of this every dinner time he came over to Hughie and said he was impressed with his oratory skills, would you fancy joining the Salvation Army? That would have been an interesting partnership.

His big pal Alastair McKillop played for Rangers when Bill Struth was the manager. They went dancing at the Albert Ballroom in Bath Street. Willie Waddell used to ask if he could go with them. So they took him along and later they got talking about wages etc., and Alastair found out what Waddell was getting as captain of Rangers, and an international player as well. So Alastair told Willie he was getting ripped-off, You should be getting a lot more. So a few days later Alastair was leaving training and going through the main foyer at Ibrox. Willie Struth, the Rangers manager, was standing at the half landing on the stair. 'Hey McKillop, can I have a word with you!'

So Alastair goes into Struth's office. 'Well Alastair, you might be the best dressed, best read, best looking guy at Ibrox but you certainly aren't the best player. I've just had Willie Waddell in here asking for a raise. He says he was at the dancing with you on Saturday night and you were telling him this that and the next thing. . . So in future McKillop you keep your opinions to yourself.' Later on Alastair moved to Morton and the last Hughie heard he had emigrated to South Africa.

The shipyard owners used to hire work detectives. One cold morning the guys decided to get this one. There were steel plates on deck and the detective had steel heels on his boots. So the guys welding managed to manoeuvre him close by them and zip zip, they welded his boots to the deck. Across from him a couple of welders started to brew-up so he starts to go over to kick over the billy-cans – that was what they did if the men were making tea, they kicked over their billy-cans. But this one was stuck to the deck, they had welded his boots, so he couldn't move. All the guys had a nice brew-up, and a good laugh.

Hughie had to meet Matt McGinn in a pub in the Gallowgate (the Canteen Bar?). Matt was getting a wee bit famous. So his old pals start quizzing him about how he was doing and what he was up to these days. So Matt has a pint and a pie from one of these old pie-heaters, it was the only food you got in pubs back then. So Matt says he's working at the Edinburgh Festival then he buys another pie which he duly wires into. 'Yes, I'm understudying Duncan McCrae in Macbeth,' Matt says, kind of proudly. And at that one of the guys pipes up, 'Hey Matt, never mind Macbeth, if you have any mair of these pies it'll be fucking Dalbeth* you'll be in, they've been lying there since last Monday.'

Just after the war the Tories sent Winston Churchill up to Glasgow to do a bit electioneering. So he was in an open-top car expecting crowds of adoring voters but to his dismay, due to Hughie and his comrades, as he was driving down London Road towards the Tory headquarters in Bothwell Street, people started throwing garbage out of their windows onto Churchill's motor car. So the drivers all started speeding up but Hughie and his pals had phoned the fire department to say there was a fire at the Tory headquarters. So there was Churchill sitting in his motor covered in stour and ashes and there was the fire brigade outside the Bothwell Street building preventing them getting into their headquarters.

One night there was a concert at the old St Andrews Hall, it was Josh White, folk-protest singer. It was a good concert but it lacked the politics. So after it was finished Hughie and Les went round to the stage-door to dig him up about it. They weren't allowed in and they started a wee bit of a commotion. Josh White heard them and he told the stage-door hands to let them into his dressing room so they could talk, and he explained the only way he could get a visa from the USA to play in the UK was to cut out the politics from his concerts.

When Hughie was in the Party the house in Montieth Row was always full of people, obviously from the CP. I'm not sure when he left but I remember suddenly all the people who were round having cups of tea disappeared overnight. The people in the photo taken at the Gorbals Branch, especially the wee guy who looked like Jimmy Clitheroe, I never saw again, they all disappeared.

---

*Dalbeth Crematorium

Hugh Savage outside the People's Place on Glasgow Green

INTRODUCTION
JAMES KELMAN

I MET Hugh Savage on a picket line one Saturday morning in February 1990. It had been organised to protest an exhibition that ran for nine months and was central to Glasgow's year as European City of Culture.[1] The overall cost of 'Culture Year' to the people of the city was rumoured in the region of £50 million. Of course the people of the city had no say in the matter. The decision was taken by the political authorities in conjunction with their own advisors. 'The European City of Culture'! What a magnificent title! There was a glorious ring to it. How could Big Business fail to invest in such grandiosity? And private investment was the main objective. The media went along with it as did 'popular opinion'. Fun is always popular. This would be a year of fun. Opera, theatres, ballet, and art galleries: art with a capital 'a'. Plus popular entertainment: street celebrations and face painting for the masses. It all fits under 'culture'. Even the art was democratic; Pavarotti *and* Sinatra! Old Blue-eyes was a must, given he was the epitome of cool for most male politicians.

In 1990 £50 million was an extraordinary sum for a city to spend on a public relations exercise. A couple of years later Dublin held the title and their outlay was only £5 million. The political hierarchy of Glasgow would not discuss the finances. But when trapped into a comment their notion of culture was revealed as a peculiar confusion of taste, manners and etiquette. The media and arts establishment were content to allow the confusion. A year-long jamboree was what they wanted, plus whatever else was going on, or going out. Pavarotti and Sinatra did venture into the city, £1.6 million went out.

---

[1] See Hugh Savage's 'Campaigns' and the other essays and writings of *The Reckoning*, edited by Farquhar McLay [Clydeside Press 1990].

How to reconcile 'European City of Culture' with the notorious municipality whose relative rates of asbestos cancers, alcohol-related diseases; infant mortality rates, male mortality rates, and so on are a byword throughout Europe? It was a major public relations exercise. Thus the political authorities called in a major public relations company. Saatchi and Saatchi marketed Margaret Thatcher on behalf of the Tory Party and were now employed by Glasgow's Labour administration, and paid with money belonging to the people of the city. Business is business. The Labour Party is adamant about that.

But the PR job succeeded to the extent that Glasgow has come to be seen as the exemplar for any city wishing to purchase the title of European City of Culture. The phrase 'New Labour' was not yet in use but what happened in 1990 Glasgow was a precursor to what has taken place since. The sanitization of the radical past was to the fore of the Labour Party agenda.

A few critics condemned the enterprise as a charade, as a financial nightmare.[2] For some it was an actual assault on art and culture, principally working-class culture. To pay for the jamboree 'the public funding of libraries, art galleries and museums; swimming baths, public parks and public halls [was] cut drastically. . . '[3] and cut altogether for many local community projects. The authorities rejected criticism and condemned the critics, especially those who used the phrase 'working class'. They described them as philistines and kill-joys. It was an odd line of attack since a few of the critics were well-known writers, artists and musicians. One list of critics attacked publicly by the Labour politicians and arts administrators, then held to ridicule by the media, contained the names of some fifty artists, including Alasdair Gray, Liz Lochhead, Billy Connolly,

---

[2] 'When one heard the phrase 'culture city' bandied about by the politicians and media commentators 'one thought of. . . the new Sheriff Court, the largest in Europe, with cell space in its bowels for 2000 prisoners in emergencies. Of the Scottish judiciary which imprisons a higher proportion of the population than any European country except Turkey. . .' see Farquhar McLay's Introduction to *Workers City* [Clydeside Press 1988]

[3] See my essay 'Art and Subsidy, and the Continuing Politics of Culture City', contained in *Some Recent Attacks, Essays Cultural and Political* (AK Press 1992).

Archie Hind and Tom Leonard.[4] But that hardly mattered. And what did they have to do with 'Culture Year' anyway?

Media figures and arts administrators joined the attack alongside the politicians and it proved effective. Artists whose politics are perceived as left-wing by the establishment are occasionally condemned in the same fashion nowadays, occasionally in the same clichéd language. Meanwhile the arts administrators have consolidated their hold on power; backed by political authorities and most of the mainstream media. They have become the most important cog in the Scottish art machine; the true creators of the country's art. They may not paint the pictures or write the books but they set the conditions for that to happen and what comes first: making the art or making the art possible?

They hired people with little knowledge of Scottish art and history. This is an old tactic. Ignorance at higher management level has been a feature of postwar political economy. Local communities might depend on one industry for survival: the steel, fishing and coal industries are obvious examples. When the authorities – state or 'captains' of industry – have to make harsh decisions about job losses it is better not to know of potential consequences for the local communities. A way of life might be wiped out: so what? This is why hatchet men are hired from the outside. The jobs can be taken from these communities more easily when personal attachments are nonexistent. The lessons of imperialism help. That same logic is applied when Scottish soldiers go marching as to war in India, Ireland or Iraq. The history of art cannot be kept separate from radical history for long, and indigenous art is always radical in cultures under siege. Scottish culture has been in that position for many many years.

A journalist acquaintance of my own *confessed* to enjoying 'Culture Year'. Surely some of it was enjoyable? Of course some of it was enjoyable. But when £50 million is spent somebody gets something. The cleverest of thieves and conmen could hardly net such a sum without giving something in return.

People were surprised by the ignorance and lack of sensitivity directed by the Labour authorities towards their own radical tradition and socio-political history. But a handful of politicians

---

[4] These and another forty artists and writers signed a protest letter published in a *Glasgow Herald* of 1990.

were all too aware of that same history and tradition and were intent on marginalising it, even re-writing it. One prime sector of Glasgow's old town had already been christened 'Merchant City'. This blatant manipulation of the city's history was at the core of the critique offered by Hugh Savage and others within the group known as Workers City.[5]

> The name Workers City carries obvious connotations but it was chosen to directly challenge 'Merchant City', highlighting the grossness of the fallacy that Glasgow somehow exists because of the tireless efforts of a tiny patriotic coalition of fearless eighteenth century entrepreneurs and far-sighted politicians. These same merchants and politicians made the bulk of their personal fortunes by the simple expedient of not paying the price of labour. . . Those legendary (Scottish) heroes our children are taught to honour – Buchanan, Miller, Ingram and so on – were men who trafficked in degradation, causing untold misery, death and suffering to scores of thousands of men, women and children. Yet this myth is perpetuated by the. . . Labour authorities who see themselves as far-sighted and fearlessly donate financial and other inducements to the (present-day) 'merchants'.[6]

Slave-owners are praised as heroes to generations of young

[5] In 1988 an open meeting was held in a social club at St George's Cross, Glasgow to discuss the proposed 'City of Culture' year and its relation to writers and artists. It was organised by the Free University Network and attended by a variety of writers, magazine editors and artists, including Eddie Boyd, Cathie Thomson, Dominic Behan, Tom Leonard, Farquhar McLay, Freddie Anderson, Alasdair Gray, William Clark, Keith Miller, James Kelman, Malcolm Dickson, Peter Kravitz. Hugh Savage and Ned Donaldson were also present. Some were associated with the anthology Workers City and formed a central part of the group. It should be noted the anthology and the group were distinct. As indicated by the open meeting and McLay's Introduction to the *Workers City* anthology, people held different opinions and perspectives on 'Culture Year'.

[6] See foreword to *Some Recent Attacks, Essays Cultural and Political* [AK Press 1992].

people, a mythology peddled by our education and political authorities. There have been plenty of heroes in Glasgow and the central belt but most have figured in the struggle against injustice; their names are not just forgotten but ignored, marginalised, occasionally suppressed.

When I met Hugh Savage on the picket line that February morning in 1990 he was alongside Leslie Forster and Ned Donaldson. The three had been close friends for forty five years. Hugh regarded highly his involvement in the Workers City group. And he enjoyed it. After a break of a few years it was a return to political activism. Others present included Isabel and Freddie Anderson, writer and editor Farquhar McLay and Jeanette McGinn, widow of the late great Matt McGinn, close friend and former comrade of some of those present. All were activists of long-standing and all were in at the start of the Workers City campaigning group. Around them was a wider circle of friends and acquaintances, young and old. Some were ex-members of political parties; some remained members of political parties. Present in abundance were experience and energy, physical and intellectual. Individuals held and expressed different opinions. In common was a left wing sensibility, an impatience with humbug and a distrust of professional politicians and arts administrators.

Workers City was a non-sectarian formation and did its best to remain that way. The group's critique of the European City of Culture produced the greatest wrath from the political authorities and their apologists within the media and arts establishment.

What angered the authorities most was that there was no way to stop people talking. Had the political machinery failed? Surely it and the media were there to control debate? What the hell was happening here!

One thing that did upset them was the appearance of an irregular scandal-mongering organ entitled *The Keelie*, produced anonymously and distributed freely. For decades in Scotland, the name 'keelie' has been applied pejoratively to Glaswegians, denoting 'low class, vulgar beings'. Absolutely appropriate for the Workers City group.

The Keelie became its heart. The appearance of this free newspaper coincided with particular campaigns and demonstrations. Its primary targets were Labour politicians and where possible named names and used photographs. *The Keelie* featured snippets of local history and occasional lampoons in the form of poetry or cartoon. Everybody associated with Workers City was encouraged to contribute and some of the writings produced by Hugh Savage for *The Keelie* are included here in the addenda.

The Labour authorities knew they were in a fight and along the way they suffered some defeats. The most notable followed their bungled attempt to sell a third of Glasgow Green to private developers. They were unprepared for the depth of revulsion felt by Glaswegians. And of course they underestimated the opposition. That mistake derives from a failing common to politicians: arrogance, but an arrogance that thrives on ignorance. The sad truth is that contemporary Labour politicians have little or no knowledge of the origins of their own party. If so they might have approached the Workers City group with more caution.

The group received strong outside support and solidarity but rarely featured more than fifteen or twenty individuals.[7] There were no leaders within it but Hugh Savage was the pivotal figure, and he greatly enjoyed his participation. Until the late 1980s his main involvement had been with the Friends of the People's Palace. 'The Friends' were a group of volunteers who existed to support and raise funds for the People's Palace Museum on Glasgow Green. Money raised by them went from assisting in the purchase of historical relics and art objects to buying a photocopying machine for the Museum office.

Hugh's relationship to the People's Palace museum was an important factor in the Workers City campaigns. The museum's curator Elspeth King and her assistant Michael Donnelly had transformed the old place into something quite special.[8] It had become a proper people's museum whose existence gave the lie to the politicians' fantasy of Clydeside as historical home to budding billionaires and global entrepreneurs, whether in kilts or 501s. King and Donnelly knew the past and they treasured it, literally, on behalf of the people of Glasgow.

So the authorities wanted rid of them. They wanted people brought in from outside, preferably with no knowledge of the city's

---

[7] 'We just seemed a lot,' said Ian McKechnie, a regular participant.

[8] See *The People's Palace and Glasgow Green* by Elspeth King [Richard Drew Publishing, 1985].

radical past and definitely without any personal attachment; they wanted people who would grasp the nettle, do the council's bidding, carry on the purge. By all means allow a place for working class culture but not on its own terms. Forget Willie Nairn, John Maclean, Harry McShane, Guy Aldred, bring on Harry Lauder, Rab C Nesbitt, Oor Wullie and the Broons. What about disease-ridden slums, state repression, police brutality, rent strikes and racism; sectarianism, the struggle for adequate living conditions; a proper life for our children? Forget it, not unless there is a happy ending. Tourists prefer to exit 'cultural outlets' – art galleries, theatres and museums – with a smile on their face. Financiers and prospective employers are better not to hear about militant suffragettes, socialists, anarchists and communists from Glasgow's radical past. Nor need they be reminded about that from Clydeside writers and artists. Where is their patriotism? Surely they could do more to help 'our' revival, 'our' regeneration.

Even the Calton district location of the People's Palace Museum presented the municipal authorities with a problem. As late as 2005, fifteen years after the mammoth costs of the 'European City of Culture' project, the life expectancy of males in this district was less than 54 years of age. It is an incredible statistic. For the UK as a whole the life expectancy of males was 75.9 years.[9] If the Labour Council could have uprooted the People's Palace and set it down in a prosperous suburb like Bearsden they would have acquired the funds from somewhere. Unfortunately for them Bearsden is not in Glasgow.

In their customary ruthless manner the Labour authorities sacked Michael Donnelly and denigrated his work. They tried to force Elspeth King's resignation by humiliating her publicly, then they forced her to apply for her own job. And then they gave her job to a man she had trained. Hugh Savage and the Workers City group campaigned to safeguard their positions. And the Glasgow citizenry rallied in support. Who ever heard of such a thing! A public campaign to save the job of a museum curator and her assistant?

Elspeth King's professional reputation extended way beyond the Scottish border. News of the campaign and of the treachery of the Labour authorities reached as far as Australia. More letters reached the *Glasgow Herald* newspaper than for any news event

---

[9] According to a *Guardian* report by Audrey Gillan, 21.1.05

since the evangelist Billy Graham's tour in the 1950s. Finally the authorities succeeded in ousting Ms King but not without a lengthy struggle.

Following the end of 'Culture Year' the activities of the Workers City group wound down but individuals remained in touch. For a period a few continued to publish *The Keelie*; some became involved in the struggle against industrial and environmental disease with *Clydeside Action on Asbestos*. Around this period Hugh Savage flitted from the east end of Glasgow to Rothesay on the island of Bute. But two or three times a week he travelled into the city's Mitchell Library to meet and research with Leslie Forster, Ned Donaldson, and other friends.

He and Leslie Forster were members of the Glasgow Labour History Workshop. Radical history and political affairs, whether historical or contemporary; those were passions. They worked on projects before, during and after the time of Workers City and published *All for the Cause,* a book on Willie Nairn, 'Stonebreaker, Philosopher, Marxist'.[10] And they played a crucial part in the publication of others: *The Singer Strike Clydebank, 1911;*[11] *Militant Workers: Labour and Class Conflict on the Clyde 1900 – 1950;*[12] *Roots of Red Clydeside 1910-1914 – Labour Unrest and Industrial Relations in West Scotland.*[13] Forster published his own memoir, *Rocking the Boat* and with Ned Donaldson, wrote *Sell and be Damned, The Glasgow Merrylee Housing Scandal of 1951.*

Reclaiming history, exhibiting the radical tradition; the work they accomplished is inspirational, packed full of information: to read them is to come into contact with a roll-call of outstanding men and women. They were more excited by the unknown or forgotten names, 'the unsung heroes who toiled to enlighten the

---

[10] *All for the Cause: Willie Nairn (1856-1902); Stonebreaker, Philosopher, Marxist* by Hugh Savage and Leslie Forster, published by themselves in 1991 [printed by Margaret McQuade McAuslan, assisted by Clydeside Press]

[11] Published by Clydebank District Library 1989

[12] *Essays in Honour of Harry McShane (1891-1988)* edited by Robert Duncan and Arthur McIvor [John Donald, 1992]

[13] Edited by William Kenefick and Arthur McIvor [John Donald, 1996]

workers without any thought of gain other than the spreading of the word of Marx and Engels.'[14] Both in their memoirs and other work what becomes apparent is not only their knowledge of Glasgow's radical tradition, but their grasp of its political significance.

For all that, Hugh Savage was an activist first, and the writing came down the list. Yet he was always working on one thing or another. Beside the research, the campaigning copy and features there were angry letters to the powers-that-be. Such writing is done for immediate use, and not much of Hugh's output remains but some does, and in the addenda here are a few of his contributions to campaigning features from earlier times, published in *Socialist Revolt* and *New Commune*, two radical journals that he and his friends and comrades produced back in the 1950s and early 1960s.

It is unclear when he began on his *Memoir*. It was not something he discussed easily. When he saw reviews for the publication of another 'life of an old socialist' he gave a shake of the head, No another one. . . He considered such projects an embarassing aspect of the ageing process. And here he was doing the same thing. He described himself as 'a foot-soldier' and worried about being presumptious. His family and friends encouraged him and he stuck to the task.

When he moved to the flat in Rothesay he did most of the heavy graft himself. He gutted the place and put in a new central heating system which meant boring through the sandstone wall of a tenement building. Then he redecorated completely, renovating all the plasterwork, the lot. Hugh was a plumber and welder to trade and had always been a fit, active man, a teetotaller and nonsmoker. But he was then into his 70s. When he did find time to get on with his writing he experienced acute back pain. It became impossible to stay at the keyboard for long.

The stress he suffered from that move to Rothesay was not only physical. The political atmosphere on the island he found stultifying and anachronistic. This was the 1990s yet he saw religious sectarianism dividing a community still in thrall to the local aristocracy. He was not entirely joking when he said the Masonic Lodge controlled anything not already controlled by the Marquis of Bute.

---

[14] See their Preface to *All for the Cause*.

Everybody living in the place had to pay the aristocracy ground rent. The Marquis was a feudal lord. This side of Rothesay life was like a shameful secret. Hugh found it embarrassing. And nobody was doing anything about anything; they were just taking the punishment. That was the worst of all. Nobody was fighting back.

If an injustice was afoot it preyed on his mind. A battle was being waged against two of his elderly neighbours by the factors of the Marquis of Bute. Hugh took up the cudgels on their behalf and got sucked into the mire of civil disputation that occasionally masquerades as politics in this country. It was over a drainage or sewage problem. The sort of weighty affair the Home Rule movement and formations like the current Scottish Parliament were set up to process. At the same time he was tackling the authorities on his own behalf with his continued refusal to pay the Poll Tax. One skirmish led to his appearance at the High Court in Glasgow. It was over his refusal to have his name entered onto the Electoral Roll. He refused to pay all or any part of the fines levied against him and was prepared to do a couple of months 'porridge' if so required. When he was called to the dock he bewildered the court by addressing them on the theme of 'freedom'. Who was this old guy, this ghost of the radical past?

Each skirmish meant more time wasted in the composition of letters to the authorities. Life was getting in the way of the *Memoir*. His work was laid aside. He had taken it beyond boyhood, young manhood and the start of World War II. This was when he began work on the Clyde, joined the Communist Party, became a labour activist and militant trade unionist, got married, started a family. After the war he was blacklisted by the shipyards, and much of the building industry. He could not get a job because of his commitment as a CP activist, to the trade union cause and to the socialist movement in general. Within the party he had a growing reputation. A by-election had been called for Glasgow-Gorbals and the party offered him temporary work as an election agent. He writes of this in the *Memoir*; the one occasion in his political life that he accepted paid employment as a party official.

But that was that, for different reasons he was unable to continue the story. He had reached the year 1948.

The by-election of that year had been called because of the resignation of George Buchanan of the Labour Party. He had been promoted to a junior ministerial position and was standing down. Tom Johnston was Secretary of State for Scotland and Buchanan became his junior. On the one hand this was thought too lowly a position for someone of Buchanan's standing. He had been a close friend of James Maxton, John Wheatley, the Reverend Campbell Stephen and members of the early Independent Labour Party (ILP). On behalf of the Labour Party he had introduced a Home Rule for Scotland bill. In those days the ILP was affiliated to the Labour Party. A little digging into radical history shows he was one of the original Red Clydesiders who stormed the Westminister barricades back in the early 1920s. In fact Buchanan was resigning the seat he had held since 1922.

The man who held the seat before Geordie Buchanan was George V. Barnes. He took the seat back in 1906. Thus, during that 42 year period only two MPs occupied the seat. But the bare facts conceal some extraordinary times. A little more digging reveals that the Glasgow-Gorbals constituency has been associated with some of the more significant election battles of the first quarter of last century.

Radical history is more complex than others. Not only is the history itself repressed, so too is the radical movement. Repression is exercised by any ruling authority, left or right. Individuals are marginalised when it appears in the interests of a party hierarchy. Names are marginalised, glossed over, forgotten. So too are the issues, the disagreements and arguments. And conversely, the names of those who did nothing to advance the socialist and labour movement have been venerated.

The Communist Party of Great Britain (CPGB) was quickly corrupted intellectually, but not from beginning to end. There were thousands of individuals within who acted in good faith and struggled on. Activists could and did involve themselves completely in the issues of the day, strikes, demonstrations, parades and commemorials such as May Day. There was much being done but it took place in a sort of intellectual vacuum. For any 'freethinker', the closer one got to power, the more demoralising it must have become. Without access to their own history and traditions how can people breathe? Every culture has its own traditions. How did people come to form the Communist Party and how did they fare beyond? Almost since its inception, before Stalin succeeded Lenin, the Communist International (Comintern) was crushing the life out of the socialist movement, and destroying its intellectual development.

The source of that development is the lives of other people and the closer we are to those lives the more vital is the development. This is why indigenous history is primary. In an occupied country indigenous history can only be radical. It is a class issue. The intellectual life of working class people is 'occupied'. In a colonised country intellectual occupation takes place throughout society. The closer to the ruling class we get the less difference there exists in language and culture, until finally we find that questions fundamental to society at its widest level are settled by members of the same closely knit circle, occcasionally even the same family or 'bloodline'. And the outcome of that can be war, the slaughter of working class people.

The generation who joined the Communist Party during World War I did not have access to the information we have today. They would have been familiar with aspects of the wider history of the socialist movement but rarely of their own radical tradition. Much of it had yet to be unravelled. A little of it had but remained obscure, deliberately or otherwise. Some is still unknown and mysteries exist that will plague us forever. The British State has secrecy orders placed on material from the nineteenth never mind the twentieth century. The establishment refers to it as 'politically sensitive'. What they mean is that if exposed it might damage them, by revealing clear evidence of their duplicity and involvement in the worst crimes, whatever it took to retain power.

For the Communist Party membership, socialists from earlier times were taken seriously but for those who died before the formation of the party it was more difficult: they came from a sort of twilight period and their status for many communists was similar to that of Socrates, Plato or Cicero for Christians. Somehow they were guilty. But of what? Being born out of time? Could somebody be a genuine socialist who was not a member of the Communist Party? Semantics enter the argument: how do we define 'socialist', what features distinguish 'socialist' from 'communist'? And what about those born in time who had the option to join the party but rejected it? From the mid 1920s the Communist Party hierarchy had to deal with McShane and a few other renegades from within, let alone John Maclean, John S. Clarke or Guy Aldred who were never party members in the first place.

The Communist Party of Great Britain was only formed in 1920, two years before the great 'Red Clydeside' victory at the 1922 General Election. Prior to then male and female activists had come through struggle together, over many years. Syndicalists, suffragettes and reformist socialists; anti parliamentary communists, Catholic socialists, presbyterian socialists, anarchists, industrial unionists. Those and more were around and easily confound an older assessment that 'the always parochial character of Clydeside politics offered only two competing ideologies, that of the Marxist SLP and that of the ILP.'[15]

There may have been sectarianism, political as well as religious, but on the left there was also a general commitment to certain tenets, eg, the anti-war position, universal suffrage, adequate housing, a proper education, health care, etc. That commitment extended to a common political end and the acceptance of the validity of much Marxian theory.

But there were other elements to that shared perspective. Marxism was not then institutionalised within power structures. On different fronts it would become so, emptied of much of its philosophical and ethical – or humanist – base for the sake of its 'use-value'; the economic and micro-political employed as a sort of managerial strategy. On Clydeside and elsewhere people lived by a set of principles and were prepared to confront the full might of the British State, they were prepared to go to prison, and some were prepared to die for what they believed. There were divergences; some thought religion and Marxism mutually exclusive, others that they might be reconciled. But the fact remains that for many working class people in Scotland an alternative way of life was on offer, it was not just a matter of economics.

The early socialists had almost no relevant literature at all. They had to create it then publish and distribute it themselves. Nowadays there is a great deal but it remains obscure, unavailable in bookshops, except secondhand ones. And radical history itself is never taught outside of specialised areas in departments of higher

---

[15] p46 Robert Keith Middlemas *The Clydesiders: a left wing struggle for Parliamentary power* [Hutchinson 1965, reprinted August M. Kelley, New York 1968]

education; and only then as a function of the interests of individual academics. At ordinary school level there is hardly anything; children are still force-fed the establishment diet of imperial victories and monarchical lineage. In the 1960s and 70s a short-lived attempt came about through the subject known as Modern Studies. Eventually it was dumped. 'Ordinary' radical history is virtually unknown to the wider public.

Hugh Savage and Leslie Forster write that their own interest and eventual excavatory work in radical history would never have happened but for. . .

> the enthusiastic guidance and encouragement of Harry
> McShane. For years he told us of the early pioneers of
> the socialist movement, most of whom he had met,
> spoke with, worked with, and even gone to jail with.[16]

For a quick idea of the world that opened up go to the index of *No Mean Fighter*.[17] This is not a written autobiography. It was dictated by McShane. Through regular conversations with him forgotten names from Clydeside's radical past became familiar to Savage, Forster and friends, also a familiarity and knowledge with a tradition that was under severe attack, and continues to be so. The names of these early socialists peppered their own conversation and their ease with radical history is evident in their writings.

The fifty year span from the Paris Commune through the formation of the CPGB into the mid 1920s was a spectacular period in socialist history. On Clydeside a rare collection of individuals came and went. Some names remain familiar: Keir Hardie, Maxton, Connolly and Maclean. Others are less familiar: Guy Aldred, Willie Gallacher, R.B. Cunninghame-Graham, John Wheatley, John McGovern, John Muir, Eunice Murray, John S. Clarke, Maggie Moffatt; Bob Hutcheson, Dr Elizabeth Chalmers-Smith, James McDougall, Jane Rae, John Murdoch, Neil Maclean, Harry Hopkins; William Haddow, J.Bruce Glasier, Mary Barbour, Agnes Dollan, Patrick Dollan, J.R. Campbell, George Barrett, Emmanuel Shinwell; William Nairn, George S. Yates, James Messer; William Paul, Helen Crawfurd, Tom Bell, Arthur McManus.

---

[16] See their *All for the Cause: Willie Nairn 1856-1902*

[17] *No Mean Fighter,* Harry McShane and Joan Smith [Pluto Press 1975]

This list of names is not exhaustive. Most of the people are of an ordinary working class background, similar to that of Hugh Savage and friends. Some would have figured as heroes to their generation, as they would to the youth of the present day, if they knew of their existence. It would not matter to which party they belonged. But their ideas would have mattered, the motivation, what brought them there, the nature of the struggle, how they responded, the sacrifices they made along the way. People died for what they believed.

In 1922 George Buchanan's left wing rival for Glasgow-Gorbals was John Maclean. Maclean had contested the previous General Election in 1918. It was the first postwar General Election and Maclean was then a leading member of the British Socialist Party (BSP), a forerunner of the CPGB. In that year, much to the horror of Labour's National Executive the Gorbals Labour constituency selected Maclean as their prospective candidate.

The BSP was affiliated to the Labour Party so such a thing was possible. Beyond Parliament the Labour Party was hardly a 'party' at all, but a loose group of left wing bodies, ranging from the BSP to the Fabians, by way of the ILP and assorted trades unions. MPs could be sponsored by any one of these different formations. George Buchanan had been nominated to represent the pattern-makers trade union although he was a member of the ILP.

When the Gorbals nominated Maclean for that 1918 election he was in prison doing five years hard labour for sedition. This when 'the Scottish system was probably one of the most inhuman in Europe.'[18] Maclean was known internationally, a hero within the wider socialist movement, recently appointed by Soviet Russia as their first British Consul. On Clydeside he was one of a group of major left wing activists; a leading figure and by far the most prominent, but not *the* leader. There was no leader in that sense.

Within the left there were conflicting views. Among factories and shipyards on the Clyde few were as effective as Arthur McManus, Davie Kirkwood and Willie Gallacher; each a shop steward, each a member of the Clyde Workers Committee. The ILP's John Wheatley was as influential as anyone, more so in some quarters. He said of Maclean 'John's ability and fearlessness. . . have singled him out as

---

[18] p126 Nan Milton's *John Maclean*

one of the great rebel leaders of our time, and consequently one of the first subjects of persecution. Our rulers fear Maclean more than they do the whole Labour Party.'[19]

Clearly the state authorities wanted rid of him, and managed to imprison him on six occasions. Their cynical, often brutal treatment, had its effect and finally Maclean was dead at the age of 44. When they had him on trial in July 1918 the legal procedure and severity of the judgment was blatantly biased: 'In the officers came, one after another, with parrot-like repetitions of carefully coached and memorised 'stories'. On the most appalling testimony of little 'patriots', led by a 'patriot' judge. . . [Maclean was] sentenced to five years' penal servitude.[20]

For some within the Coalition Government it was a political embarassment but they got away with it. And while Maclean was incarcerated they did not interfere with the procedure. Maclean was held in contempt and subject to vile treatment by the prison authorities and by their medics. He was imprisoned in April of that year and sentenced in July, and he embarked on an immediate hunger strike. He was refused all visitors and the prison authorities force-fed him. They used two warders to restrain him physically while rubber tubes were inserted by the medical staff.

At the end of October his wife Agnes was at last granted access. She discovered that he was being 'fed by a stomach tube twice daily' which was 'forced down his gullet or up his nose.' She had been advised earlier that such a thing would never happen unless the relatives were forewarned. The authorities ignored that. They were after Maclean and '[the] most worrying aspect of [his] imprisonment down to 1918 was the collusion between the State, the Secretary of State for Scotland, the Lord Advocate and the army generals in Scotland to defame and misrepresent their vulnerable prisoner.'[21]

The Clydeside left had few illusions about the political sympathies of the British State, that 'invincible alliance of aristocrats and capitalists, with its overwhelming control both of the Houses

---

[19] Written for 'Catholic Notes' in 'Forward' cited by Nan Milton, p49 *John Maclean*.

[20] p199 Willie Gallacher *Revolt on the Clyde*, p212 [Lawrence & Wishart 1936]

[21] See James D. Young p207 *John Maclean: Clydeside Socialist* [Clydeside Press 1992]

of Parliament and of the courts of law.'[22] Nevertheless, even radicals
highly experienced in the workings of domestic security could not
have known the extent of the collusion between the Whitehall
Government and private 'right wing groups such as the Navy League
and the Anti-Socialist Union [also] the British Empire Union. . . '
During World War I these formations. . .

> helped Special Branch and MI5 by attempting to locate
> German agents, spies and saboteurs. This assistance
> continued when surveillance was extended to include
> pacifists, the anti-war movements, socialists and those
> engaged in war-time strikes. These informal
> arrangements carried over into the post-war years when
> the Security Service became alarmed at the dramatic
> upsurge of industrial unrest and political militancy. . .
> Militant trade unionists, radical socialists, and
> communists were now seen as the new enemy. [23]

John Maclean was not suffering delusions. He was targeted.[24]
State surveillance is one historical element rarely remarked upon
anywhere, except by those who endure it. Individuals who suffered
personal harassment during the time of John Maclean were far
more sympathetic to his plight. Tom Mann, James Larkin and Guy
Aldred are three outsiders who were so targeted and each was
acquainted with the radical scene on Clydeside. Each lived to an
old age but unlike many of Maclean's Clydeside comrades none of
the trio changed his opinions on Maclean. None charged him with
delusions or behaviour that might have arisen from a source other
than the extreme victimisation to which he was subject. And where
Maclean's behaviour might have been open to such criticism
outsiders such as Mann, Larkin and Aldred, knew from their own
personal experience the extent of state surveillance. Even then,
none of the trio suffered the same physical hardship.

People around Maclean were aware of the problem but ignorant

---

[22] p90 *The British Working-Class Movement 1787-1947* G.D.H.Cole
[Allen & Unwin 2nd edition 1927]

[23] See *Lobster 22*

[24] See James D. Young's *John Maclean: Clydeside Socialist* for good
information on this.

of the extent to which he was targeted and generally underestimated the effects such targeting can have on the individuals and their families. In retrospect the case is typical. The language used by contemporaries to describe his later behaviour is consistent with what we know on the subject nowadays. Their willingness to seek fault in the individual, in other words 'blame the victim', is also consistent. Coupled with that was the political reality. In 1919, the time of the 40 hour a week strike and the massive demonstrations in George Square, Maclean was back in prison, and by 1920 his time had gone. There was no longer room for singularity. The October Revolution altered the course of the socialist movement and the intellectual influence of Lenin was pervasive, for better or worse. 'The Communist Parties are dead: long live the Communist Party.'[25]

It is ironic that this was stated by Maclean's old comrade Arthur McManus. The irony is heightened by his personal experience of the power of the British State. McManus had good reason to know about the spy system and the work of *agents provocateurs*. The anti-war movement had been strong among the Clydeside left, in particular within the Clyde Workers Committee of which he was a leading shop steward.

> Throughout the war the Government resorted to the old practice of sending spies amongst the militant workers as informers and provocateurs. The ammunition shops were riddled with them. The Workers' Committees were pestered with them.[26]

In early 1916 the Coalition Government stepped up its attempts to nullify the anti-war movement on Clydeside and destroy the power of the Clyde Workers Committee. They took the drastic step of imprisoning leading radicals such as Maclean, Patrick Dollan, Maxton, John Muir and James McDougall. Then they deported McManus and other shop stewards, all leading members of the Clyde Workers Committee.[27] In radical history he remains an

---

[25] Arthur McManus cited by Pelling, Henry *The British Communist Party: A Historical Profile* [A & C Black Ltd. 1958] p13

[26] McShane in *No Mean Fighter*

[27] including Tom Bell, James Messer and Davie Kirkwood

enigma. By contemporary accounts he was a strong personality, for some a hard-liner, and first Chairman of the CPGB. Nevertheless, at that earlier period, still a member of the Socialist Labour Party (SLP), he was one of the few who 'succeeded in breaking through the paralysing influence of De Leonism.'[28]

> When war was declared [John Maclean] held a big
> meeting at Nelson's Monument to state his revolutionary
> anti-war position. The meeting was notable also because
> Arthur McManus spoke alongside John. . . Arthur was in
> the SLP and until then it had been almost impossible to
> get anyone from the SLP on a platform with any other
> socialist organisation.'[29]

But there was an additional reason why McManus was more knowledgeable than most about the machinations of British State 'domestic security'. During the enforced exile McManus travelled south from Edinburgh and in England he met his future wife, a young woman whose mother kept 'open house' for anti-war activists and militant socialists on the run. She was Hetty Wheeldon, younger daughter of the great 'Alice Wheeldon, a militant suffragette and socialist [who] along with [her elder] daughter and son-in-law were sentenced to ten years' penal servitude, five years and seven years respectively for 'plotting' to assassinate Lloyd George.'[30] Of course it was an outrageous and shameful lie by the British State.

While in prison the Wheeldon family embarked on a series of hunger strikes. Political prisoners used hunger strikes then as now to draw attention to the injustices perpetrated by the state authorities. Imprisoned women of the early suffragette movement were to the fore in that, as were Irish prisoners. The Government passed the 'Cat and Mouse' Bill to help them defeat the suffragettes. The authorities felt that a group of dying women was unsound politically. This legal move allowed them to release female hunger strikers shortly before their predicted death. While at home their friends and family would look after these women, they would feed them

---

[28] p26 of Gallacher's *Revolt on the Clyde*

[29] McShane, *No Mean Fighter* p67

[30] See the same 1998 issue of *Statewatch* Vol 8, No 2 as referred to above.

up and care for them, try to get them strong again. If they survived and regained a degree of physical strength the police would come back and re-arrest them. If the women died at home it would not look so bad.

The state authorities used this tactic with other anti-war activists, for example Guy Aldred. They were concerned that the public might be sickened by the logical outcome to a hunger strike, ie, death of the prisoner. They were less concerned by Irish deaths. Irish people were considered hardly people at all. If they were, they were indistinguishable. In the midst of their ruthless assault on Ireland and the Irish people highly-placed individuals within the British establishment thought that nationalists and republicans were a part of the Home Rule movement. This is the essence of racism, where the possibility of individual difference cannot be distinguished.

In August 1920 Terence MacSwiney, the Lord Mayor of Cork was 'arrested in Cork City Hall.' The Royal Irish Constabulary had already murdered the city's previous mayor, Tomás MacCurtain, while the British looked on. Now they brought MacSwiney to England, and to Brixton Prison where '[he] went on hunger-strike, thus focusing world attention on the Irish cause. He died in October 1920 on the seventy fifth day of his hunger-strike.'[31]

Alice Wheeldon and her family served a couple of years in prison and then were released, following a series of hunger-strikes. Alice died a few months later. Her eldest daughter and son-in-law contracted pneumonia and were close to death for several weeks. This is the affair that Arthur McManus would have known about intimately. It was through him that Tom Bell got to know of the case.[32]

That contemptible action by the British State was only compounded by the fact that it took Her Majesty's Government until June 1998, a period of seventy one years, to finally confess what had been known all along, that it was a complete 'set up' from beginning to end, that the family were 'entrapped by Alex Gordon and Herbert Booth, both agents of a MI5 branch known as PMS2.'[33]

At the time of the events the left was outspoken in its attacks on

---

[31] See p33 Meda Ryan's *Tom Barry: IRA Freedom Fighter*

[32] See p 126-7 Tom Bell's *Prioneering Days*

[33] Information in *Statewatch* Vol 8, No 2 or *Lobster 22*

HM Government. In the socialist newspaper, *Worker*, its editor, John S. Clarke, was particularly scathing, and accused Lloyd George of personal responsibility.'There are several ways of murdering our valiant women comrades. There is the straightforward, brutal way of sheer murder, which killed Rosa Luxemburg. And there is the secret, sinister, cowardly and slower method which killed Mrs Wheeldon.'

Seventy one years of official denial could not have occurred but for the collusion of highly placed individuals within the Labour Party. This allowed British offialdom, spies and *agent provocateurs* to escape exposure. It further allowed a network of far right, private enterprise formations to strengthen covert operations domestically. Contrary to conventional wisdom the main target of domestic security is not foreign infiltrators and terrorists, it is the left wing public, and it always has been. Secrecy is the nature of these operations. The obfuscation of radical history embraces the role of the domestic security forces, and further conceals it. MI5's involvement in Ireland is no secret but what is less well-known is the extent of the spy operations that were activated, not only in Ireland but in Britain itself. An organisation known as National Propaganda 'functioned as [its] central co-ordinating body.' Only a few outsiders knew of the network's existence. No matter how extreme these far right bodies were, including the openly fascist, they were given access to 'confidential intelligence material' belonging to HM Government. It was to this network that Lloyd George appealed in 1919 'to defeat the Railway Strike'.[34]

The Clyde Workers Committee was composed of some of the more committed activists of the time and there is no question how they were regarded. This was demonstrated when shop stewards were deported and others imprisoned under the Defence of the Realm Act. Many were employed at the more famous Clydeside factories and shipyards, and almost all had attended classes organised by Maclean and comrades.

A few of these same shop stewards had worked previously at Singer's factory in Clydebank and were involved in a major industrial action that took place in 1911, and ranks as one of the most crucial 'in the History of Labour alongside the Dockers' Strike

---

[34] *ibid.*

of 1889, and the Engineers' Lock-out of 1897.'[35] It began as 'a spontaneous outburst of rank and file aggression, initiated by women workers [and led] by a democratically elected Strike Committee [which] brought together workers across a broad spectrum.'

The Singer management had honed its UK industrial relations from its US-based operations. Here at Clydebank they responded with a ruthlessness that shocked the workforce: 'the resultant victimisation. . . [was] quite extraordinary and the militancy of the workforce. . . countered by mass sackings of between 400 and 1000 workers. . . [including] the whole of the almost 200-strong Strike Committee.'[36] Many were blacklisted and would have remained so except for the outbreak of the 1914-18 War. Skilled and semi skilled workers soon found employment on the Clyde. A few became members of the Clyde Workers Committee, whose

> . . . militant use of the strike weapon, of direct action. . .
> owed much to the strategies previously formulated by the
> revolutionary industrial unionists on the Clyde. . . The
> CWC was in essence a federal industrial union, constituted
> of representatives of all firms involved in munition
> manufacture thus [replicating] the structures promulgated
> by the IWGB and initiated in practice in Singer. [37]

The syndicalist influence of the SLP is here in evidence and shop stewards from Singers who became members of the CWC include McManus, Bell, Paul, Messer and Neil MacLean.

But their influence during the Singer strike should not be overemphasised. Tom Bell was the archetypal 'party' man. A founder member of the CPGB and one of its two first paid full-time officials [the other was Harry Pollitt]. Even after Bell was kicked aside in the upheavals of the mid-1920s he remained a loyalist to the bitter

---

[35] See *The Singer Strike Clydebank, 1911* by the Glasgow Labour History Workshop, published Clydebank District Library, 1989

[36] The last quote is from Tom Bell, p135-6 cited by McIvor and Paterson in their discussion in Knox's book

[37] See Glasgow Labour History Workshop's *The Singer Strike; Clydebank, 1911* by the [Clydebank District Library 1989]

end. He was a shop steward during the 1911 Singer industrial action but expressed misgivings personally. He thought a strike inevitable but that 'we were not yet ready to exercise firm control and discipline.' The female workforce made their own decision. '[The] spark which ignited' the action was struck not by a politically-motivated caucus or vanguard action of party members but by 'the stand taken by the women polishers.' [38]

Shop floor activists at the Singer factory included Jane Rae and Frances Abbott and neither were members of any political party. Several months after the strike Rae joined the ILP, 'after hearing Keir Hardie.' Frances Abbott was also in the ILP and 'involved with . . . the Women's Section of the Labour Party,' and fifty years later 'was given a testimonial by the Labour Party for her. . . 'services to the people's cause.'

It was the activity itself that politicised the workforce. Members of the female contingent later were involved in the Glasgow rent strikes of 1915 where Agnes Dollan and Helen Crawfurd were to the fore. Agnes was the wife of Patrick Dollan, friend of John Wheatley and an early participant in meetings of the Catholic Socialist Society. He was imprisoned in 1916, along with Maxton, Maclean, McDougall and John Muir. Agnes was. . .

> . . . involved with the Women's Labour League [and] committed to the struggle for obtaining political status for women. . . [She] joined the Women's Social and Political Union [and with] Helen Crawfurd. . . was instrumental in forming the Glasgow branch of the Women's International League in 1915, and the Women's Peace Crusade in [1916].[39]

She and her husband moved far to the right in later life and along with John McGovern became enmeshed in Moral Rearmament, a 1950s anti-communist formation that received funding from the CIA. But in earlier times they contributed greatly to the

---

[39] *ibid.*

[30] See Helen Corr's introduction to *Rent Strikes; People's Struggle for Housing in West Scotland 1890-1916* by Joseph Melling [Polygon Books 1983].

socialist movement. Manny Shinwell described Dollan as 'perhaps the most conscientious and hard-working propagandist the Scottish Labour movement ever had. His capacity for work was amazing and there was hardly an agitation in which he was not in the front line. . . '[40] Eventually he became the 'first Catholic Lord Provost of Glasgow.' But Agnes was very highly regarded by, amongst others, Harry McShane who felt that she was 'held back' by her husband.

Following the end of the war the Coalition-Government sought a return to power at the 1918 General Election. The conflict with the left continued. John Maclean had been arrested in April and sentenced in July. There had been mass protests and demonstrations, including an historic Mayday. It fell on a weekday: tens of thousands of people took the day off work and held a mass rally to demonstrate their outrage at the authorities' victimisation of Maclean.

But when his wife Agnes was finally allowed in to visit him she discovered that he had been on hunger strike since the sentencing. The authorities were supposed to inform a prisoner's family when hunger-strikes and force-feeding took place. Instead they kept it secret. They managed this by not allowing in visitors. He had been isolated and without a visit since July. Agnes Maclean was badly shocked by his condition: he had. . .

> . . . the look of a man who is going through torture. . .
> Seemingly anything is law in regard to John. I hope. . .
> the atrocity [will be made] public. We must get him out
> of their clutches. It is nothing but slow murder.[41]

Before his wife's visit to the prison there had been tremendous expressions of public support. Following publication of her letter this intensified and news of the scandal became widespread. Friends

---

[40] p44 Manny Shinwell's *Conflict Wthout Malice* Odhams Press 1955

[41] Nan Milton's *John Maclean*. See also Maclean, John *In the Rapids of Revolution* p115, his wife's letter was published in the BSP's *The Call* and other socialists journals reported on his condition.

and family worried about the effects of his hunger strike and the deterioration in his condition. An approach was made to the appropriate MP who happened to be George N. Barnes, and he 'flatly refused to raise a finger to secure his release.'[42]

But the situation presented a quandary for the Coalition Government who wanted to ensure Barnes would be returned as Gorbals MP. How would it look if his only serious challenger for the election was a political prisoner now into his third month on hunger strike, a genuine local hero to a large part of the working class population?

Granting Maclean an early release would scarcely have been unprecedented. He had been gaoled for sedition in February 1916 and sentenced to five years hard labour under the Defence of the Realm Act. He believed it was no 'coincidence that he was arrested before he could take part in the Conference organised to form a Scottish Labour College.' He remained 'convinced that the 'greatest' crime that he had committed' as far as the British State was concerned 'was the teaching of Marxian economics to the Scottish workers.'[43] The Conference went ahead anyway and according to a report in *Justice* [17 February] comprised: '412 organisations and branches of organisations, including Cooperative Societies, Trade Unions, Trades Councils, BSP, ILP, Women's Labour League, etc.'[44]

Many agree with Maclean's own assessment. His summary of the State-sponsored higher education system bears repeating:

> The professors of political economy in the universities claim to be impartial men of science. But nobody believes them; their attitude is recognised as a necessary, professional pose. Their teaching has become a mere system of apologetics, by means of which they reveal the moral reasons that justify the plundering of the working class.[45]

---

[42] *ibid.* p178 Nan Milton's *John Maclean*

[43] *ibid.* p118

[44] See p119 Nan Milton *op. cit.*

[45] p118 *In the Rapids of Revolution*

Following his imprisonment in 1916 he was released less than halfway through the five year sentence. This because Lloyd George was set to arrive in Glasgow. The local authorities were to present him with a 'Freedom of the City' award and it would have looked bad if thousands of angry Glaswegians turned up at the ceremony to protest the continued victimisation and barbaric treatment of a local hero. So they released him. If the state wants something it finds a way.

On the approach to the first postwar General Election the Coalition Government did not want a working class socialist martyr, certainly not one renowned internationally and whose work as an educator was proving as politically significant as his general activism. Had Maclean stayed on hunger-strike and experienced much more of the force-feeding he would have died. The authorities knew that. They were very experienced in the grand fight against hunger strikers. Although there were arguments for allowing Maclean's death it made sense to release him, and protect the Coalition Government from a sympathy vote against their candidate. After all, they could re-arrest him for 'sedition' any time they liked. Once he recovered some of his health he might endure another bout of prison.

Now into December and with a few days to go before polling day, the authorities released him. He had served only seven months of a five year sentence.

It was a flagrant admission of culpability by the authorities and a demonstration of the value they placed on Maclean's influence. He had been foremost among the anti-war campaigners and a leader of the anti-conscription campaign in early 1916. For the past decade he had devoted himself to educational as well as propaganda work, in the tradition of Willie Nairn, Bob Hutcheson and George S. Yates, his old mentors from the Glasgow branch of the Social Democratic Federation (SDF). Aided by comrades like James McDougall the success of his work was illustrated by the quality of the younger Clydeside activists who had attended his classes. Not only was his educational work providing a theoretical basis for their militancy, his presence had become emblematic. He carried something of the aura that student circles create round a gifted teacher. And add to that the victimisation he had endured from the authorities. Those who doubted Maclean's wider political significance simply had to look at his treatment at the hands of the British State.

A crowd of thousands assembled in Glasgow to greet his release from prison. Those with no experience of prison life nor of the damaging effects of hunger-strikes failed to appreciate the deterioration in his physical condition. Maclean was too ill even to speak, and far too ill to conduct an election campaign. His deputy candidate was Willie Gallacher who would have 'refused' to stand on his own behalf but agreed to deputise for Maclean.[46] At that time Gallacher was opposed to parliamentary involvement by the left. He was 'a member of the Scottish Workers' Council, whose function was to promote 'communes', not Party communism.'[47] He had yet to discover tricky Bolshevik concepts like 'revolutionary parliamentarianism.' In those days Clydeside socialists would have guffawed at an obvious contradiction. Later Lenin would point out to them that it need not represent a contradiction at all.

When the results of the 1918 General Election were known Maclean had polled 7500 votes. But the sitting member for the Coalition-Government, George N. Barnes, doubled that number and hung onto the seat he had held since 1906.

Back then Keir Hardie had come in person to canvas on behalf of Barnes. Keir Hardie was very aware of the situation as it applied in a constituency like Glasgow-Gorbals, or Blackfriars as it then was. It is an additional element and, while not to be exaggerated, can never be discounted. On Clydeside, particularly in a district like the Gorbals, political affairs are complicated by issues affecting the Irish diaspora. Like any other immigrant group the Irish population and their descendants are also concerned with the politics of the 'mother' country.

By the turn of the twentieth century the Irish Home Rule Movement had gathered momentum throughout Britain and the Irish National League (INL) thrived; Glasgow 'branches [affiliated] to the Workers' Municipal Election Committee. . . and this cooperation proved important in building up Labour and working-

---

[46] See p212 Willie Gallagher's *Revolt on the Clyde* [Lawrence & Wishart 1936]

[47] See Calkdwell, J.T. *Come Dungeons Dark: the life and times of Guy Aldred, Glasgow Anarchist* [Luath Press 1988]

class representation in the government of the city. . . ' In 1900 the INL '[merged] with the new United Irish League. . . to become part of. . . a new and stronger Home Rule campaign on either side of the Irish Sea.'[48] Keir Hardie wished to influence the Gorbals electorate on behalf of the Labour candidate, so he made an appeal to John Redmond, leader of the Irish Home Rule movement.

What happened was slightly complicated. Redmond did not reject the appeal from Keir Hardie, but 'gave an understanding in such guarded terms that it was almost useless. However, the local. . . United Irish League rebelled against Redmond and the clear advice of the [Roman Catholic] Church, and told its members to vote Labour.'[49]

And a majority did vote Labour, thus Barnes was elected. Their reasons and motivation would have varied. The Gorbals population was not solely composed of an Irish diaspora but perhaps as much as 60% belonged to it. The district had been the traditional home for assorted immigrants, notably East Europeans in the nineteenth century, and a strong Jewish community lived there still. However, even had it been a purely Irish population what difference would it have made to the result? Of course the Catholic Church exercised a huge influence but other voices existed. In the early days of last century Irish socialists were advising their English, Welsh and Scottish comrades not to vote Home Rule at all.

Not only socialists opposed Home Rule. For a great many it was self determination, independence or nothing. Connolly and a few Irish comrades sought the establishment of an Irish Socialist Republic. But a far larger number favoured independence and gave allegiance to the 'Sinn Féin leadership [who] resolutely opposed. . . the republican movement developing a socialist character.'[50] There was even a small but significant group in Ireland prepared to fight to preserve Whitehall rule and their secondary status as a people, not only Protestants. And not all Protestants were Loyalists. They

---

[48] p12 Wood, Ian S. *John Wheatley* [Manchester University Press 1990], part of the Lives of the Left series

[49] p34 Middlemas *op. cit.*

[50] p165 John Newsinger *Rebel City: Larkin, Connolly and the Dublin Labour Movement* [The Merlin Press 2004]

could be met under any banner, as had been the case since the days of Wolfe Tone and the United Irishmen a hundred years before.

The variety of political opinion found in Ireland was found to some extent within the Irish communities of Central Scotland, and in their sister communities elsewhere. In 1902 Connolly was visiting USA, attending meetings and lecturing under the auspices of Daniel De Leon's Socialist Labour Party. He spoke to Irish immigrants on the need not for Home Rule but for an independent Ireland. Later he would return to live and work in USA, taking his wife and family with him. But in 1903 he was back in Scotland addressing meetings formally and informally. A few of the Glasgow branch of the SDF had lately been expelled or had moved away, including his old friend and comrade from Edinburgh, George S. Yates.

Yates made a telling contribution for the SDF as an educator. He held his classes at 62 Adelphi Street, Gorbals. Among those in attendance were Willie Paul, Arthur McManus and Tom Bell who later expressed his 'deep depth of gratitude to [Yates] who saved me endless floundering by leading me direct to the sources of the knowledge I desired. . . the basic theoretical works of Marxism and the writings of the great masters of science and literature. . . ' [51]

His close friend and comrade Willie Nairn was a vital influence of that period and did most of his educational work around the St George's Cross area. The local SDF branch was at 17 Cromwell Street. John Maclean came to these meetings. He was then teaching at a school in Lambhill, to the north of the city. For his political activitites he was disciplined by the education authorities and removed to Lorne Street, Ibrox. Soon he was removed altogether, nobody else would employ him. He 'founded the Pollokshaws branch of the SDF. . . in 1906. . . and took a weekly evening class, from 1908 until his first imprisonment in 1915. . . ' [52]

The SDF's push on propaganda and education impressed Maclean greatly and he later held meetings in this area himself. Nairn, Yates and Hutcheson operated classes on political economy for young and old, everybody welcome.

---

[51] Tom Bell in *Pioneering Days* [Lawrence & Wishart 1941]

[52] p10 the introduction to *In the Rapids of Revolution*

> Long before Comrade Keir Hardie we had Comrades
> Willie Nairn and Bob Hutcheson – two veteran members
> of the SDF – to name two only – in the Jail Square who
> held meetings on the Sundays, from ten o'clock in the
> morning till ten o'clock at night. The meetings were
> carried on in the relay system and were well-known.
> Comrade John [Maclean] had often listened to these
> comrades, and it was from them he received his first
> lessons on scientific socialism.[53]

At one such meeting he met his future wife, encouraged by Willie Nairn's daughter at a meeting at the corner of Shamrock Street and New City Road.

Besides his SDF activities Nairn was an organiser of the early Co-operative movement. Assorted guest speakers now arrived in the city. Names integral to the international socialist movement visited; among them Emma Goldman, Voltairine de Cleyre, Ben Tillett, Tom Mann and Leo Melliet, then domiciled in Leith, a veteran of the Paris Commune. Visitors were put up by the organisers and their friends. One of Nairn's guests was Peter Kropotkin, around 1895, and Nairn's daughter, Annie Gordon, remembered 'sitting on the great man's knee when she was an infant.[54]

There were a few anarchists on Clydeside at that time. Annie Gordon remembered that the Russian revolutionary was not the anarchist who impressed her the most; this was Guy Aldred, whom she met later. By then she had become a regular activist in the anarchist federation.'[55] One anarchist group seems to have formed in Glasgow the year after Nairn's death which would put it around 1903. It was from the Socialist League that the early anarchists

---

[53] See Nan Milton, p28 citing her father's first biographer, Tom Anderson.

[54] See the fuller account in Annie Gordon's recollections of John Maclean also in *All for the Cause: Willie Nairn 1856-1902* by Hugh Savage and Leslie Forster. Mrs Gordon was Willie Nairn's daughter. She gave Michael Donnelly a taped interview in 1979. The tape is lost but a short transcript remains. Donnelly allowed Savage and Forster access to it.

[55] *All for the Cause: Willie Nairn 1856-1902* by Hugh Savage and Leslie Forster.

emerged.[56] The Socialist League itself formed from a split in the SDF ranks in the 1880s.

Beside their educational work these early Clydeside radicals '[held] seven and eight meetings per week, as the old files of *Justice* show. . . [and] debating, lecturing, writing and propagating Socialism. . . [organising] great demonstrations, numbering sometimes 12,000 persons on Glasgow Green.' All of this they were achieving in their 'spare' time. In those days they worked a minimum ten hour day, doing the heaviest manual work. Nairn worked as a stonebreaker. Like many of his comrades he was a parent; he and his wife had to ensure the survival of their family in conditions of severe poverty, and 'these years of open-air toil and [activism] told heavily. . . [Nairn] died in 1902 at the age of forty six.' Even so, he outlived two of his own children. His wife lived until 1940, and 'worked as an attendant in the [public] toilets in West Campbell Street.'[57]

George S. Yates gave a fine oration at the funeral of his friend. The text is given in the addenda to Hugh Savage and Les Forster's biography of Nairn. They make the point that the Glasgow branch of the SDF was 'composed mainly of workers [whereas] the leadership was strongly in the hands of middle class and upper class intellectuals [and was] purely elitist: emancipation would come from the top and be ushered in by educated leaders.' Throughout his life Yates remained. . .

> an unswerving revolutionary socialist and the scourge of right-wing traitors. In 1910 [he] attended the Paris Congress of the Second International at which his voice was heard denouncing backsliders and reaffirming his belief in a socialist goal. He returned. . . carrying an English translation and music of *The Internationale* thus, for the first time, that stirring ballad was introduced to the British working-class.[58]

---

[56] But for a slightly different look at the origins of the Glasgow Anarchist Group see p219, and p200 for the ILP in 1906, Paton, John *Proletarian Piligrimage* [Routledge 1935]. See also John McGovern in *Neither Fear nor Favour*.

[57] See addenda to *All for the Cause* by Savage and Foster.

In the same year of 1910 the Fourth International and Trades' Congress took place in Copenhagen and Scottish delegates included the ILPers Keir Hardie, Bruce Glasier and William Haddow who records 'that the Government thought us sufficiently important to send one of their secret agents to keep an eye on us.'[59] From the end of the eighteenth century the British State led the way in the espionage industry, and its impact was conspicuous during the first quarter of the nineteenth century, culminating in the State murder of three weavers that ended the Scottish Insurrection.

Hugh Savage and Les Forster were led to research and publish their book on Nairn's life through the influence of Harry McShane who was a boy at the time of Nairn's death. He had become familiar with his lifework as educator and propagandist through word of mouth, via such as Maclean and James McDougall.

---

[58] The title of Nairn's biography is a hymn by William Morris. Hugh Savage and Leslie Forster took it from the tribute to Nairn by close friend and comrade George S. Yates. The hymn was sung by the mourners at Nairn's funeral.

[59] William Martin Haddow's *My Seventy Years* [Wm McLellan 1943]

Each generation of working class activists has had to learn mainly through its own experience and by what is passed on by 'tradition-bearers' – older activists, unembittered parents and grandparents. Any learning to be done takes place as a personal or community project. The early radical socialists were well aware of that and much time and effort was expended on educating themselves and each other through discussion groups and meetings. One crucial element of Nairn's educational practice was his ability to '[pass] on the message in language understood by workers thirsting for knowledge . . . ' This was a feature of the old Common Sense tradition in Scottish philosophy. It was never enough simply to know the subject, one had to pass on the information. This was at the heart of its political significance.

Any history that cannot distinguish the intellectual traditions within Britain cannot succeed. Harry McShane knew this and refers to the distinction between the socialist movement in this country and that of England, writing of the debates in Glasgow prior to the 1914-18 war:

> Scotland had a tremendous reputation for theological hair-splitting. As well as the Catholic v Protestant debates, the arguments about church government were very important here. Calvinism was still very strong and to get people away from it, or from Catholicism, meant a big fight about secularism. The free-thought fight was very good for the Scottish socialists. It sharpened them and led them into thinking about socialist principles more deeply, whereas in England some elements of the socialist movement formed a rival faith, more or less, to the Christian Church. . . . [60]

Although respect was accorded the regard for ideas and first principles that existed in Scottish socialist circles, some saw it as a

---

[60] p20 *No Mean Fighter* by Joan Smith and Harry McShane

drawback to actual struggle; too much energy being dissipated in the theoretical argy-bargy. Once on Glasgow Green Bronterre O'Brien advised an incredible assembly of '130,000 people' that 'he would not give a fig for all their clamouring and clapping of hands, unless [they] were prepared to do something effective. . .'[61] An echo of this critique of the Scottish predilection for discussion was voiced some seventy years later at one of John Maclean's lectures on Marxian economics, meetings that attracted massive audiences. The overseas visitor who was less than impressed was known in Glasgow. . .

> . . . as Jack White the Irishman, who wanted to be in on any possibility of a fight. John [Maclean] had been explaining marxist economics; the roof of the hall was broken off into segments, and he had the whole audience looking up at the roof and using it to sort out marxist categories. White stood up and said: 'Every time I come to Glasgow I feel like a child alongside the Clyde workers. The Clyde workers know all about economics. I know nothing about economics. In my opinion there's too damn much education and too little action.'[62]

He was the same 'Captain Jack R. White DSO, a Protestant Ulsterman', committed socialist and republican and founder member of the Irish Citizen Army during the Dublin lock-out, alongside James Connolly. It is important to note here White's familiarity both with Glasgow and the radical left. Twenty years after the Easter Rising Jack White was as completely committed as ever. Then based in London, he was dispatching illegal shipments of arms to the Spanish anarchists'.[63]

On Clydeside education was an essential area of activity and the fruits of that were self evident. Intellectual activity was not confined to Clydeside, through in Edinburgh 'Helen MacFarlane,

---

[61] p118 *History of the Chartist Movement 1837 - 1854* by R C. Gammage [facsimile edition by Merlin Press, London 1969]

[62] See p122 *No Mean Fighter*.

[63] See Stuart Christie's *The Albert Memorial: The Anarchist Life and Times of Albert Meltzer, 7 January 1920 – 7 May 1996* [The Meltzer Press 1997]

Window notice used in the 1915 Rent Strike.
From an original in the People's Palace.

In bygone days the Labour Party
supported many of the struggles fought by
working class people

[made] the first English translation of the *Communist Manifesto*.'

But the primacy of education was not a Scottish peculiarity. Education was central to the SDF at the wider British level and it was central to the socialist movement in general. The list of activists who attended classes run by the old SDF socialists contains legendary names on Clydeside and many of them became educators, as well as activists. Maclean and MacDougall came through the SDF educational tradition, as did McManus, Bell, James Messer and Willie Paul who also took classes on aspects of Marxian theory, and from Maclean's classes throughout central Scotland came a host of activists, some from the ILP, including Jimmy Maxton.

The need for appropriate literature was recognised. There was just about no left wing literature available. The early socialists had to do it themselves, not only the printing and publishing but the actual writing. In the latter years of the nineteenth century 'the Labour Literature Society established itself in premises in London Street. In the backshop they installed a printing machine and from this small beginning emerged. . . the Civic Press.'[64] Members of the ILP opened a bookshop in Bothwell Street, flitting to Buchanan Street when larger premises became necessary. Here they published pamphlets, the first by John Wheatley, entitled *How the Miners are Robbed*.[65]

Wheatley's father had been involved in the Irish National League and he himself read widely. Robert Blatchford rather than Karl Marx was his initial influence.[66] Apart from writers of the Rationalist Press, he seems to have read Tolstoy whose influence on the socialist v. religion debate extended worldwide. Could there be such a thing as a Catholic socialist? Many Christians thought so.

---

[64] William Martin Haddow, *My Seventy Years* p32

[65] *ibid.*

[66] p36 Middlemas said that 'Like most ILPers [Wheatley] read Marx critically, and though he accepted the theory of value he rejected the materialist conception of history.' But John Hannan, a biographer of Wheatley, dismisses this peremptorily; see p11. But in her biography of John Maclean, Nan Milton says that 'Wheatley was influenced by Marxist teaching, except by the materialist conception of history.' p47

In 1906 Wheatley formed the Catholic Socialist Society and also held meetings in his home, attended by young men mostly of an Irish Catholic background. Among them were McManus, Bell, Dollan, Willie Paul and John McGovern who met people of a background similar to their own, in particular James Connolly, Irish Scottish working class Catholic socialist republican.

Even arranging the order of those terms is a tendentious affair. This attempt to reconcile Christianity and socialism was attacked on all sides whether by Christians or by those who became or remained atheist.

Tom Bell argued that Wheatley was 'gathering. . . a large following of young Catholic workers and keeping them out of the main stream of the militant workers' movement, under the pretence of reconciling socialism with the Church.'[67] Wheatley's son replied that while Bell 'enjoyed the debates. . . [he] came to fear his host's ability to win over to the ILP cause waverers from the other socialist groups.'[68] Wheatley favoured the ILP and certainly opposed the abolition of all private property but he was a socialist all his days.

Political debates were extremely popular on Clydeside and people packed into the meetings. Given that 'the restriction of [CSS] membership to Catholics was reaffirmed'[69] many non-Catholics attended the larger meetings. One was the young Emmanuel Shinwell who was loudly critical of the attempted reconciliation of socialism and religion. At another meeting the talk was on 'Awakening Womanhood. . . [and] a Mrs J.D. Pearce [pleaded] not simply for the vote but for a society of true partnership between men and women. The *Glasgow Observer* noted the presence of 'many ladies in the audience on this occasion.'[70]

Tremendous pressure was brought to bear on socialist-inclined Catholics by the priesthood, and not simply spiritual. In Shettleston Wheatley's local priest promoted demonstrations against him.[71] Among Catholics there were spirited arguments for and against

---

[67] p79 *Pioneering Days* [also confirm that McManus went to these meetings]

[68] See Ian Wood's biography p43.

[69] *ibid.*

[70] p23 see Ian Wood's biography *ibid.* citing *The Glasgow Observer* 3O.11.1907

[71] *The Glasgow Observer, ibid.*

the CSS, and letters to and from newspapers. 'A considerable number of the opponents came from members of the teaching profession who were anxious to demonstrate their loyalty [to the Church] because they depended upon clerical favour for advancement.'[72]

Fighting his own corner in Ireland, Connolly had to contend not only with the clergy but with members of the independence movement, nationalists and republicans, who wished to steer clear of the socialist taint. His analytic response, here outlined by Peter Berresford Ellis could be offered generally:

> socialism was a practical and economic question, a
> science like pure mathematics, whose validity could be
> discussed without involving questions of theism, atheism
> or the dogmas of institutionalised Christianity. Politics. . .
> was a question of the stomach and not the brain.
> Socialism and religion could and must coexist.[73]

The argument remains of value, though nowadays a great many socialists reject it, as they rejected it then. James Maxton of the ILP thought. 'Socialism was a complete philosophy of life extending to all spheres of human relationships and with particular emphasis upon the development of human personality.' The anarchist Guy Aldred also rejected the attempt to reconcile socialism and Christianity. He argued that socialism and religion were mutually exclusive: 'socialism. . . was founded on a materialism which explained all abstract ideas and institutions in terms of mother earth. To embrace its teachings was to war against every myth 'from God to captains of industry.'[74] Aldred was much influenced by another Englishman, Richard Carlile, who spent ten years of his life imprisoned on charges relating to sedition and blasphemy. Back in 1820-21, while in prison Carlile essayed on 'the tyranny practised

---

[72] p35 McGovern, John; *Neither Fear Nor Favour* [Blandford Press 1960]

[73] p38 of Ellis's introduction to Connolly's *Selected Writings*, edited by Ellis himself [Pluto Press 1973]

[74] p117 number five of Aldred's *No Traitor's Gate! The Autobiography of Guy Aldred* in twelve monthly numbers [The Strickland Press 1956]

on Ireland by the English Government' and concluded that. . .

> nothing will seriously benefit her that does not root up
> every part of the system that degrades her, which may be
> brought under two heads, that of government and that
> of religion. . . [and] the Protestant Religion of Ireland is
> as bad as her Roman Catholic Religion, equally
> persecuting, equally degrading, equally pernicious to
> the minds of its followers.[75]

Neither Connolly, Wheatley, Maxton nor Maclean appears to have read Carlile. They might well have known of him but where would they have had access to his work? Eventually Aldred published some of it and wrote a biography of him, but he did not come to live in Glasgow until after the 1914-18 war. However, no matter what anti-socialist republicans, anti-socialist Christians or even anti-socialist atheists might have had to say on the subject, vital members of the radical and socialist movement were practising Christians. At the ILP celebrations following the 1922 General Election thousands sang *The Red Flag*, but finished with *The Lord's Prayer*, both Catholics and Protestants. And among the latter was the new MP for Glasgow-Gorbals, ex-Boys Brigade boy George Buchanan.

Among those who condemned Wheatley's project were a number of Catholic socialists. They thought formations like the CSS would split the socialist movement along sectarian lines. James Larkin was critical but later changed his mind. In 1906 he was in Scotland on behalf of the National Union of Dock Labourers (NUDL), sent north to organise the ports. Larkin had performed good work in Liverpool and lost his job in consequence. The NUDL had given him this temporary post. In Glasgow he met many people, and became friends with a few. He invited John Maclean to Nothern Ireland 'through the Belfast Socialist Society,'[76] to address the workers during a major industrial action.

This extraordinary strike had a lasting effect on Maclean. No wonder. During the summer of 1907 Larkin 'united the people of

---

[75] Robert Carlile p46 in his essay 'Ireland', in his *Jail Journal, and Other Writings*, edited and arranged by Guy Aldred [Strickland Press 1942]

[76] p34 Nan Milton's *John Maclean*

Belfast into an effective Labour movement. He had the Catholics and the Protestants, the Orangemen, Hibernians, republicans and socialists all marching together.'[77] It was one of the most significant strikes in British and Irish labour history. 'For generations before Larkin came into their city the working people of Belfast had been murdering and maiming one another in the name of religion.'[78] Not only were Catholic and Protestant workers now marching together, an Orange flute band was leading them off.

News of this would have astonished the whole of Ireland and Scotland, never mind the Glasgow socialists, 'against [whose] meetings. . . the delinquent wing of the Orange order campaigned vigorously and violently. . . '[79] The British State, the shipyard owners and other Loyalist authorities were aghast. They believed the Protestant working class was their property, the 'Orange card', to be dealt on behalf of the British ruling class wherever and whenever they chose.

But there had been one remarkable outcome to that first postwar General Election: across the Irish Sea, out 'of 105 seats Sinn Féin won 73 [thus] two-thirds of the people. . . had given a clear mandate for the affirmation of the 1916 Republic. . .'[80] And in accordance with that mandate the Sinn Féin MPs did not go to the 'London House of Commons', they formed their own government, Dáil Éireann.

It was a major victory for Sinn Féin and the republican movement and a tremendous blow against British Imperialism. It was a blow also to the supporters of Home Rule. Yet within the British State many authorities, including high-placed members of MI5, found it 'virtually impossible to distinguish between' the republican and Home Rule movements. That would have presented difficulties within Whitehall, given that Home Rule was the ILP position.

Only one year after Sinn Féin had formed Dáil Éireann, in accordance with the wishes of two thirds of the Irish electorate, the British authorities 'suppressed. . . [it] as an 'illegal assembly'. And they sent in the army to destroy the Irish bid for freedom; they

---

[77] Boyd, Andrew p79 *The Rise of the Irish Trade Unions* [Anvil Books 1972, reprint 1985]

[78] *ibid.*

[79] p34 in McShane *No Mean Fighter*

[80] p243 Peter Berresford Ellis's *A History of the Irish Working Class* [Braziller Inc. NY 1973]

'poured into Ireland, with tanks, armoured cars, motor lorries and other weapons.'[81]

Solidarity for the Irish people was expressed on Clydeside when thousands 'joined the campaign for a British withdrawal and an end to the excesses of Crown forces. . . ' Countess Markiewicz was the main speaker on a platform shared with John Maclean, John Wheatley and others. She had created her own history: the first woman ever elected to the House of Commons. As a member of the Sinn Féin contingent she never took up the seat.

That huge demonstration took place on Glasgow Green 'at the 1919 May Day Rally. . . when Irish tricolours were carried openly among a crowd of 100,000 and the 'Soldier's Song' was sung, as well as 'The Red Flag'.'[82] Maclean visited Dublin soon after and 'witnessed the solemn farce of 15,000 soldiers with bayonets fixed, machine guns and tanks, marching through the streets to celebrate peace. . . '[83] The city was full of spies and *agents provocateurs*. 'Everything conceivable has been done to stir the Irish to open rebellion. . . '[84] The army was waiting for any sign of revolt to crush the Irish people. It was this invasion that led to the birth of the Irish Republican Army, formed from the older Irish Volunteers, and the remnants of the socialist Irish Citizen Army.

It took until the next General Election to get rid of Barnes. This time, in 1922, there was no possibility of Maclean being selected by the Gorbals Labour group. He had been 'slipped out' from the BSP previously. The BSP and the SLP formed the nucleus of the new CPGB. Maclean opposed it. He was not alone in that but his was the most prominent name. But he still fought the Gorbals seat. Now as 'a Bolshevik, alias a Communist, alias a Revolutionist, alias a Marxist.'[85] A fair degree of solidarity existed within the Clydeside left but it was important to be clear about where you stood. In the final part of his election address he urged the Gorbals' voters: 'if you cannot agree with me then vote for George Buchanan.'[86] He

---

[81] *ibid.* p 247-9

[82] See p 29 Ian Wood's biography *John Wheatley.*

[83] p161 John Maclean, *In the Rapids of Revolution*

[84] *ibid.* p164

[85] *ibid.* p234

[86] *ibid.* p238

Arrests at the 1919 'Bloody Friday' demonstration in Glasgow.
Willie Gallacher is in bandages and David Kirkwood is held by police.

polled more than 4000 votes which was not a bad result in the circumstances.

By now Maclean had endured five terms of imprisonment and still had one to go. He had been granted political-prisoner status on the fifth occasion, thus food and clothing were allowed in from the outside. McShane organised that until he too was imprisoned. Jimmy Maxton of the ILP was supposed to take over the duties but it never worked properly because Maxton 'was never any good at organising.'[87] While in prison McShane had much to think about. He was impressed by the support given to prisoners by members of the newly formed Communist Party. When eventually released he had made the decision, he joined the Party. It caused a major breach between himself and Maclean, his close friend and comrade. A year later Maclean was dead, at the age of forty four. The photographs taken of him from this period show a man who looks twenty years older.

If the Gorbals electorate had returned Maclean in 1922 he would have taken the Sinn Féin route and not gone 'to the London House of Commons.' He would have stayed home and fought for 'a Scottish workers' republic.'[88] Most Scottish socialists favoured a form of self government. This had been the case since the early days of Keir Hardie and 'Don Roberto' Cunningham-Graham, although the latter moved from the Home Rule position to Scottish Nationalism. When the ILP 'introduced the Government of Scotland Bill' it was the new MP for Gorbals who performed the introduction.

Geordie Buchanan was a local man, and popular; ex-Boys Brigade, known for his prowess at billiards and his skills on the poker table.[89] While in London he, Maxton and Campbell Stephen shared digs for years. They were members of the ILP group that stormed Whitehall, winning ten out of fifteen Glasgow seats. Two Communists were returned as MPs that same year: 'Shapurji Saklatvala, a Bombay Parsee who won Battersea North. . . as an official Labour Party candidate [and] Walton Newbold. . . for

---

[87] according to McShane in *No Mean Fighter*

[88] p238 Maclean *In the Rapids of Revolution*

[89] See essay in *Scottish Labour Leaders 1918-39, A Biographical Dictionary* edited and introduced by William Knox [Mainstream 1984].

Motherwell' who stood 'as a Communist but without Labour opposition.'[90]

Buchanan had been a Councillor before going to Whitehall and had gained very useful experience 'representing the most impoverished and disabled of his constituents at welfare and pension tribunals. . . [and became] a master of the intricacies of the codes and regulations governing the payment of welfare benefits.'[91] Eventually he was 'accepted by the Labour Party and sometimes by the Government as the spokesman of the unemployed.'[92]

But he had to deal capably with the day-to-day issues confronting his constituents. One of whom was Harry McShane. The ILP man had the reputation of being 'fearless', except when it came to McShane.[93] He remained Gorbals MP until 1948. By then he had resigned from the ILP and become a member of the Labour Party. It was his acceptance of a ministerial position that caused the by-election that resulted in Hugh Savage becoming a paid official for the one and only time in his life.

Shortly before the 1922 election a final decision was taken to form the CPGB at a Unity Convention held in 1921. The two main parties were the BSP and the SLP. A cautionary note on the adulation then heaped upon Lenin was urged by Willie Paul, a well-kent figure from the 'impossibilist' days of the SDF: 'Lenin is no Pope or God.'[94]

Following an earlier Unity Convention in Glasgow comment appeared in the *Worker* published in October 1920, and the writer probably its editor John S. Clarke: 'It is fairly evident that to many Communists Russia is not a country to learn from, but a sacrosanct Holy of Holies to grovel before as a pious Mohammedan faces the Mecca in his prayers.'[95] Clarke's 'notion of socialism as a crusade of liberation made him among the first to be disenchanted with Russia as Stalin rose to power. . . He would ask questions such as: have peoples' lives become easier? do workers control production? are

---

[90] See p25 Pelling, Henry *The British Communist Party: A Historical Profile* [A & C Black Ltd. 1958]

[91] p71 Knox *op. cit.*

[92] p280 Middlemas *op. cit.*

[93] p190 Middlemas *op. cit.*

[94] p10 Pelling

[95] p11 Pelling cites *Worker* (Glasgow) 2 October 1920

they free from exploitation? When the answers he received were unsatisfactory he broke with his old pal Willie Gallacher.'[96]

After Lenin came Joseph Stalin but in the early 1920s, even before Lenin's death, the numbing intellectual control by Comintern was already being exercised. In fact it had been institutionalised: 'All the decisions of the congresses of the Communist International, as well as the decisions of its Executive Committee, are binding on all parties belonging to the Communist International.'[97] It was like a form of death to the intellect for radicals from the earlier period and a far cry from the great debates heard on Clydeside.

Nevertheless the CPGB 'reshaped' itself accordingly.[98] Sylvia Pankhurst's voice was one of the loudest in condemnation of what was happening. She was well-known on Clydeside and friendly with local socialists. She and Helen Crawfurd teamed up for the visit to Moscow in 1920 for the Second Congress of the Communist International. But as Hugh Savage tells us, Sylvia had other connections to the area, her brother lived in Glasgow and was known within the east end weaving community.

> I wonder how the owners of Strang's cotton-mills in Greenhead Street would have reacted if they had known that the well-spoken woman who spent some time with the weavers, taking sketches of them at their looms, was Sylvia Pankhurst and that the senior tenor in their mill was the brother of the famous – or infamous – suffragette, depending on your point of view.[99]

One grandfather of the Pankhurst children had been a cotton spinner in Salford, Lancashire. Their father Richard was a member of the ILP from the earliest years. Their mother was Emily. 'When other children were demanding a pretty doll or a lollipop. . . the cry of the Pankhurst children was 'Take me to a meeting!' '[100] Emily

---

[96] McShane in *No Mean Fighter*

[97] p18 Pelling, citing Degras (ed.) *C.I. Documents*, 1, 171

[98] p21 Pelling

[99] p91 Hugh Savage's *Born Up a Close*

[100] p106 Roger Fulford's *Votes for Women: the Story of a Struggle* [Faber & Faber 1958]

Pankhurst spoke at a meeting in Clydebank, chaired by the 'redoubtable' Jane Rae who had been to the fore at the great Singers' strike of 1911.

Sylvia Pankhurst was expelled from the CPGB. Meanwhile Comintern continued its criticism of 'the British party [where] there is a sort of special system which may be characterized thus: the party is a society of great friends.'[101]

But those forming the leadership of the party had come through much together and bonds forged through earlier struggle remained crucial. People like Maxton, Agnes and Paddy Dollan, Maclean and Wheatley were accorded respect. '[The] old Clydeside group, especially McManus, Campbell, and Bell, formed a hard core of influential officials, controlling the party with the assistance of. . . Albert Inkpin [and] a few newcomers. . . [including] Arthur Horner.' Other Clydeside party members were Helen Crawfurd, Willie Gallacher, Harry McShane and Willie Paul. They had to become accustomed to shifts in policy or tactics at a quite fundamental level, not to mention an organisational structure which was, quite literally, foreign. But some took to it, and most coped; very few resigned.

Although he was the CP's first Chairman Arthur McManus fails to rate one solitary mention in the most recent history of communism in Britain.[102] He occupies a primary position in the radical history of Clydeside. Following a period of imprisonment he died at the age of 38 and his ashes are buried in the Kremlin Wall. He was on the executive committee of Comintern but was already being seen as awkward, as somebody who asked questions. During the 1914-18 war, when James Larkin was domiciled in the US, he published the US edition of the *Irish Worker*. News from the Clydeside industrial and anti-war front reached US socialists through this and other channels.[103] One account published in a US socialist journal 'offered the observation that Arthur McManus and John Maclean stood 'at the left of the Left of the British Labour

---

[101] p46 Pelling

[102] Neither does Tom Bell rate a mention in *Under the Red Flag; a History of Communism in Britain* by Keith Laybourn & Dylan Murphy [Sutton Publishing Ltd. 1999].

[103] See p15-24 on James D. Young's Introduction to his *John Maclean, Clydeside Socialist* [Clydeside Press 1992].

Movement.'[104] His short life is the stuff of legend and it is suprising no biography of the man has been undertaken. Maybe it has and just never been published. His good friend Helen Crawfurd wrote her autobiography which exists in manuscript form only.[105]

By 1928 'the Comintern officials. . . were already fashioning an alternative leadership for the British party [and] wished in particular to reduce the influence of Campbell, who. . . had become the party's most prominent member, especially after the death of McManus in 1927.' The membership of the CP had peaked at nearly 11,000 the year before. From now on it dropped and did not recover until the outbreak of the Spanish Civil War.[106] Comintern sought to impose a more malleable leadership and made use of the Young Communist League 'which had assumed the role of Comintern watchdog.'[107] The older brigade did not capitulate at once but eventually were removed from power; one of their 'serious errors' was to have 'been too sympathetic to non-Communist 'left wingers' such as Maxton and [A.J.] Cook'[108] the miners' leader.

A new breed of party workers came to the fore and some would be employed as full-time officials. These were 'for the most part ambitious young men of working class origin who had never had any other political allegiance than that of International Communism. . . very different types from the Scottish artisans.'[109] Peter Kerrigan was one such. He became Scottish Secretary, National Organiser then Industrial Organiser. He had been Chairman of the Glasgow Central Strike Co-ordination Committee in 1926[110] then on the executive1927-29, 1931 to 1965. There were rumours about his conduct when 'a political commissar' during the Spanish Civil War and he was said to have taken part in some dubious practices.[111] John McGovern suggested 'that Peter Kerrigan was

---

[104] Crystal Eastman, sister of Max, cited by James D. Young p18 *ibid.*

[105] in Glasgow's Mitchell Library

[106] p192 Pelling's Appendix A

[107] p50 Pelling

[108] p51 Pelling, citing *Inprecorr*, ix, 885

[109] p51 Pelling

[110] Succeeding Jock McBain, another CP founder member.

[111] I heard this said about him myself, directly from Ned Donaldson.

never in the International Brigade, never fought in Spain and was there only representing the *Daily Worker*.' [112] However, Harry McShane went out of his way to refute the worst allegations.[113]

During the Spanish Civil War period 'the Catholic Church was speaking up for the. . . fascists' and McShane debated the issue on numerous occasions, including 'four. . . with H.W. Henderson around 1936.'[114] 'H.W.' was the brother of Arnold Henderson, a highly respected member of the CP and well-known on Clydeside. Hugh Savage came to know Arnold personally when he worked beside him on the Clyde. But his brother H.W. was editor of the right wing *Common Cause* magazine and wrote pamphlets and tracts such as *What Are Russia's Ultimate Aims?* He published the pamphlets himself, printed by Burns of Buccleuch Street, then publisher for the Roman Catholic church in Glasgow.

The 1939-45 war was a difficult period for CP members with its major shifts in policy. During the 1930s communists and the left in general had been to the fore in their denunciation of fascism. Many fought and died to defend the Spanish Republic. But now the Moscow hierarchy 'denounced the War as an imperialist war'. It caused consternation in Britain and the breaking of ranks in the most senior positions. Harry Pollitt, a paid official since the formation of the party, was relieved of his full-time position. The same happened to another veteran, John R. Campbell.

But the shift in policy was a grave problem for young activists like Hugh Savage. His 'first political activity as a new Communist was advancing the call for a People's Peace, with negotiations with Germany and Hitler.' Unfortunately most men around the Clyde shipyards, including communists, had relations, friends or acquaintances in the armed forces. Some had suffered bereavement. Now the CP was as good as telling them it was in vain and Hugh had to dodge when a heavy spanner was flung at his head.

Ironically, had this policy not then been in operation one of the turning points on Clydeside would not have occurred: the great apprentices' strike of 1941. Moscow's opposition to the war at that

---

[112] p113 McGovern, quoting Fred Copeman

[113] p233 *No Mean Fighter*

[114] See *No Mean Fighter*

particular period *allowed* the CP membership to support the striking apprentices.

Hugh downplays his own part in the strike. He was not an apprentice but a young journeyman plumber and welder, and his role was governed by that. Aged 23 he was close to the apprentices and pals with a few, including young communists like Johnnie Moore, a strike leader. Strategical matters were the business of the apprentices' own strike committee. Hugh is very clear on that point. However, he was crucially involved. This was demonstrated by the shameful behaviour of the British State, acting on behalf of the shipyard owners. Hugh and Johnnie Moore were conscripted into the army and destined for the front line. This happened to other militant workers when employers wanted rid of them. It made no difference that they worked in a prescribed industry. The political authorities were as attentive to the demands of big business then as they are now. Hugh had little doubt that he and Moore would have been killed had older and more experienced trade unionists not challenged the authorities on their behalf:

> I really did not suspect a thing if it had not been for the others, maybe especially when I saw the determination on Bob McLennan's face that morning and then when he said to us 'The bastards are not going to murder any workers from John Brown's.'[115]

The apprentices' strike of 1941 may have been the most significant industrial action during the war years but another took place in 1943-44, again on the Clyde. A youth by the name of Robert Lynn was involved. He was serving his time as an engineer in Yarrows shipyard. Unfortunately for him and the other striking apprentices, the 1943-44 dispute followed another 'complete turn-about in the Communist Party's policy'. The German army had advanced on Russia and the Moscow line immediately returned to 'resistance to Fascism'. Now 'the CP vied with the employees in the ferocity of their denunciation of workers taking industrial action'[116] and. . .

---

[115] See p179 Hugh Savage's *Born Up A Close*

[116] See p29 essay by Peter Bain and Tommy Gorman, 'Keeping the Home Fires Burning: the Albion Shop Stewards in the Second

entirely supported war production in favour of
increasing capitalist production [and] didn't support
strikes. . . By the end of the war the. . . Party was
completely tied up in supporting the Coalition
Government's policies [and] demanded the continuation
of a National Government including 'progressive' Tories
like Churchill and Eden [which] was an amazing
suggestion [because] Churchill had always been the
villain of the socialist movement.[117]

The apprentices who did not belong to the Communist Party
were left battling the shipyard employers on their own. The absence
of solidarity meant none of the Party's leading young members
could lend support to the strike, even though many were apprentices
themselves. Hugh never alludes to the 1943-44 strike in his *Memoir*.

But that turn-around in party policy had a long-standing affect
on the apprentices of the time. Lynn said that 'the Communist Party
. . . opposition alienated me and numerous other young people.'[118]
From then until his death he remained a stalwart of Glasgow's
anarchist network, a familiar figure around the Glasgow Cross and
Calton area.[119] Lynn was never a regular in the Workers City group
but he came along to a few of their activities. I met him on Glasgow
Green in the late 1990s, not long before he died. He was on his way
back from a Sunday Mayday. Other socialists too were leaving early.
The platform had been dominated mainly by Labour Party hacks
or trade union officials. When Workers City was around a couple of
years earlier Hugh and others had organised an open platform, so
anybody could speak, a most unusual concept then as now. They
also organised an alternative Mayday, one that took place on the
first working day of the month.

World War', in Fighting the Good Fight? Socialist History 7
[Pluto Press 1995].

[117] p236-38 *No Mean Fighter*

[118] 'Not a Life, Just a Leaf from it', essay by Robert Lynn; *Workers
City* [Clydeside Press 1988]

[119] See also Stuart Christie for further information on Lynn in Vol
1 his autobiography, *My Grannie Made Me An Anarchist: The
Christie File: Part 1, 1946-1964* [Christie Books 2002].

When Geordie Buchanan finally resigned the seat for Glasgow-Gorbals in 1948 the CPGB put up an unsuccessful fight against the next Labour candidate. The man whom the CP hierarchy selected as candidate was Peter Kerrigan. Hugh Savage became his election agent.

In that capacity Hugh was often in Gorbals and there met up with Harry McShane, then living in a room and kitchen flat attached to the local CP office. McShane was a nationally-known figure, and had been for twenty years. Within socialist circles he had been known as an activist for much longer than that. Until making McShane's acquaintance Hugh Savage described himself as 'a good wee Stalinist.' It is no exaggeration to say that the course of his life now altered. A friendship developed that lasted all of forty years, right until McShane's death at the age of 96.

Peter Kerrigan also had been involved in the Hunger Marches. He and McShane had known each other since the mid-1920s and the pair had collided on numerous occasions. At this late stage McShane remained a thorn in the flesh of the CP hierarchy, whereas Kerrigan had been a party man through and through. Another Irishman, Dominic Behan, brother of Brendan, lived in Glasgow for many years and tells of the time he, Freddie Anderson and Matt McGinn. . .

> noticing that the comrades in London had made a mistake in their all-embracing philosophies, went to London to put the matter to rights. At King Street we asked to see the leader to point out that the 'British Road to Socialism' said nothing about Maclean or self determination. And that grand old Scottish rebel, Peter Kerrigan, who had fought for the Spanish Republic, met us at the door and said 'Fuck off you chauvinist anti-British bastards!'[120]

The successful Labour candidate at the 1948 polls was Alice Cullen, nicknamed 'Silent Alice' through her ability to say nothing, a respected quality in Labour Party circles.

In 1950 Hugh Savage was nominated CP candidate for Dalmar-

---

[120] See his essay 'Call me Comrade', in *Workers City; the Real Glasgow Stands Up* [Clydeside Press 1988].

nock in the city's municipal elections. Two years later he, Leslie
Forster, Ned Donaldson, Matt McGinn and Bill McCulloch had
resigned from the Communist Party. McShane followed soon after.
Forster refers to one significant incident that had occured during

> . . . a keynote speech made by Bill Lauchlan, the Scottish
> Secretary. . . at a Scottish Congress of the CP held in
> Glasgow. When he finished his peroration, delegates
> stood up clapping again and again in praise of the
> Messiah. During this display of adoration Ned
> Donaldson and Hugh Savage remained seated. . . [121]

Such behaviour was seen as subversive. Anyone who asked the
'wrong' question was subversive.

Roundabout then Forster travelled to England as a delegate
from the building workers to the Trades Union Congress in Black-
pool. During the trip he palled up with two delegates from Glasgow,
one a Trotskyist the other an Anarchist. They had long conversations. What a freedom! It could not have happened at home. To
chat to another socialist who was not in the CP! Somebody who saw
the world differently yet still from a left perspective. It was exciting.
It had never happened before. Meeting left wing activists from
outside the party was an unusual event, being able to talk to them
was even more unusual, to discuss theoretical mattter was just not
done. The memory of the conversations Les Forster shared with
the two men stayed with him. He felt he 'owe[d] them a debt for
blowing the cobwebs from my mind.'[122]

Sectarianism among socialists, where it is not based on selfish
motivation or in blind allegiance to a leadership, can derive from
straight ignorance. But this ignorance is not necessarily the fault
of the individual.

But it was McShane's resignation that caused the furore. Even
in Scotland's populist press, news of it was carried as a front page
story. McShane was a journalist on the Communist *Daily Worker*
and a nationally-known figure, one of the more prominent Communists in the UK. His role on the Hunger Marches and within the
NUWM especially brought him to national prominence. He was

---

[121] See *Rocking the Boat* p50 [Clydeside Press 1996?].

[122] *ibid.* p50

now over 60 years of age and forced to seek manual work:

> For eight months after. . . I couldn't get a job. One was
> at a place I had applied to before the first world war,
> when I was put on a short-list of six out of fifty
> applicants [and] asked what school I went to; it was a
> Catholic school, and of course I didn't get the job. [Now]
> in 1953 they took me round and showed me the engine
> and I was quite entranced with the job. Then they asked
> me where I had been employed before and I said the
> *Daily Worker* – and that was it for the second time. . . [123]

It was a very difficult time for him financially and at one stage he had a run-in over a matter to do with pensions and the social security department of the time. He challenged the findings of the officials that had led to an unfair cut in his income and very soon a decision came in his favour. The decision had come from the very top, and the man who held the top ministerial post at that time was his old adversary, Geordie Buchanan.

The resignations of the group caused a sensation in left wing circles. Les Forster tells of 'a meeting in Bill McCulloch's house, along with Hugh Savage, Matt McGinn, Harry McShane. . . we were paid a visit by the Trotskyist leader Gerry Healy. . . to recruit every one of us into his Movement. He even had in his pocket a Press statement, announcing that we had thrown in our lot with The Workers' Revolutionary Party.'[124] They met with bitter hostility from the CP itself. Forty years later they still faced hostility. And exactly the same question was being put to them: 'Why did you leave the Party?' Such 'disloyalty' was unforgiveable. Meanwhile others on the left were condemning the group as Stalinists. For the purposes of this *Memoir* there is included as its final section an essay Hugh wrote for a commemorative work on McShane.[125]

1948 was the same year Eric Heffer was expelled from the CPGB. He wrote to McShane following his resignation. . .

---

[123] p255 *No Mean Fighter*

[124] p60 Forster *Rocking the Boat*

[125] *Militant Worker, Labour and Class Conflict on the Clyde 1900 - 1950, Essays in Honour of Harry McShane [1891-1988]*, edited by Robert Duncan and Arthur McIvor [John Donald 1992]

> indicating that I agreed with his public statement and
> [McShane] came down to Liverpool and stayed a few
> days at my house. . . Harry [had] left the CP with a
> number of younger colleagues and they formed the
> Clyde Socialist Action Group. On Merseyside a number
> of us had got together and we had formed the Socialist
> Educational Group. . . comrades like I. P. Hughes, Neil
> Beresford, R. G. Bale and S. Sheldon. When Harry
> came. . . we discussed the political situation and what we
> thought should be done. We agreed that efforts should
> be made to get the various groups together and that we
> should organise a conference to this end in Liverpool.
> This was ultimately held on 17 – 18 July 1954.[126]

At the age of 63 McShane was 'back on the tools'. He returned to Marx, especially the first volume of *Kapital*, to look at things on the basic level again. Surely 'Marxism was nothing if not a theory of liberation' and has to offer working class people a different way of living. McShane was a great reader of Adam Smith. In Hugh's effects was a well-thumbed copy of an essay by Ronald Meek. In it Meek comments on Adam Smith that 'the more narrowly economic views of *The Wealth of Nations* have usually been emphasised at the expense of the general sociological system of which they were essentially a part.'[127] It is consistent with McShane's argument on the need to remember the humanist side of Marxism.

In USA the philosopher Raya Dunayevskaya had been developing her own thinking, '[showing] Humanism to be the red thread connecting all four decades of Marx's development. . . ' McShane was intrigued by her ideas and corresponded with her: 'I kept reading all I could get my hands on and finally came to the conclusion that you were correct.'[128]

> The preoccupation with what Leon Trotsky called 'the
> small coin of concrete questions' has ever been the road

---

[126] *ibid.* p20-21

[127] Ronald L. Meek's article was published in pamphlet form in the mid-1950s.

[128] See p8-9 Peter Hudis *Harry McShane and the Scottish Roots of Marxist-Humanism* [John Maclean Society 1993]

away, not from the Mystical Absolutes of Hegel, but from the revolutionary principles of Marx. It was so during the life of the Second International. It characterized the Third International following the death of Lenin. The theoretic void in the Marxist movement has persisted to this day, when mindless activism thinks it is the answer to today's hunger for theory. . . It has always been my belief that in our age theory can develop fully only when grounded in what the masses themselves are doing and thinking.[129]

The correspondence between McShane and Dunayevskaya endured from 1959 until 1983 and provides the core of The Harry McShane Collection 1959-1988: Scottish Marxist-Humanism's Development in Dialogue with Raya Dunayevskaya, which is deposited at The National Museum of Labour History in Manchester.

Dunayevskaya, former secretary of Trotsky, was Chairperson of *News and Letters* Committees and occasionally, when in Britain, she stayed at Hugh Savage's home in the east end of Glasgow. Amongst Hugh's personal effects is her card of condolence following the tragic death of his youngest son.

In recent years good work has been done in reclaiming aspects of Clydeside's radical history. Of course the history-revision industry is also an employer. Some have 'denied the existence of Red Clydeside', which is rather a peculiar action. Others have denied the deniers. This debate is little more than a red herring and takes us from the history itself. It is of more value to get a proper line on that. Nor should we let the academics do it alone, even well-intentioned academics, those whose quackatatory travails in paradigmatic and contextual connotatory provinces can leave the rest of us gasping.

For people such as Savage, McLaren, Forster and their contemporaries the socialist tradition was fundamental; without a good working knowledge of this, really, there was no place to go. There in an extensive bibliography offered here and other sources should be accessed.

---

[129] See Dunayevskaya's introduction to her Philosophy and Revolution; From Hegel to Sartre, and from Marx to Mao [Delacorte Press, 1973].

On a personal level Hugh Savage had a great regard for performance art-forms like music and drama, and a fondness for
show-business and show-business characters. He enjoyed anecdotes
and stories about individuals, whether hearing them or narrating
them. He was known also for his 'strong tongue' and you were
advised not to get on the wrong end of it. On one occasion a
newspaper carried a report on a confrontation the City administration had suffered with Workers City; the headline read 'Savaged'.

He had another close friend, close canine friend. Even for a
Rotweiler Rory was massive. Hugh had trained the dog to be
suspicious of anybody wearing a suit. That helped when Poll Tax
officers and other authority figures came unannounced to the door.
Also the Rotweiler was prone to jealousy. If anybody looked twice at
his pal one of those deep gurgling growls came from the dog's
throat. It was a distinctive gurgle, like the last drops of some poor
guy's blood swirling about. On one occasion during the Workers
City days *The Keelie* was targeting suspected political corruption in
a Glasgow district. It was rumoured that a few heavies were going
to disrupt one of the editorial meetings and sort everybody out.
Hugh shrugged. When the night arrived he brought along Rory.
When the heavy squad came in he would shut the door and let
loose the dog. None of the local heavy squad arrived so who knows
what would have happened.

On occasion one had to travel as a passenger in Hughie's car;
humans on the front seat, Rotweilers to the rear. And the tongue
lolling a few inches from your neck. If forced to speak you tried to
do so without moving your jaw. His method of restraining the dog
was to call at him and grasp him by the neck. He was a strong man
but in view of his age there was an outside chance he might be
unable to restrain Rory's almighty lungings.

I included footnotes to his *Memoir* to give additional detail to
the political context, and a bibliography that contains material
readers unfamiliar with local radical history will want to discover
for themselves. Like his close friend Leslie Forster, Hugh's conversation was crammed full of the names of known and unknown
socialists. Their knowledge has been inspirational for myself.

Leslie has been a constant support throughout the long period
I took to deliver the finished work. Other friends who have aided
its progress include Laureen and Scott Savage who found patience

to cope with the delays; also my wife Marie, Tommy Gorman, Brendan McLaughlin, Euan Sutherland, William Clark and the late Ned Donaldson.

Many of the books used in reference come from Hugh's own library and this includes some from James McLaren's fine collection. McLaren died from tuberculosis back in 1947, still in his 20s. Included in the addenda is a short section on him. He and Leslie Forster belonged to the Central Branch of the CPGB. McLaren was a high-flyer and already holding office. He was Treasurer to the City Communist Party Committee while Secretary of his local branch, and an all-round activist according to his friends: organiser, motivator, orator, campaigner, as well as theoretician and educator. Hugh cherished scraps of his friend's lecture notes and commentaries.

Hugh wanted a title for his *Memoir* that would detract from the idea that he himself was of any importance and suggested we call it, 'Born Up a Close' for that very reason. Les Forster disagreed vehemently and chose a quotation from Thomas Paine, and Tommy Gorman backed him up. But finally we remained with Hugh's original choice.

It nagged at Hugh he was writing such a thing. His life was no more worthy than anybody else's. He described himself as a 'footsoldier'. Sometimes he was reluctant to discuss the project, it embarassed him. At rare times it excited him. The political years during World War II is of obvious interest but so too is the story of Hughie's early years. It is a fine account of what it was to be an ordinary boy growing up in the 1920s and 30s. He had little interest in his own feelings, at least not in print. This account of his early years was never to do with his importance or otherwise, it was for the historical record; it is the information that is crucial, part of our radical history here on Clydeside.

Born up a Close

memoirs of a Brigton Boy

Blessed are those that expect nothing
because they won't be disappointed

Eugene Debs

PREFACE

I T WAS not without a great deal of persuasion that I decided to put my experiences into print, going back over a fifty year period in the social, industrial and political field. I am not a great writer, not even a writer at all, but it is time the voices of the footsloggers were heard rather than the generals. Like hundreds of other workers I never had the ambition nor desire to be any kind of leader. It was always exhilarating for me when the ordinary working class won even a small victory over the employing class, more so when there was an advance of democratic rights.

My philosophy has always been that the struggle to emancipate the people from the rotten and corrupt chains of the present system is greater than the personality or ambition of any leader, or any party, or indeed any government. I have the greatest hatred for a system that denies there is any such thing as society in the real sense of what that means; a system that denies responsibility for millions of unemployed people, that accepts no liability for a million homeless people, that discards school-leavers, forcing them onto the scrapheap without any means of support, that deprives old-age pensioners of more than £80 million by changing the method of assessment so that eleven million pensioners now have the lowest pensions in Europe. It is a system that shows absolutely no concern for the health of the people, no concern that diseases such as tuberculosis are once more back on the agenda, that practises the philosophy of greed and encourages the triumph of the powerful. Those responsible have squandered our oil and gas resources before selling them to their friends in the city, creating private monopolies in Telecommunications, Gas, Water and Electricity.

These are the same Houses of Parliament that legalised the plundering of a quarter of the world's territories, colonised India, Australia, Canada, the West Indies and America. They enslaved millions of African people, took them in chains to their plantations in the American continent. Ethnic cleansing did not begin with Hitler, Stalin or in the former Yugoslavia, the British aristocracy and ruling class started it more than two hundred years ago – ask the Scottish, Irish and Welsh people. Not only did they steal whole countries and continents they now stand exposed as having sent children from Britain after World War I to Australia, New Zealand and Canada, both to work on farms as slave labour while at the same time trying to populate these colonies with 'good white people'.

The most damning hypocrisy of all came from the various religious orders, churches and organisations who participated in enslaving whole nations. They blessed the troops before they went abroad to plunder the world, and built their churches on the captured soil. Christian organisations were further entangled in schemes to steal these young children and the deceit they used cannot be allowed to be covered up. The same organisations wonder why people have turned their backs on religion, why a variety of denominations and churches are closing down, why there is such a dearth of priests within the Roman Catholic church, why many of those who begin fail to complete their training.

After such damning exposure of religion down through the centuries one would think another way could be tried by people. What is wrong with the humanism of the early socialists, the syndicalists who preached cooperation rather than confrontation, those who sought truth rather than miracles. Along with religion, nationality and race have been used deliberately to divide and keep people apart.

Above all I despise the so-called Labour leaders who give credibility to a corrupt parliamentary system. This system only functions because the Loyal Opposition participates, giving the cloak of respectability to reactionary laws that have set the Labour movement back by a hundred years or more. Is it not a fact that the purpose of creating the Labour Party was to abolish capitalism, not to save it? One thing is for sure, it was never intended that the workers should make sacrifices to defend a system that robs them from the cradle to the grave.

I am a Marxist and was a member of the Communist Party for a number of years, and some reference has been made here to Russia. While I was educated at the various classes I attended after joining the Party, I was never happy about the continual worship of everything that emanated from there. I joined the Party through struggle, because I believed its members were involved in fighting for the working class, and I had difficulty in defending aspects of Russian policy. I did not visit Russia and never had the inclination to do so. But hundreds of thousands, maybe millions, of trade union delegates and party members did do so, and returned lavishing praise on its achievements. I wonder what they have to say at the present time? We became familiar with the following quotation of Lenin. How does it stand now in light of the collapse of the Soviet Union?

> Man's dearest possession is life, therefore you must so live as to feel no torturing regrets for years without purpose, so live that you can say all my life is dedicated to the liberation of mankind.

Hugh Savage with Rory

Photo taken outside in the street at the conference of the
Socialist Labour Party in Edinburgh in 1935. Note the street children
at either side of the member group. Glasgow was a major centre of activists in
the SLP.

Part I

LOCAL HISTORY, FAMILY HISTORY

BRIGTON (or Bridgeton) is one of the oldest districts in Glasgow and many city institutions began there. In 1461 James Lord Hamilton bestowed a grant of property and Glasgow University was created on the site which is nowadays the disused College goods station, right on the Bridgeton boundary. It is ironic that James Watt, inventor of the steam engine, had a workshop within its halls. The university survived the ravages of the Reformation and in later years Professor Adam Smith taught there. The rafters in the old Common Hall rang to the voices of the famous, and Lord Rectors Burke, Peel and Macaulay addressed the students.

While James Watt was born in Greenock he will always be associated with Glasgow Green, one of the oldest common greens[1] in the land. It is generally accepted that the grant by James II to Bishop Turnbull in 1450 was the beginning of Glasgow Green as we know it today. But there is evidence that the tract of ground known as Kinclaith was church property prior to 1116 and was used by the people as a common green. Kinclaith is opposite Monteith Row – now Weavers' Court – and reaches down to the Clyde, lying between the Doulton Fountain and the gymnasium, extending north to Charlotte Street via the People's Palace.

James Watt first visited Glasgow at the age of 13. Later he started as an apprentice spectacle-maker and set up business in the Saltmarket, selling maps and making fiddles, flutes and guitars. He did not have an ear for music although he was familiar with harmony. He could turn his hand to anything and among other work was commissioned to build a barrel-organ for a Masonic Lodge. In 1766 he built an organ for St. Andrews Church. It was only used

---

[1] The Records of Glasgow Green are among the oldest existing records of Glasgow. The earliest known document is the *Notitia*, or Inquest of David, attested before the judges in the year 1120. (see John Taylor Caldwell's essay 'The Battle for the Green' contained in the *Workers City* anthology.)

once, on the 23rd August 1807, when it was interdicted by the Presbytery. The invitation of Adam Smith for Watt to occupy a small building on the grounds of Glasgow University in High Street was extremely important. It was there he met Joseph Black, lecturer in chemistry. Black's discovery of the principle of latent heat could be held to have led to the breakthrough for Watt's theory of a separate condenser which resulted in the successful invention of his steam engine.

Bridgeton was an industrial district. The growth of the Colonial trade and influence of Glasgow's merchants saw the booming imports of raw materials like tobacco and cotton which, in the eighteenth century, led to a tremendous growth of factories and weaving mills. Apart from the district of Anderston there were more cotton mills in Brigton than anywhere else in the city. Later more industries arrived, names like Beardmore's and Dixon's iron and steel manufacturers; White's chemical works, Mavor and Coulson's engineers, Sir William Arrol's bridge builders, Templeton's carpet-makers; along with leather works like Dick's balata belts, the Scotia works in Boden Street etc. All were within walking distance of the thousands of workers pouring into the city from the Scottish Highlands and from Ireland.

The population of Glasgow rose from 42,832 in 1780 to 274,324 in 1841, a large proportion of whom were Irish refugees escaping from the Famine. It was reported that of the 1000 destitute people sleeping on the streets 30% were Irish. The Irish population in the Calton in 1819 was 21.73% and in Bridgeton 12.1%. People from other parts of Scotland amounted to 54.84% of the Calton population and 40.59% in Bridgeton. The living conditions of the people in the city's east end were described in the following terms:

> I have seen human degradation in some of its worst
> phases both in England and abroad, but I can advisedly
> say that I did not believe, until I visited the wynds of
> Glasgow, that so large an amount of filth, crime, misery
> and disease existed on one spot in any civilised country.[2]

The Gallowgate was first mentioned in 1325 and in 1544 the

---

[2] The source of this quotation is lost but it may have been Dr. J.B. Russell, Glasgow's Medical Officer of Health, see p76

Battle of the Butts took place on the ground occupied by the old Barracks and the Cattle Market to the north of the Calton. The Earls Lennox and Glencairn, supported by the townsmen, fought against the Earl of Arran's army. Three hundred were killed on either side and sixteen leading citizens were hanged afterwards. At the Battle of Vittria in 1813, during the Indian campaign, Colonel Cadogan led the HLI regiment (the Highland Light Infantry) with the cry: 'Come on lads, charge them down the Gallowgate.'

As early as 1175 King William the Lion opened a market at the Glasgow Cross end of Gallowgate, and another later on the old Glasgow Green, between Saltmarket and Stockwell bridges. A painting by William Walton of the fair held there could be seen hanging in the Banqueting Hall in the City Chambers.

The Calton (which means Hazel-grove) is one of the oldest districts in Glasgow and was first named in 1722. Its original name was Blackfaulds and until the Glasgow Council development around 1977 there was a street of that name facing Abercromby Street. Although small, this was one of the busiest streets in the Calton, housing the premises of Dunn & Moore, the soft drinks' manufacturer. It ran into Canning Street which nowadays is called London Road.

The lands of Blackfaulds were owned by the church until annexed by the Crown in 1587, passing through several hands before reaching John Walkinshaw, a Renfrewshire laird. Walkinshaw's daughter was the famous Clementina, mistress of Bonnie Prince Charlie and she went to France in 1745. John Walkinshaw's grandfather was imprisoned during the 1715 rising.

There was a Calton Loch adjacent to Hunter Street and the rear of the old Glasgow University. Hayracks were seen in the Trongate in 1795 and as late as 1890 pigs wandered Tontine Close. The boundaries of the Calton village were indefinite but in 1817 George III granted a charter to Esther and Martha Ray, and Robert and William Pollock, creating the Calton into a Barony, but not of Regality.

In 1819 Mile End was annexed to the Calton by an Act of Parliament, then in 1846 the Calton was itself annexed to Glasgow. There had been four Provosts during the time: Robert Struthers, a Calton brewer; Nathaniel Stevenson who held office for 21 years; and Robert Bartholemew and Robert Bankier were the others. The

Burgh Buildings stood at the corner of Struthers Street and Stevenson Street. The Provost's House, a substantial two storey building, was situated in James Street. Later it became a stable and it stood until 1930 when it was burned down. I was there the night it happened and will never forget the screams of the poor horses trapped in the blaze.

The demand for political reform was taking shape in 1793. Thomas Muir, Advocate of Huntershill and born in the High Street, was tried for sedition then transported to Botany Bay. The Calton was a village of weavers in the late eighteenth century and when the mill-owners introduced a massive wage-cut which, in some cases, meant pay was halved, there were strikes and demonstrations. On the order of Provost Liddell troops were called out under the command of a Colonel Kellet. The Riot Act was read and the soldiers opened fire, killing six weavers and seriously wounding twenty; dozens of others were injured.

No history of the Calton could ever be written without reference to this.[3] It was one of the most vile acts against workers in a long history of foul deeds. The weavers' only crime was to defend themselves against the wage-cuts carried out by the mill-owners. In 1787 they marched down Barrack Street in an orderly procession to demonstrate their opposition, only to be met by the military. Three of the dead were buried in the old Calton cemetry in Abercromby Street.

Provost Liddell was a prominent merchant of the day and his uncle was John Glassford of Douglaston, probably the most famous merchant in the city. After Colonel Kellet's brave act of shooting into a crowd of unarmed workers Provost Liddell deemed it appropriate to give him the Freedom of the City of Glasgow, and he granted all the troops a toddy and a free pair of boots and stockings.

The Calton Weavers have become legends in the trade union movement for laying down their lives for a basic human right. Memorial stones were erected in the old Calton cemetery.[4] They have been renovated and renewed down through the years by the

---

[3] See the Calton Weavers' Memorial 1787: the first recorded industrial strike in the history of Glasgow [pamphlet published by Glasgow District Trades Council, 1957]

[4] In 1991 another commemoration took place in the old Calton Cemetry at Abercrombie Street, led by Hugh Savage on behalf of the Friends of the People's Palace who had been instrumental in raising the funds for a commemorative stone.

Glasgow Trades Council and the Friends of the People's Palace. This brave movement of weavers and other workers later on led to one weaver by the name of Andrew McKinlay being arrested in 1817 and charged with treason. His trial in Edinburgh came to an abrupt end when it was seen to be a conspiracy led by spies of the state.[5] The Rising of 1820 was a real threat to the state authorities and the weavers played a central part in that.[6]

The biggest social problem in Glasgow has been bad housing. For a period of more than a hundred years successive local councils and governments not only failed to solve it, they made no attempt to tackle it. The only politician of any stature was John Wheatley, MP for Shettleston.[7] He succeeded in getting basic housing legis-

---

[5] Lord Cockburn refers to 'the case of McKinlay' in *Trials for Sedition in Scotland*, Vol. 1 p244 (Douglas, Edinburgh 1888 in two volumes; reprinted as one by Augustus M. Kelley, 1970).

[6] During the Scottish Insurrection, the Strathaven weavers and other radicals were much to the fore, including 63 year old James Wilson who was executed by the authorities at Glasgow Green in 1820. The other two weavers were executed at Stirling; Andrew Hardie from the Townhead area of Glasgow and John Baird from Condorret. See the seminal *The Scottish Insurrection of 1820*, by Peter Berresford Ellis and Seamus Mac a'Ghobbainn [Pluto Press 1971]

[7] John Wheatley (1869-1930) was born in Co. Waterford, Ireland; his family moved to Scotland in the same year and he was brought up in Bargeddie. 'Maxton was an orator and nothing more; it was Wheatley who had actually built the ILP in Glasgow. . . None of the [Clyde Workers' Committee] shop stewards ever criticised him – he was the only man in the ILP who was never attacked by the revolutionary left – because he did a lot of work behind the scenes for them.' [McShane in *No Mean Fighter* p198].
But later others were critical of Wheatley, his support for Davie Kirkwood at the expense of the other six Clydeside shop stewards, following their deportation from Glasgow in 1916; his lack of support for John Maclean during the latter days of his imprisonment. Leon Trotsky was dismissive, condemning Wheatley alongside David Kirkwood and George Lansbury; that 'their radicalism is bounded by democracy and religion, and poisoned with a national conceit that completely subjects them to the British bourgeoisie.' see Raymond Ross *Trotsky Among the Scots*, published in *Cenrastus* 28 in which he explores Leon Trotsky's connections with Scotland.

lation through the House of Commons which allowed local authorities to address the problem.

At one time if you walked from Glasgow Cross along the southside of the Gallowgate beyond Moir Street you would have come to several large openings in the grey sandstone tenements. These were called 'pens'. At the back of them you would have seen as many as four closes leading to three landings, with six or four doors on each. In one particular pen – locals called it the 'Pudding Pen' – at least a hundred people resided, including children and pensioners. It happened a lot. Tenements were built directly in front of the older buildings, they became known as 'back loans'.

Hundreds of them abounded in Brigton and Calton. Most of the ground floors were single-ends and the people had to burn light night and day because no daylight, let alone sunlight, ever came through any windows. Their backcourts were very small. In a whole number of cases the middens were pressed right up against the ground floor windows, so there were all kinds of vermin, the houses were rat-infested.

Despite the efforts of the tenants the insides of these hovels were horrific. Some of the single-ends hardly measured 8 ft by 4 ft. They had set-in beds which in some cases slept two adults and four children. Some set-in beds had a door that could be shut. In 1818 typhus fever raged unchecked for a year and raised the death-rate for the city 42% higher than the average for the previous five years. Cholera first appeared in Glasgow in 1832. The virulence of the disease terrified people. In the Albion Street cholera hospital 79% of all victims died and three thousand people died between February and November. In the whole of the city south of the river there was only one doctor, and none at all in either Brigton or the Calton. In his report on the children whose deaths were so numerous, Dr. J. B. Russell, Glasgow's Medical Officer of Health at that time, stated:

> Their little bodies were laid on a table or a dresser so as
> to be somewhat out of the way of their brothers and
> sisters who play and sleep and eat in their ghastly
> company. From beginning to rapid-ending the lives of
> these children are short. One in every five of those who
> are born there never see the end of their first year.

The most important pastime for a large section of the working class was social drinking in public houses. This was as true in Brigton or Calton as it was elsewhere. According to G. B. Wilson (quoted by T.C. Smout in his *A Century of the Scottish People 1830–1950*) the average consumption of spirits between 1830 and 1839 was 2.55 proof gallons per head of population per year. Considering the terrible housing conditions – the worst in Europe – it is not too surprising that drink might have been seen as an escape.

It is also true that Brigton and the Calton had the largest number of public houses in Glasgow so the people would not have had to travel far for a drink. In most streets and particularly the main roads there was said to be a pub at every lamp-post. There certainly was one at nearly every corner. My father told me that between Glasgow Cross and Parkhead Cross there were at least one hundred and fifteen. There were five pubs in my own street alone which was only about 900 yards long, and less than 20 yards away London Road had another ten. And of course it was never difficult to find a drink in any of the tens of dozens of shebeens in the district.

It may seem a contradiction to some but the growth of the Chartist movement in the Glasgow of 1838 also saw a growth in awareness of the evils of alcohol. On Monday 21st May there was a Chartist demonstration in Glasgow Green that drew a crowd of 200,000. Seventy trades unions marched in that procession. All public works were stopped. One newspaper sympathetic to the Chartists said that if Parliament refused to hearken to the call of the unenfranchised then the people would 'abstain from all liquor and tobacco and thus cripple Government revenue'.[8]

---

[8] There were two journals based in Glasgow around this period, the *Scottish Patriot* and the *Scottish Chartist Circular* but Hugh Savage may be referring to the earlier, *The True Scotsman*, which was Edinburgh-based. In his *History of the Chartist Movement 1837–1854* (facsimile edition by Merlin Press,1969) R. C. Gammage tells us that: 'Edinburgh the seat of learning and refinement was determined not to lag behind in so important a matter as that of the Press. There was not a democratic paper in Scotland and it supplied the deficiency. A journal marked by respectable talent and of imposing appearance, was started under the editorial management of Mr. John Fraser, an inhabitant of that city; it bore the title of *The True Scotsman*. It devoted itself more particularly to a record of the movements of the Scottish Democracy. With respect to the questions of moral and physical force, it was the exact counterpart of the *London Despatch*.'

Alongside this agitation grew a strong temperance movement.[9] Temperance hotels began and the Chartist leader Robert Cranston began the temperance tea-rooms which lasted over a hundred years. Most of the religions played a part, except the Roman Catholic Church which remained aloof. There were individual exceptions. One Catholic priest, Father Theobald Matthews, was a passionate supporter of the temperance cause and in 1842 he addressed 30,000 people at Glasgow Green. While the non-Catholic churches led the temperance movement in Scotland the skilled craftsmen and their trades unions played a large part from among the working class.

There were Chartist shops and Chartist churches and hundreds of demonstrations and working class people were hearing alternative voices. One of the greatest was Bronterre O'Brien who once spoke to an assembly of 10,000 at Monkton Moor in Fifeshire.[10]

---

[9] In 1829 Glasgow saw 'the first Temperance Society in Britain, founded in Maryhill by John Dunlop, an unpopular absentee landlord and Mary Hill's grandson.' (see Guthrie Hutton's Introduction to his *Old Maryhill*, published by Richard Stenlake, 1994)

[10] James Bronterre O'Brien (1805-?), editor of the radical journal *The Operative*; see Gammage for some good information, in particular Chapter IV(p19): 'a man of great and singular talents. He had for many years been before the public. . . and had contributed a larger share in moulding the minds of the British Democrats than any other public writer (p77) . . . he detained his audiences longer than any other public speaker. Three hours was about the usual time he occupied a meeting; but he sometimes spoke for four, and even five, hours. . . ' He also spoke on Glasgow Green, once to an extraordinary assembly of around 130,000. At nearly every sentence [he] drew forth a burst of laughter or cheering, or both. . . [then advised the audience that] he would not give a fig for all their clamouring and clapping of hands, unless [they] were prepared to do something effective. . . ' (p118)

THAT YOUR family and your environment are fundamental to your development into manhood and your socialisation goes without saying. I was born after the first World War into a family of two girls and two boys. My father was a railway worker employed by Wordie Ltd., a subsidiary of the LMS, the London Midland & Scottish Railways. He was a carter to begin with but later on he became a checker in the goods' yard at the old Buchanan Street Station. He was a staunch Roman Catholic, attending Sacred Heart chapel every Sunday. My mother had been a cotton weaver in a few mills in the east end of Glasgow. When I arrived she worked in Wilson's, alongside her sister Jean who died when I was quite young. My sister Peggy worked there too. The mill was around the corner from our house in 118 Bernard Street. It was owned by the Shaw family who acquired a great deal of fame through one of their sons, G. D. Wilson, one of the greatest rugby players seen in Scotland.

My paternal grandparents came from the north of Ireland in the 1850s, among the thousands that flocked to Scotland to escape from the collapse of the agrarian economy and the potato famine. But they seemed to prosper in Glasgow and had a small fish and chip shop in French Street, right in the heart of the cotton mills. Our family stayed in Solway Street in those days, just round the corner. This was before I was born. I never met them and have no recollection of them. I don't think they were tycoons as the only one of the two girls and three sons that made up their family who did not take up a manual job was my Uncle Hugh whom apparently I'm called after. My maternal grandparents' family came from the north of Scotland much earlier, fleeing from the Highland Clearances so the roots of my working class background were deeply entrenched.

My father was the eldest son. Including my Uncle Hugh he had two brothers and two sisters. His other brother James lived in Canning Street. They were not close but we did get visits from James's two sons, and he also had at least one daughter. She was engaged to be married to George Geddes Junior, son of the famous

Georgie Geddes who founded the Humane Society, responsible for rescuing people in difficulty both in the River Clyde and other waters in and around Glasgow.

The death of George Junior was one of the worst tragedies in Glasgow. Apparently a woman had tried to drown herself by jumping from the suspension bridge in the Glasgow Green. Young George managed to get a hold of her from the boat but she was quite a heavy woman and they were drifting near the wear gates. He jumped into the water to try to lift her in but she immediately grabbed hold of him round the neck and despite him being a champion swimmer she pulled him under. They were sucked towards the wear and both were drowned. Despite that old Georgie Geddes carried on with the rescue service well into his eighties.

My father kept in touch with his family from time to time and he usually took me along to their nice corporation house in Riddrie. I thought that anyone who had a garden lived in a palace as the nearest grass we saw was the Glasgow Green half a mile away. My mother never came as she never went anywhere with my father, although she did feel that my Auntie Agnes was a bit of a snob. My dad's eldest sister Mary stayed in the house and she was a very nice person. She was a mistress [supervisor] in Strang's mill in Greenhead Street and was a sweet lady. She was a regular visitor at our house in Bernard Street and she never missed giving us all a penny. I faintly remember visiting my Uncle Hugh's house in Riddrie and the frosty atmosphere there, you were hardly allowed to leave your chair and I do not recall ever being spoken to by either aunt and my uncle or any of his family. Although I was named after him and all our family went to Sacred Heart school in Bridgeton where he was a teacher – my sisters Peggy and Elizabeth were in his class – he never acknowledged our presence. There was always an air of superiority about him. Many years later when my father died, the very night his body was being taken to the Chapel, Uncle Hugh came to our close but he waited at the bottom and didn't come up to the house. He never did enter our house. Yet if the older members of his family had not taken ordinary jobs to supplement the family income my grandparents could not have afforded the fees to put him through university.

However I most certainly remember my Granny Scott, my mother's mum who lived further along Bernard Street. She had been widowed very young. My grandfather was called Walter Scott, he became the chief superintendent at the Philadelphia gas works in America. Their son, my uncle Andrew, was only a baby when Walter was killed outright by an explosion. As far as I know my gran had been planning to go out and join my grandfather in the USA. It must have been a terrible shock for her, a young woman widowed with three children. But she did not sit back feeling sorry for herself. There is no doubt she received generous compensation because in no time she opened up three or four 'oil and colour' shops in the Calton and Mile End.

This type of shop was a necessity in Glasgow in those days, selling candles, gas-mantles, paraffin and firelighters. Most of the tenements were gas-lit, perhaps with the occasional paraffin lamp. My grannie prospered for many years but when I came along she had remarried and all the shops were gone.

My step-grandfather was called McDairmid. He had been the coachman to the Caldwells, the family who owned the famous Scotia leatherworks in Boden Street, Bridgeton. Up till recently if you were going down Dunn Street you could see the large water steel-tank still standing with the name Scotia emblazoned on it. According to my mother when Granda McDairmid was dressed in his livery and driving the Caldwell coach with its pair of grey horses he was a handsome sight. He was a very tall man and must have cut a dashing figure. Then of course it is obvious that my grandmother, being a young, quite well-off widow, must have been regarded as a very good catch. However when I remember Granda McDairmid he was retired and working as the watchman in the Scotia works. I used to go along with him to keep the boilers going and feed the Airedale watchdog that I played with. I had the time of my life wandering through the empty works and offices followed by the large dog.

Grannie Scott was one of the most capable and able woman I ever met. Even although I was quite young I knew she feared no one, despite her size. Not that she was physical in any way but her commanding voice and capable manner made people twice her size shrivel. She had developed a cancer on her forehead and she had to travel by tramcar to the Royal Infirmary twice a week to have it burned, without any pain-killers. My mother used to come home crying yet my grannie never said a word. She kept an immaculate house with two horse-hair rocking chairs that I used to play on although because of my short trousers my bare legs got jagged whenever I slid on or off them.

The real attraction, as I got older, was using her stairhead toilet. This was my pride and joy, my reading room. There were only two houses on her landing and only three people used it so it was scrupulously clean and you had all the time in the world to do your business, which for me meant being able to read.

I used to buy my favourite comics and make a beeline for my granny's carsy and if it was dark I borrowed a wee candle and a match. I read in peace and solitude, until one night I had retired there with my Rover comic, the candle and a box of matches, and I heard footsteps halt outside. I was settled back enjoying the exploits of Morgan the Mighty. I wondered what to do. I was ready to chap the door and say there was somebody using it when whoever it was seemed to lean against it. I immediately doused the candle then horror stricken I heard two voices. It was the lassie upstairs with her boyfriend. I waited in silence, afraid to breathe or even pull up my trousers. After a few minutes I knew I could not declare my presence, it was going to be a serious winching session. I looked around to see if I could squeeze out the wee window but as it was one stair up it would have been very difficult and probably quite dangerous so I waited in silence. Then my granny came to the rescue, she opened her door and shouted 'Hughie! hurry up out of that lavvy!' And to my relief I heard the lassie saying a hurried goodnight and running up the stairs. I was out that toilet and diving into my grannie's house faster than the favourite at Shawfield[11] could get out its trap. After that, whenever I passed that lassie, I always kept looking away.

My grannie's cancer got worse and she eventually died. I cannot recall a great deal about her actual death but I can remember her funeral. She was buried in Sandymount cemetery and I went regularly with my mother on a Sunday to put flowers on her grave. I also know that she had made my mother promise to take in Peggy Park, the second daughter of my Auntie Jean who before she died worked in Wilson's cotton mill alongside my mother. After she died her husband emigrated to Canada and her daughter Peggy Park

---

[11] Shawfield Greyhound Stadium which at that time and up until the 1980s was home to Clyde FC. Greyhounds continue to race there four nights per week.

had stayed with Granny Scott. So despite the terrible pain and agony my granny was suffering she made certain that when she herself died my cousin Peggy Park was still sure of a home.

Our house at 118 Bernard Street became quite crowded with three boys and now three girls. Unfortunately my mother was dealt a terrible blow, my sister Lizzie died when she was only 13. My mother never recovered from this. Despite the fact it was diagnosed as meningitis my mother always felt it came because Lizzie had got a fright from the man next door that she never got over. I was just a wee boy and cannot remember much about that period.

But despite the cramped house it was a happy house most of the time, with plenty of people coming and going. The week-ends were very cheery. On Saturdays my mother's brother, my Uncle Andrew, came down from Germiston. He walked all the way there and back again. While we were not wealthy there was always plenty of good homemade soup, with stew or mince and tatties or stovies. My uncle Andrew had not worked for years so my mother used to give him a shilling for a wee punt with the bookie that lifted the lines in our close. He really was a good laugh. He used to bet 'thruppny' doubles and trebles. We always said if his line came up the bookie would have to do a runner as he would not have enough cash to pay out. My Uncle Andrew was really a poor soul but he was so nice and warm he lit up the entire household.

Then of course we had always a great night on Sunday. When the tea was finished there was a domino school with all of us in the game, including a distant relation of my mother's, Davie Fairley. We called him Uncle Davie. He was a top-class cabinet maker, an artist. He made beautiful, hand-carved mahogany tea-trays and any kind of furniture. He was a modest and quiet man and he loved his game of dominoes every Sunday night. Although the stakes were only coppers he had a good laugh when he put down his last domino to win the pot and he always shouted 'domino for Dovid'.

We did not have a wireless in those days. We made our own entertainment. Our house was only a room and kitchen with an outside toilet and there were seven of us living in the place. Even so there were hundreds of people worse off than us, living in much more overcrowded conditions. When you are young it does not seem to matter though, I never felt disadvantaged. It was a very happy home. Before James, my older brother, got married there were four wage earners in the family. This made us better off financially than most of our neighbours. Of course my father's pay was only £1/12/0 per week and my mother's was 15/-, my sister Peggy earned only 10/- and James got 12/-, so it was not exactly a fortune.

There were two busy cooperative societies, the Glasgow Eastern and the London Road. They played a very important role in the social fabric of those days. It is important to stress the role the Cooperatives played in things like the organisation of day-trips to the coast for children. They always had choirs for males and females and these choirs were usually available for weddings and socials. When the May-Day parades came around you could be assured that the largest and most colourful section would be the Cooperative Society and they would have dozens of decorated lorries. Children would be seated inside and they would be drawn by magnificent Clydesdale horses that were owned by every Cooperative Society; and leading many of the contingents would be their massed bands.

Another aspect of the Cooperatives was the dividend they paid on your purchases. As well as providing everything from dairy produce to clothes and furniture the dividend could be large enough to buy school clothing. It was paid on a quarterly basis and if you left it lying it came in handy for your Christmas and the New Year, or even as a help towards your holidays if you could afford them. We were quite fortunate in that regard as my father worked in the railways at Buchanan Street goods' station. He could get passes for his family every year. For over thirteen years we went to the granite city of Aberdeen and the co-op dividend made a major contribution to our expenses. It also helped to purchase clothes out of what they called the drapery department.

But none of any of that would have been possible if it had not been for my mother. We could never have managed without her. As well as bringing up a family of seven, including my cousin Peggy Park, my mother worked at the mill from 8 o'clock in the morning till nearly 6 o'clock at night. On Saturdays she finished at 12 noon and went straight to the steamie at Ruby Street. She booked for two hours and we pulled all the washing in a large wicker basket on wheels down the road, and then when her turn was up we pulled the clean clothes back to Bernard Street where they were hung out in the backcourt, weather permitting. After that they would be taken up to the house for ironing.

My mother was also a good baker and could make shortbread and a clootie dumpling for a few pennies. She made large pots of broth with a nat or hambone from the butcher plus a penny's worth of vegetables. For tenpence she could make stovies and tatties for ten people. We used to go to what was called the 'shan shop'.[12] This was opened by McFarlane Lang the bakers to sell off their mishapen loafs, buns and cakes – the ones that did not come up to standard – at reduced prices. We carried them home in a big pillow case.

None of the boys ever wore a pair of trousers bought out a shop. My mother used to buy good-sized remnants from a small Jewish tailor in Saltmarket who gave her quality material cheap. The only snag was the Singer sewing machine she had to use. She could not manage the intricate sewing on the front of the short trousers and created what she called a 'bobbie-patch', so a wee boy like myself could answer the call of nature.

My father was a very dour man. I can never recall having a conversation with him. He never read anything of substance, but then he was no different from most people in his time, your only pastimes were the pub and a wee bit gambling maybe on the horses. His wages in those days were £1-12-0 a week when he worked with the LMS railways so there was not much to go around. Then again you could get a pint of beer for a penny and a quarter gill of whisky for thruppence, and twenty woodbine cigarettes for thruppence, so I suppose everything is relative.

In most things I feel my father had an inferiority complex but he was not afraid of any of the so-called hard-men in the district. I remember my mother telling me of an incident between him and a man called Boyle when we were all very young. There was a Mrs Murdoch who lived in the wee single-end in the close. One day she came to our door which was on the third floor and battered on it quite loud and she was shouting 'Hurry up Mrs Savage, wee Boyle is going roon the Booly[13] to fight your man and he'll get murdered.'

My mother opened the door and said, 'If my man is daft enough to fight let him get murdered, that's his problem' and she shut the door. Old Mrs Murdoch who was fond of a drink leaned against the

---

[12] shan or shang: a Scots word for food, especially a bite between meals; still current in Glasgow and district.

[13] The area known as 'The Booly' was in Walkinshaw Street, Bridgton.

wall and shouted 'Whit kind of wummin are you who's no worried about yer man.'

Apparently what happened was down in Flynn's pub wee Boyle, who had a bit of a reputation as a fighting man, demanded that my faither buy him a drink. My faither told him to get lost or words to that effect, so the challenge was issued, and it was accepted. The whole pub more or less emptied and made their way to the Booly for the square-go.[14] My father finished his pint then followed them. Wee Boyle led the crowd. As he passed a group of men standing at the corner of Dunn Street and Bernard Street he saw a well-known fighting man called Willie Lamont and he said to him, 'Are you coming roon the Booly to see me giving Savage a doing?' Willie Lamont looked at him and said, 'Ah widny bet on it'.

When they reached the Booly wee Boyle stripped to the waist and started sparring around, practising. My faither, who had arrived later, finished his fag and stepped into the centre of the man-made ring. As Boyle approached him he pulled the skip of his bonnet to the back of his head then grabbed Boyle's arm and butted him right on the nose with his forehead. He continued to do that with wee Boyle's nose spurting blood and the crowd booing, until the man slumped to the ground. My faither made an attempt to give him a hand up but Boyle's supporters pushed him away shouting, 'Savage by name and Savage by nature'. Apparently when my faither came home he washed his hands, took his tea and went to bed without saying a word. But he never spoke about anything that happened outside the home.

It seemed like our house was always packed with people. My mother must have been the Mother Teresa of those days as she never turned anybody away. She took pity on one of my father's workmates who worked as a carter with the same firm of railway contractors. The man had no family in Glasgow and he had lost his digs, so my mother fitted him in.

Then of course when her step-sister had to run out in the middle of the night from her husband, she had to take her in as well. This was my Auntie Nellie, escaping a beating when her man came home drunk. She was one of the first lady conductors on the Glasgow trams and had been a skilled shoemaker in Galleries' factory in

---

[14] 'square go' is a 'fair fight', ie. no weapons

Dalmarnock Road. She was a tall lady and very good-looking when she was young. She also had a nice soprano voice. She could have had her choice of young men. One of the boys that she went with was called Kenny Campbell. As far as I know he played for Dundee United and was capped for Scotland. However, Auntie Nellie had married a plumber called Walker and a sore face was a regular occurrence when he came home drunk at the weekends. My mother used to tell her she did not have to take it because she had no family to hold her back.

But Auntie Nellie was not alone. When I was a baby my mother had the same problem when my own father came home drunk. When he was out drinking on a Saturday night she had to take all us kids downstairs to a nice woman called Mrs Elborn. We all waited there until after the pub doors closed and he had come home and went to bed. One time he found out where we were taking refuge and he came up the stairs and burst open her door and confronted all of us. I was in my mother's arms. As he made to grab her my brother James who was only sixteen stepped forward. James was an apprentice joiner and had taken up a wee bit boxing, he was very well-built. He said to my father, 'No, I've watched you hitting my mother for years and you've hit her for the last time.' My father moved to hit him but James hit him first and he fell to the floor. James pulled him outside and sat him down on the stairs. Most of the family went back up to the house. But Mrs Elborn made my mother a cup of tea and when the girls came to take their mother up the stairs they said their dad was still sitting on the stairs crying, 'My boy hit me.' But it is a fact that that was the last time my dad ever raised his hand to my mother.

Clydebank showing the huge Singer factory after it moved from Brigton.
This picture from the deck of a ship in John Brown's yard shows industry all
around

Employment, Unemployment; Living Conditions

MOST WORKERS were within walking distance of a job in Brigton. Sir William Arrol's steel and bridge building-works was right in Bernard Street and there was the other factories like I mentioned earlier on, plus several cotton-mills including Wilson's where my mother was a weaver along with my sister Peggy. I knew the inside of Wilson's very well as I had my dinner in it every day. My mother had it laid out for us alongside her loom. After eating it there I had to rush back to school. Of course there were many famous mills in the vicinity, including Anderson's shirt-mill which became Hollins, manufacturers of the famous and expensive Vyella shirt.

The first motor car in Scotland, 'the Argyle', was built in Brigton at a factory located at the corner of Baltic Street and John Street. Later on the same site Singers began their first sewing-machine factory before moving onto Clydebank.[15] There was also the Acme wringer-works in Fielden Street on the north side of London Road. Their products were a boon to those women who could afford to buy one. A large number of backcourts had uncovered middens and in the summertime, because of the lochs of human excrement, many tenants could not even get into the backcourts. This meant the women could not hang their washing out to dry. The Acme wringer meant their clothes could be wrung out at the sink and would be dry enough to hang up in the pulley inside the kitchen.

Further along London Road in Fordneuk Street was Claude Alexander the tailor. It was some name for Brigton but he had many shops throughout Glasgow. Going towards Celtic Park and two streets before Kerrydale Street there was McPhee's sawmills. Across the London Road on the southside you had Connell's ginger-

---

[15] There was a very significant strike at the Singer's sewing machine factory in Clydebank For detailed information see *The Singer Strike Clydebank, 1911*, compiled by the Glasgow Labour History Workshop and published by Clydebank District Library in 1989; Hugh Savage and Les Forster were among the Workshop contributors.

works.[16] In the next street you had one of the largest haulage contractors in the business, Gavin Wilkie's. They hauled all the tubes from Stewart & Loyds in Rutherglen to all the shipyards, and to the other tube works in Tollcross and as far as Coatbridge, all horse-drawn. It was some sight to see, four big Clydesdales in pairs, pulling tons of tubes miles in a day all over the west of Scotland. As wee boys we used to sit outside the stables in Boden Street waiting for the horses to come back in the evening.

There is no doubt that Brigton was one of the city's key industrial districts. Yet at nearly every street corner where I stayed there were dozens of unemployed men and boys. Hardly one of them had a suit on his back; they wore odd jackets and trousers. In most cases they wore hand-me-downs, clothes passed from one person to another. There were no dry-cleaners in those days, and no money to use them if there had been.

Unemployment was particularly bad among the young men over twenty. Many had to leave their homes due to the imposition of the means-test. The local parish officers calculated the total income from the parish and if it was over a certain figure, just like today, then any single person's benefit would be stopped, and that person would have to leave home. While hundreds went abroad, many more had to join work-schemes. Thousands could be seen hanging about the street corners in Glasgow. You could tell them because they were sorely clad. Many of them did not even own a suit, and if they did it was in the pawnshop. Their trousers and jackets were mostly torn or stained.

I remember one of the above young men, he had been idle for over two years and then got a job in Martin's leather works which was situated at the end of our street. Within a few weeks he had saved enough money to purchase a complete new suit. Unfortunately his pal, big Andy, was knocked-back for a job. In better times they had exchanged suits as they were more or less the same build. The purpose of this caper was to creat the impression that they had an extensive wardrobe or, as they said in those days, to show they were 'well geared-up'. During this period a few of the Glasgow dance-halls, like the Locarno, ran matinee sessions and it only cost 3d or 4d to get in. So big Andy got into the habit of going up to his

---

[16] In Glasgow lemonade and other aerated waters occasionally are referred to as 'ginger'.

pal's house and taking a loan of the suit to go to the Locarno and returning it before his pal came home from work.

But here I have to admit I cannot remember the outcome of that story, but I do know that long-term unemployment is degrading and should play no part in a civilised society. It is remarkable, when you look back, that in a district teeming with works and factories, at every street corner from morning till night groups of unemployed men of all ages spent their time hanging about.

Most of these world-famous firms paid starvation wages and woe betide any of their workers who happened to mention unions. Another feature of the employment policy of firms such as Templeton's, Sir William Arrol's and others was the strict veto on Catholics. This was never admitted and the bosses concealed it by asking school-leavers which school they attended. In the case of adults they checked their record and religion by contacting their previous employers. The number of firms that did not employ a religious-bar was so small that just by naming his previous place of work the applicant provided that necessary information.

I wonder how the owners of Strang's cotton-mills in Greenhead Street would have reacted if they had known that the well-spoken woman who spent some time with the weavers, taking sketches of them at their looms, was Sylvia Pankhurst and that the senior tenor in their mill was the brother of the famous – or infamous – suffragette, depending on your point of view.

In school you were shown maps of the world coloured in red sections indicating the countries that formed the Empire. You were never told that the natives of these lands had been dispossessed and then enslaved by their captors, the British ruling class. This was only one of thousands of facts and truths that you were not told as you made your progress through school. In the 1930s Glasgow was still the second city of the British Empire and the sixth city of Europe but to wee boys playing about the streets it was just places like Brigton with street after street of smoke-grimed grey tenements, with the occasional red sandstone one where we thought the toffs lived. These grey tenement buildings consisted of three stories with three houses on each landing and with an earthenware w.c. on the half-landing, providing one toilet for all the occupants of the three houses in that particular landing. In a tenement close like the one our family stayed in at 118 Bernard Street probably twenty two people including children used that one bog. In the twenty odd years I lived there the w.c. was never renewed and nor was it ever painted. Neither was the close.

The above example was not the worst. There were some tenements in Brigton where as many as thirty or forty folk were all using the same so-called toilet-facilities, up closes in Baltic Street and Nuneaton Street for instance, and in some of the back-loans of London Road where there were six doors on each landing, and that meant six families.

Bernard Street ran parallel with London Road and had five public houses with another ten nearby. A pub consisted of a public bar and a 'family department' that catered for anyone wishing a carry-out of liquor. In those days the publicans did not cater for women. Outside the ground floor windows and at the mouth of most of the closes groups of women would congregate. None of them wore coats, they all wore shawls of various colours and sizes. In most cases they were carrying weans. You could look along the whole of Bernard Street and never see a pram. The women carried their children everywhere in a shawl. They just had to get out of the houses. No wireless, no washing-up facilities except the kitchen sink, no furniture other than several beds, a coal bunker and a large kitchen table where the whole family dined. There was hardly a place to sit and being lit by gas the atmosphere was always very stuffy.

The women went on standing at the close and the corner till well after 10 pm. I remember a pal of mine, when we were talking about this, he told me a story about a crowd of women that used to stand outside a close in Arcadia Street. One of them had been married very young and still carried her wee boy in a shawl, right up till he was over four years of age. It so happened the young mother had a full vocabulary of the more colourful language. One evening she was standing at the close and her wee boy got tired and fell asleep, and he slumped ever deeper into the shawl. She kept adjusting it by opening it and changing the wean's position till eventually he woke up and shouted, 'Shut the fucking shawl, there's a draught!'

You can sometimes forget that in the midst of all the deprivation and poverty not only had people a sense of humour and humanity, they had a real community. There were no social services or social workers as such, you had a health visitor or green-lady, as she was called. Most babies were born at home. The death-rate was horrific but it would have been much higher if it had not been for the mid-wives who delivered a large number of these children. One such person who has never received a mention in all the records of Brigton as far as I know was Nurse Mulholland. She lived all her life in Greenhead Street facing the Glasgow Green and she must have delivered thousands of babies.

In the summer particularly it was quite a regular occurrence to have large puddles of waste water flooding the back courts, usually with human excrement floating on the surface. It got so bad that tenants could not get access to the middens to deposit their ashes and rubbish. And the women could not walk out to the backcourts to hang up the family washings, especially if it happened at weekends when a plumber was not available. Most women were like our neighbour Mrs Kerr, a clean wee soul and a very kind lady, but always running back and forward to the steamie.

The most serious consequence of the above was disease, if the drain remained choked these great big puddles were an attraction for the weans, even although they were afloat with horrible sewage waste. The backcourt was the only real place they could play so who could be surprised when an outbreak of a contagious disease like dysentry did take place? If these children stood on a piece of glass when wading with their bare feet you could be sure that the cut would fester if not immediately sterilised. It is to the credit of the ordinary people of places like Brigton that if Iodine Tincture or Boracic Lint was not available then something would still be done, and the good old carbolic soap with a bread poultice was used as the final standby.

The rents of our houses went to a house factor called R. Metcalf who had at least three offices in the district where you paid in at least once a month. I learned many years later that the actual owners of these tenements lived abroad, some as far away as the Argentine. The factors who looked after the houses for them had allowed the backcourt washhouses to fall into such a state of disrepair that either they fell down or had to be demolished.

When they did fall down they could severely injure children because the backcourt was their playground. The hundreds of delapidated old buildings that still stood in the backcourts, the remains of long-gone houses, workshops and derelict wash-houses provided active boys like me with good dykes to play on. We did what we called 'the jumps', jumping or leaping from one dyke to another. We graduated from wee jumps of maybe three or four feet to some as long as six, seven or even eight feet. It could be dangerous as it was a long fall to the ground. The dykes stood as high as eight feet and the landing would be onto tarmac or concrete or dirt and old rubble but it was usually a kind of contest and most boys took the risk.

I can recall on one occasion a wee fair-haired boy getting crushed to death when the rotten old brickwork built with lime collapsed and the solid concrete roof of the washhouse fell in on him. He came from Dunn Street, from a nice family, and they never got over their unnecessary loss.

THE CHURCH AND RECREATION;
WORKERS' CASINOS, STREET ENTERTAINMENT

THERE WERE two churches in the street and both were very well known, one of them was St Francis in the East. It provided a great deal of help to the unemployed by providing some basic training on things like assembling radios for the men, and sewing and cooking classes for the women. My mother became a member of their sodality classes. The place was known as the Pal's club and I think was quite similar to what the late Rev. George McLeod[17] carried out in Govan.

In most working-class districts were the soirees run by some of the evangelical churches. These consisted of a religious service, the singing of hymns, a bag of cakes and cups of tea, and then a sermon was usually conducted by a well-known evangelist. The famous Seth Sykes and his wife regularly came. They went all over the country, and abroad, singing and preaching. When they appeared in the Bethany Hall in Bernard Street the main hall, which held nearly a thousand people, was full to capacity.

When the tea-meetings ended at about 9 pm. there was an army of small boys standing outside the main entrance. They would be asking the congregation, mainly women, if they 'had any bags?' The women all received a bag each when they went into the meetings, with at least four or five cakes and most of them only managed to eat one or two. In many cases they took pity on the children, most of them poorly clad, and gave them their bags. I was always partial to cakes myself and I joined the chorus and shouted, 'Have ye any bags missus?' till one night my mother saw me and that was the end of my begging.

It was also a weekly event for twenty or more of the regular congregation of churches and mission halls to march from their

[17] The Very Rev. George Fielden MacLeod; Scottish Presbyterian minister in Edinburgh and then in Govan Glasgow; founder of the Iona Community and eventually Moderator of the General Assembly. He was regarded as 'extreme left-wing' by colleagues and other Christians and had an ecumenical approach which outraged many, especially when he wanted to 'introduce bishops into the kirk.' See his *Only One Way Left*.

premises to the nearest main road junction. The Bethany Hall people marched to the corner of Dunn Street and London Road, singing hymns and accompanied by musical instruments like a concertina or an accordion. When they reached the corner they carried out a prayer meeting with several speakers – men and women – telling people who were standing or passing by how they had found the glory of God. They sang their hymns and appealed for people to come forward and join their church, then they put round a small velvet bag asking for a financial contribution.

This was repeated throughout Brigton and the whole of Glasgow by hundreds of religious missions and evangelical groups. There were larger organisations like the Salvation Army who had a twenty-piece brass band performing at Brigton Cross every Sunday night. Sometimes they went all over the east end playing and collecting. There was another uniformed group from Moncur Street in the Calton who had a brass band and did the same as the Salvation Army, playing throughout the district. They also had a medical centre in their premises where they administered medical help.

So in different ways Brigton, despite the grinding poverty, had a vibrant community. But the main form of entertainment was the pictures. Talking-pictures had just been introduced and the very first one to come to Glasgow was *The Singing Fool* with Al Jolson as its star. It appeared in the Coliseum, Eglinton Street on the south side of the city. I was too young to remember but it caused a real sensation. As I got older cinemas had mushroomed all over Glasgow[18] and talking-pictures came to most of them. Many music halls changed to showing films. Some like the King's in James Street and the Olympia at Bridgeton Cross did both on the one prog-ramme, putting on a live variety-turn in between the two pictures.

I remember as a wee boy being in the King's and to the delight of the audience the one and only Victor McLaglan was introduced on the stage. There was uproar. On his way out after he went up the centre passage and as I was on the outside seat next to the passage I reached out and touched his beautiful camel-hair coat. He towered above everybody and must have been over 6' 4". He had a big grin over his face and I felt so good to know that for the first and probably the last time in my life I touched a real film star. I learned later that

---

[18] For further information see Bruce Peter's *100 Years of Glasgow's Amazing Cinemas*, Polygon, 1996.

when he left that night he was on his way to Shawfield Stadium to see the world championship fight between Benny Lynch and Peter Kane.

The area was saturated with picture-houses. Along with the King's and the Olympia there was the Royal, the Arcadia, the Star, the Strathclyde, the Plaza and the Premier which some people called the 'Geggy'. And if you cared to travel a few hundred yards to Dennistoun there were four more there, or else to Parkhead where there were another three, and so on.

This onslaught killed variety in most districts stone-dead although theatres like the Princess in the Gorbals and the Scotia in Watson Street still carried on, along with the Metropole and the Pavilion and quite a few others. Although it must be said that the closing of the Glasgow Empire in the 1960s was really the beginning of the taking-over of the city centre by the property speculators, that end of things had nothing at all to do with the growth of the cinema.

In the thirties Brigton was really a hive of activity and two other aspects of social life, particularly for the men, were drinking and gambling. At least three street-bookies lifted betting lines in our street. Our close at 118 was used by a bookie called Tommy Hyndman. He was quite a nice kind of man and many an unfortunate was given a bung by him. Then again, as it was unlicensed in those days, very few expenses were entailed and most of the runners and watchers were unemployed men. The bookies used to pay out the winners in a house up the close, usually one near the ground floor that was made available to them from the tenants for a small fee.

The bookies always made sure that the close where they operated had several escape-routes because it was a fact of life that the police always endeavoured to grab the guy who was taking the betting slips and they used all kinds of tricks to try and trap them. One favourite disguise the polis had was to pretend they were a plumber coming to fix a burst pipe. They had the usual working clothes on with a bag of tools and a water key. If the polis got near the bookie's lifter then he was taken to the jail, at that time in Old Dalmarnock Road. The lifter's betting slips and cash were confiscated and he was charged and eventually fined.

Later on it became more sophisticated. I can remember a well-known bookie with a betting shop in Cowcaddens. He got prior warning from his friendly neighbourhood cop about a raid and so warned off his good punters. Then he got several dozen occupants from the model-lodging house in Milton Street to come along to his betting shop to wait for the raid. When the model-lodging house punters were being taken into the Black Maria the bookie gave them five shillings each and another five bob to pay their fine, and everybody was happy apparently.

Hundreds of street bookies operated in Glasgow. I can remember one who lifted betting-lines in a close facing my school in Pirn Street. To get away from the polis this bookie actually dreeped from a two-storey window, which was probably about twenty feet high. It always struck me as amazing that the bookies were all well-known yet they managed to operate for years. They did get the occasional visit with a fine but they were back on the streets the next day as usual. So the legalising of it probably saved them a lot of bungs to the polis and the magistrates or whoever happened to be on the payroll.

There was another type of gambling that was rife in working-class districts, this was Pitch and Toss. These 'tossing-schools', as they were known, took place in isolated spots and the guys here also had several escape-routes in the event of a police-raid. It is said by known gamblers that Pitch and Toss was the most honest game of the lot, unless you could get away with a two-headed penny which was very unlikely. Most of the tossing schools were run by the local hard-men who also ensured that winners were not pestered or threatened. Apparently, as far as I heard, if a hard-man fancied his chances he could fight his way in to get into the running of a pitch.

I do not know if tossing schools exist today. I am sure they must. In the thirties there were three quite large ones operated in the east end of Glasgow. There was a big one on the banks of the Clyde at Cambuslang. It was run by the Tottens from Rutherglen as far as I understand. They also say that the ex-British middleweight champion Jake Kilrain did his toller at it – the toller was the man that saw things ran smoothly and prevented trouble. It was a huge school with several hundred men sometimes in attendance.

For those of you not aware of the rules, if the person tossed two pennies in the air for say £50, and the coins landed on the ground with the two heads facing up then your stake of £50 became £100. The second time you won it became £200 and the third time £400.

After that you could walk away minus your original stake of £50 which went to the guys running the game. However, if you wished you could carry on tossing the coins. After that first three-timer was done you could stop when you wanted. There were also side-bets took place amongst the crowd that had nothing to do with the tollers. A bit of come-and-go over disputed decisions was allowed to punters. All in all most regular gamblers thought it was quite a fair game and went back time and time again.

The other big tossing-school was at the side of the Clyde just next to, or at the back of, Belvidere Hospital. It was run by the McGrechans. I think the head guy was called Hughie. When I eventually worked as a fitter in the Gas Board in the 1950s my helper was Tam Durie, a toller at the McGrechan tossing school. He had been a local hard-man but when he worked with me he was quite a nice guy. But he did open my eyes to what took place behind the scenes. For a start, when we were talking about tossing-schools we were talking about thousands of pounds. First of all the polis were sorted out. They knew when a raid was to take place and all the heavy gamblers were warned not to come on certain Sundays. When any gambler did win a few hundred pounds he was always offered protection to reach the main road, sometimes even to be taken home. While mugging and robbing was not so rife in those days good gamblers did not exactly grow on trees and then the fact that you had to make your way a few hundred yards through isolated lanes meant it was better to be safe than sorry.

Tossing-schools were the workers' casinos and with mass unemployment few people strayed from their local neighbourhoods where most of their social life took place. The tossing-school I was most familiar with took place on a derelict site which had once been a pottery. It was next to Barrowfield, home-ground to Bridgeton Waverley of the Central Football League. The local hard-men who ran it included the Webb brothers, Elie and David, whose mother lived three closes down from us in Bernard Street. A third brother played football for an English First Division side. The main hard-man of this tossing-school was Neilly McHugh who had been a boxer, either cruiser or heavyweight. I went regularly with my pal, who happened to be Neilly's young brother.

Big Neilly had an easy-going attitude and was never aggressive unless challenged. I remember a young tearaway stepping into the ring and Big Neilly saying to him, 'Look son it's no worth getting a sore face for a few bob.' The young guy persisted then threw off his jacket, and without taking off his bunnet Big Neilly stepped forward and belted him on the chin. It was at least ten minutes before the young guy recovered. The big man laid a pound note in his hand and said, 'Away you go home son.'

At the top of the old pottery site was an area known as Nelson's whippet ground. Here every Saturday, and most other days too, they raced whippets. It was the forerunner to the more sophisticated greyhound racing but it still took place after greyhound racing began at Glasgow's many dog-tracks. Unlike professional dog racing the handler lifted the whippet up at the start of the race and its owner went down to the bottom of the area and flapped a hankie. When the whippet was released it ran to its owner. Of course betting took place and big money could change hands. Whippet racing remains a popular pastime in some parts of the country, particularly in the old mining villages.

In the early 1930s Clyde Football Club of the Scottish Senior First Division started to race greyhound dogs at their Shawfield Stadium. They became the fourth racing track in Glasgow to operate under licence of the Greyhound Racing Association and its rules. The others were the Albion, Carntyne and the White City. Also there were unlicensed dog-tracks like Ashfield, Clydebank, Mount Vernon and others. These unlicensed tracks were called flapping-gaffs, as far as I know because of the 'flapping hankies', the same start used by the handlers at whippet racing.

Some wee bookies could not afford the official entrance-fee into Shawfield Stadium so they started making a book outside the ground on the sodia-wastes, so called because it was a dumping ground for the notorious White's chemical works, and hundreds of others. But the outside betting enterprise was quite successful. They were called the 'thrupny bookies'. From where they stood they could see the race results on the Shawfield tote board. Payment was made after every race and they had saved their entrance fee. While they would not admit it many of the old 'thruppny bookies' ended up working inside the track.

One of the most popular and spontaneous kinds of entertainment happened on the street and came from the many musicians and singers who frequented Brigton. There was a wide variety, starting from the poor badly-clad men and boys who would sing in the backcourts for a jeely piece[19] thrown down from a tenement window, or else a copper to make up the price of a bed for the night. Dotted around Glasgow at that time were hundreds of model-lodging houses. Then you had the more professional types who would be accompanied by a fiddler or an accordion player. One fellow would keep singing or playing while the other caught the coppers in a bunnet.

But there was no doubt about the most popular form of street entertainment. This was the semi-professional jazz bands that played in all the densely-populated streets throughout the district, usually on a Friday evening or a Saturday afternoon. These jazz bands usually had one or two singers, a set of drums and an accordion, plus a trumpet or saxophone. The singers had to have a very loud voice as of course no method of amplification was available.

Then there were the step-dancers who used their own board for the intricate steps they carried out. Another highlight was the dancers who disappeared up a close and come back out wearing some outrageous costume. They could do anything, from the sailors' hornpipes to the soft shoe shuffle. And there was always a Jolson singer who would blacken his face just like the original.

The acts often lasted an hour and hundreds of pennies were thrown from the crowded tenement windows that would be thronged with people getting a grandstand view of the whole performance. But most of the audience would be sitting on pavements with all the children sitting at the front, beginning from the smallest. People even sat on the roads. This was a period when poverty was a way of life for most people. It was amazing that when the performers finished and went round with the bunnets hundreds of coins came, much of it cascading down from the high-up tenement windows.

This was the 1930s and a street that was 150 yards long could house who knows how many hundreds of people, maybe thousands. You might wonder how such big events could take place on an open street. For a start the street was closed off for the performance and also to my knowledge there was nobody who owned a motor car. The main traffic was horse-drawn. The only motor cars people ever saw were for funerals or maybe belonged to the doctor, or maybe a wedding was on.

---

[19] Bread and jam sandwich

There is no doubt the street perfomers did alright. A nice summer's Friday evening or a Saturday afternoon were the most popular times as there was maybe a copper left in purse or pocket after the broo money had been spent. Or maybe some of the punters had got a wee lift at the horses. One of the turns I remember well was the O'Leary Brothers who later went onto grace the stage of theatres like the Metropole, the Queens, the Princess and the Scotia.

Benefit concerts were also held in the extended backcourts that existed in and around our area due to the demolition of derelict buildings, the old houses, old handloom mills and even blacksmith shops that had stood on the ground before the tenements were built. I remember one of the largest concerts in the 1930s was in aid of a woman who was charged with the murder of her husband. Her name was Baillie and she had several boys, one of whom I knew. As well as the usual amateur turns who gave the woman support several well-known personalities made appeals for help to defend her. Many of her supporters were there on the day of the benefit concert with petitions which most of the people signed. I had never seen such a crowd. Me and all the other wee boys were up on the roofs of the old washhouses, we had a good view of the huge audience and there must have been five or six hundred.

That was only one of the many concerts held on her behalf, not only in that backcourt but in many more. As far as I understand the campaign was quite successful and the charge was later reduced to manslaughter. The woman had a young family and the sentence was quite lenient.

Undoubtedly the most popular pastime in that period, and the least expensive, was ballroom dancing. Most of the boys you went about with when you left school were already going to the dancing so you really could do nothing else but join in. You had to save up and get yourself a suit with long trousers and then get taught the rudiments of dancing without standing on your partner's feet. Glasgow was famous not only for the large number of venues that catered for the dancing public but for the high standards in dancing that prevailed. There were two types of dancers catered for, the younger element who took up modern dancing and the more mature dancers who were fond of what was described as 'select' or old-time dancing.

So all dressed up in my Cooperative suit I went with a boy I knew to enrol in the Dobson School of Dancing held at the Orange Halls in Cathedral Street. The lessons were given by Mr and Mrs Dobson who were quite strict and I must say within a few weeks you began to get the hang of it. And while you were no Gene Kelly at least the girls did not run away when they saw you coming up to ask them to dance.

The boy I went with was an apprentice joiner who had become a really good dancer. Then I found out he was taking extra lessons at the McEwan School of Dancing. But it was no big deal as far as I was concerned, the tanner a night lessons at Dobson's was good enough for me. We went around the more professional dancehalls. My pal could pick out at a glance the best lady dancer in the place and would try to get her up for every dance, till one night at the Dennistoun Palais the partner of one girl took exception to his continual approaches. The guy was a well-known amateur boxing champion and we had to beat a hasty retreat.

Every district had a public hall. Some districts like Brigton and Cathcart had two halls, both of them fully occupied with ballroom dancing on a Friday and Saturday night. There were three Glasgow evening papers in those days, the *Evening Times*, *Evening Citizen* and *Evening News*, and they carried several pages of adverts of all the dancing nights available in public halls. Then you had the small independent halls like the Stanley in Plantation, the Tower at the Round Toll in Possil Road, and the F. & F. in Dumbarton Road, Partick which later catered for roller-skating. Due to the popularity of dancing everybody wanted in on the act; even football clubs like Shawfield Juniors in Oatlands, the Strathclyde in Parkhead, and the Rutherglen Glencairn. Then of course you had the real status ballrooms like the Locarno in Sauchiehall Street, the Albert in Bath street, the Dennistoun Palais, and the Plaza at Eglinton Toll. All this was long before Fred Astaire was even heard of. Then too there was the other dancehall, the Barrowland Ballroom. But in talking about the Barrowland we have to talk about Maggie McIvor, 'Queen of the Barras'.

Mrs Margaret McIver

DID MAGGIE MCIVOR STEAL A STREET?

MARGARET RUSSELL started business in a wee fruit shop next to the Star Picture House in Main Street, sometime after her marriage to James McIver in 1888. They moved to Green Street, Calton then to Marshall Lane in the Gallowgate, and started to hire out barrows for 1/6d per week to hawkers and street traders before the 1914/18 world war. She carried on the business after her husband was called up to the Armed Forces then extended it to horses and eventually to property.

That she was a very shrewd business woman was beyond doubt. When she opened up her first barrow site in Moncur Street in 1920 it was based on the present Barrowland ground. Some of the houses and factories had become derelict and were demolished, so Maggie McIver extended the site of the barrows. In 1923 electric lights were installed over the hawkers' stalls and in 1926 a roof erected over the whole place; in 1928 'the Barras' were enclosed.

Many people, including hawkers and Caltonians, have wondered for years what happened to the street called Calton Entry. It used to run parallel with Kent Street and was very narrow. From the Gallowgate it went south, crossing Moncur Street where it continued to Stevenson Street. This last wee bit is the only part remaining.

Calton Entry was scarcely about fifty yards in length and had about ten or twelve tenement closes. I suppose it would have been mainly hawkers and some old cotton-weavers that occupied the houses. In the late 1920s the tenement at the corner of Gibson Street and the Gallowgate into the Calton Entry, was demolished. Maggie McIver used the spare ground to expand her operation. She hired a barrow at 6d a day, occasionally double that for a Saturday. With the barrows in Moncur Street being one of the largest and most popular it was no surprise that when the remaining tenement was demolished the plan to build Barrowland took shape.

Her husband died in 1930 from malaria as a result of his war service but this did not deter her, and she pushed on with her ambition to build a modern dance hall over the market place. It was her boast that the whole enterprise was completed without an architect, no surveyor, not even a contract but a shake of the hand. In 1934 the Barrowland Ballroom was completed and opened on Christmas Eve by the proud owner. Many local dignitaries attended, including Mr James Langmuir, Procurator Fiscal.

Maggie McIver did not restrict her activities and her oldest son Sammy opened up a secondhand car market under the Barrowland Ballroom from Monday till Friday. That it was the mecca for dancers during the whole week goes without saying when you consider how she brought in famous guest-bands like Jack Hylton, Henry Hall, Roy Fox and Teddy Joyce, and I remember seeing and hearing the jazz legend Coleman Hawkins there. Much later Lena Martell then Maggie Bell were resident singers with the Gaybirds Band.[20]

It must have come as quite a surprise to a few of the big business-men of that era, that a small, quite insignificant woman, not very young and with a growing family, could undertake such an enterprise. Those who really knew her from her early, meagre beginnings, had no doubt she would make it. In the process it could also be said of this shrewd business woman, that she managed to steal a street called Calton Entry.

My first recollection of the Calton Entry had not been of the street itself but of a gang of boys who hung about it and called themselves the Calton Entry Boys. I was a young schoolboy and along with a few other boys from Bernard Street we started to attend a gymnasium. It was situated in Saracen Head Lane, just up from the 'Sarry Heid'.[21] Dr. Cossar ran the gymnasium on behalf of a religious organisation. His main function seemed to be finding wee boys prepared to emigrate to countries of the British Empire, like Canada, New Zealand and Australia where they were employed as labourers on farms.

Dr. Cossar was a tall, grey-haired man who wore a naval cap and a navy blue jersey, and he was very strict. If we laughed or jostled each other when we had been asked to join in prayers or sing hymns he would use a large belt across our legs or bottom. On a cold night you sometimes went home with your bare skin tingling.

---

[20] Dean Ford and the Gaylords later became Marmalade and had major success in the pop charts with hits like the Beatles'-penned 'Obla dee oblada'.

[21] Or 'Sarry Heid' – the Saracen's Head, a popular pub in the Gallowgate apparently established since 1755.

I suppose we might have found the same type of gymnastic facilities nearer home but only if we joined a Boys Brigade company or a Boy Scout troop. Apart from being required to join a church the discipline and regimentation of these organisations did not appeal to me.

The only question Dr. Cossar ever asked was, 'Are you a good Protestant?'

Even though I attended Sacred Heart School and was a Catholic I had no difficulty in saying, 'Yes.'

One time we took a new wee boy from Bernard Street along with us. He kept tugging my jersey and saying to me quite determinedly 'But you're a fucking Catholic.' He only stopped when I gave his arm a good twist.

Dr Cossar spoke with great authority and conviction and he started pestering us to sign up for emigration but he never did persuade any of the boys from Bernard Street.

The Calton Entry Boys were mostly Catholics and felt it was their duty to challenge the boys from Dr. Cossar's gymnasium as they made their way home. You were ambushed when you reached the bottom of Saracen Lane with loud shouts of 'Get those dirty Protestant bastards.' The Calton Entry Boys never managed to catch me but even the ones they did grab only got a slap or a kick on the arse and if you started to greet they all ran away. Their main thing was the chase itself and the shouting of 'fuck King Billy' and the defeat of his disciples, which was a joke when you consider the religion of our wee team. I never waited to explain I was a good Catholic, I doubt if it would have been appreciated, I was too busy beating Jack Lovelock's world record. I was always a better runner than fighter.

I have since learned that Dr. Cossar's gymnasium was only one of hundreds used by religious zealots and organisations to attract and entice young boys from poor homes into emigration. One of the leaders in this mass export of children was Dr. Barnado, followed by all the main Protestant religions, from the Church of England Waifs and Strays Society to the Salvation Army, on through the Roman Catholic Church. All in the name of religion, in most cases without the parents' consent, sometimes even without their knowledge. It was slave labour on a massive scale and started as far back as 1618 when the first children were sent to Richmond in

America. And it continued right through until 1967. In excess of 150,000 children were sent to every corner of the British Empire without a voice of protest from any section of the media or establishment, and with the complete connivance of most of the churches and religious bodies.

THE ONLY public place that was available to practise gymnastics was over in the Glasgow Green across James Street from Fleshers Haugh.[22] It was an open air part of the green with a small pavilion with an open shelter. The gymnasium consisted of a few sets of bars for horizontal exercises, two sets of parallel bars, three sets of high chain rings and a vaulting horse. Apparently it had been donated by a local industrialist who felt that it would be beneficial to the young men who were unemployed. It really was a boon to them, but for the likes of younger boys like me, we had to wait until the young unemployed went home for their tea, before we could get the use of the equipment.

In the square mile about our street there was no public playing fields, no swings for weans, absolutely no facilities whatsoever for young people. There was not even a blade of grass to be seen. The nearest swimming baths were at Whitevale Street in Dennistoun and they were always busy, especially in the summer during the school holidays. There were of course Greenhead swimming baths adjacent to the Glasgow Green. It was these baths that I went to when we were taken by Sacred Heart Advance Central School where I was a pupil.

Later on it became by accident the first open-air swimming pool in Glasgow when they took the roof off to make way for an extension to Templeton's carpet factory. It remained off during the five years or so of the war and was used extensively by the people of the Calton even although they sometimes needed a bath after they had had a swim. It depended how the wind was blowing as Templeton's chimney often laid a nice film of soot on the surface. Of course a real open-air pool was planned for the Glasgow Green. The steel was delivered to the site adjacent to the present putting green, the barricades were put in place and excavations were started.

---

[22] In 1990 the Labour-controlled, Glasgow District Council tried to sell off a third of the historic Glasgow Green in the form of a 125 year lease to private property developers. For some further information see *The Reckoning*, Clydeside Press 1990.

But the only work that was ever done on that site was the red leading of the steel to preserve it until the war was finished. As one of the old wags used to say, it was a pity we didn't have a real Red Leader, unfortunately we only had Sir Patrick Dollan.[23]

Until I went to the above school at 10 years of age I never received swimming lessons but fortunately our family managed to get a holiday at the seaside during 'the Fair'[24] and I did manage to pick it up. It would have been an impossible task for our physical-training teacher at school to give any type of real tuition in the thirty minutes of our one weekly swimming period.

Most of the boys I played or went about with were football mad. While I did play on occasion I was more interested in running, gymnastics and boxing. If the game started when I was there and they were choosing teams I was not picked first although I always got a game. I was quite heavy-built and I could run. The nearest football fields were in the Glasgow Green but it was usually five or six a side with a wee tanner baw we played, and the Green was too far away, too big and too busy, so we made use of the large backcourts in Walkinshaw Street, better known as the Booly, which was what everybody called it.

It was not surprising that football was very popular in Brigton as over a hundred years ago Fleschers' Haugh in the Glasgow Green saw the birth of Rangers in 1873 and Celtic in 1888. Only five minutes walk from Bernard Street lay Celtic Park itself. However, it was not only Senior teams like Celtic and Clyde that were located in the Brigton area you also had Intermediate teams like Bridgeton Waverley who played in Barrowfield Park next door to Parkhead. Other teams in the same league as Waverley were Strathclyde and

---

[23] Sir Patrick Joseph Dollan (1885-1963); 'ex-miner; activist in labour and temperance movements. . . first Catholic Lord Provost of Glasgow. See William Knox's *Scottish Labour Leaders 1918-1939*.

[24] 'The Glasgow Fair' – the last fortnight in July; when Glasgow closes down for the summer and goes for its annual holiday. For decades the carnival and sideshows have always come to Glasgow Green for this period; during the European City of Culture fiasco in 1990 the showpeople were supportive of the struggle to save the Green from the Labour Council's attempt to sell it off to private developers.

also Parkhead Juniors who played at Helenvale Park and although Helenvale Park is still there Parkhead Juniors have disappeared along with the other two. There are two teams in the east end who were in the old Intermediate league and still exist; Rutherglen Glencairn and Cambuslang Rangers.

Events like Wimbledon or the Open Golf championships never came into our world. There was not a single wireless in the whole of Bernard Street as far as I knew. In those days we were out in the backcourts after a cup final or an international with our tanner ball. There was no chance of us with our 'Setirday-penny' ever affording to buy a football strip. Although we could not afford to pay the entrance we had a very wide choice of games to watch. The fourpence you paid at the boys' gate to watch Clyde or Celtic was beyond us but back then it was allowed for the paying public to lift young boys over the turnstyle gates without them having to pay. Most fathers took their sons to games but if my big brother James was not going to Parkhead I usually stood at the pay-in entrances along with dozens of other wee boys. We would keep asking, 'Gonny gie us a lift mister?' and seldom were we refused. Of course we could always get in at Bridgeton Waverley's ground at Barrowfield which was easy access and nearer home. Their stadium was only protected by corrugated steel sheeting and it was always quite loose and not very well maintained.

It would be inappropriate when talking about football in the 1930s not to mention the Churches League teams. They also played at the Fleschers' Haugh on Glasgow Green along with so many Juvenile and Secondary Juvenile teams, and also countless school teams and factory and works' teams. Sometimes there were not enough football pitches to play on. Other times some of the teams had to use the wash-houses in local backcourts to strip off their clothes. And then the players would race across to the pitches on the Fleshers' Haugh. All kinds of teams began life here, professional and amateur, senior and junior, and thousands of footballers, from Patsy Gallacher to Kenny Dalglish, cut their battling teeth in the tough conditions.

Like most wee boys you went through the usual phases and when your favourite player or team was doing well you always wanted to emulate your idols. I was a Celtic follower and I can still rhyme the players of my favourite team off by heart.

John Thomson,
Cook, McGonnigle,
Wilson, McStay, Geatons,
Thomson, Thomson, McGrory, Scarf and Napier

It was probably one of the most famous teams ever, maybe more famous than 'the Lisbon Lions,'[25] not because of footballing achievement but the fact that John Thomson was accidentally killed when playing against Rangers.

During that period a few of us decided to start a team of our own and as we all lived within a few closes of each other there did not seem to be any problem. So we called in a big boy, Neilly – I am not sure what his surname was – but he was quite a decent boy and known as being very honest. We extended the contributors till about ten or so boys were putting in money to the kitty. After a few weeks we began to wonder when we would be buying a real football as we knew there was over £1 in our funds. We kept asking Neilly about the ball and he kept saying 'All in good time' till eventually some of the boys wanted their money back. We were flabbergasted when he told us he had spent it. What on was what we wanted to know. When we asked to see the ball or the strips all he could show us were bandages and liniment. That was what he went out and bought with the money. Big Neilly was in the Boys' Brigade so no wonder I never joined, although he went on to be a Captain.

It would not be possible to speak about street football in Bernard Street without mentioning a girl by the name of Tillie Cunningham. She stayed up our close and was older than me. She was not only the best girl footballer in the whole district, she was miles ahead of most of the boys. As a matter of fact when the boys were picking a team if Tillie was there she was usually chosen first. Although well-built she was a typical girl wearing a dress. No such items like jeans were available in those days. While her hair was always short she could head the ball with force and direction and she could kick the ball with both feet. As far as I recall she played for a ladies team from Rutherglen called Kelly's. I do not think Tillie's football career

---

[25] 'Lisbon Lions' – the name given to the Celtic team who won the European Cup in Portugal 1967. All bar one of the eleven players were locally born and raised within hailing distance of Celtic Park.

lasted long. The last I remember she was married with a growing family.

There were a few good players in our district, but they had to play on dirt pitches and not many made the major leagues. There was one boy who signed for Celtic but I doubt if he survived a season. Another young man, Willie Webb, did make it to senior football but it was for an English club. Of course there were many Intermediate and Junior players around.

The type of sport that did attract a large number of boys, including myself, was boxing. It was the era of the Benny Lynchs, the Jake Kilrains, Johnny McGrorys and many more. Boxing clubs were sprouting up all over Glasgow and old premises like churches and factories were being converted into boxing clubs. Also there were arenas like the Grove Stadium at Finnieston which were under the auspices of Johnny McMillan, ex-featherweight champion. Then there was the LMS Rovers club where amateur championship contests were held.

Apart from the glamour of the ring it was a fact of life that if you lived in a tough district fighting was thought the best way to defend yourself. I did very little about it myself until one of my pals got a set of boxing gloves for his Christmas and our stairhead lobby became a ring for the half a dozen boys who lived up the close. Despite the complaints of the neighbours it kept us out the cold during the long winter nights. And it never got out of hand because the boxing gloves were too big to really hurt you.

Later on, when I was a young apprentice plumber working on a building site, I met an apprentice bricklayer called Hughie Finnerty. His brother was the Scottish lightweight champion. Hughie did a little amateur boxing himself and was a member of McGhee's club in Parkhead. He took me along to join. I attended for quite a while and began to get the hang of the equipment, particularly the punch-balls and the skipping-ropes.

It was a very busy club and there was quite a number of boxers who fought regularly, both amateur and professional. There was not much tuition took place unless you were capable of entering a competition. The trainer was called 'Cumshy' Cameron. After taking part in a few wee club contests he asked me to enter a small competition in the LMS Rovers. I jumped at the chance. On the Saturday night I turned up with a new pair of baseball boots which was the cheap alternative to the real McCoy, actual leather boxing boots. The baseball boots were quite a tight fit but I thought they would ease off.

When I went into the main hall where the ring was I got the fright of my life. There were several hundred people from all over, shouting on the boys from their own clubs.

My opponent was a boy much smaller than me and apparently he had won a few fights due to his boxing skills. I was very nervous but the man in my corner told me to relax. This I could not do as my baseball boots were hurting my big toe and it made me flatfooted. I walked around the ring chasing that wee fair-headed boy. He danced about me like a fairy although his powder-puff blows were not hurting me at all. However, I was getting very embarrassed. No matter how many punches I threw at him he dodged them with ease, and in front of all these supporters of the noble art I felt a real dumbbell.

As the third and last round was reached my Second sponged my face and said, 'Grab him and hold him in a clinch son, and then belt him.'

So as the bell went for the last round and my opponent danced towards me I managed to push him against the ropes and hit him a glancing blow. The referee stepped in and awarded the fight to the wee boy. I left the ring with a few shouts from the crowd ringing in my ear. I was sick with embarrassment and both my big toes were killing me with pain. Within a week both my big toenails had fallen off, so I could not attend the club for a few weeks. When I did return Cumshy Cameron told me he was quite pleased with my performance.

Well that was not my opinion. My bitter disappointment with my baptism at the noble art had disillusioned me. I got the feeling that perhaps my temperament did not equip me for the rigours of the boxing ring.

But when my feet returned to normal I attended the club again, although not so often. One night a trainer asked me if I wanted to give a boxer called Jim Devlin a short spar. He was a bantam weight so there did not seem much harm in it. We sparred around for a short time and I thought I was doing alright, having managed to hit him a few times. Then the trainer shouted, 'Last three minutes.' Now when I moved towards Devlin he caught me one on the nose with a very hard right-hand punch. I tried not to show it but there was no doubt it had hurt me. I tried to land a blow in his direction but Cumshy Cameron stepped into the ring and stopped the fight. I was about to ask what was wrong when I felt the taste of salt in my mouth and discovered my white training vest was covered in blood, blood streaming out from my nose,

I do not remember what Cumshy said to Devlin although he did indicate his displeasure at the power of his punch and the fact that the guy had broken my nose. I was cleaned up and two cotton-wool pads were put on my nostrils. I did not say a word when I got home. My nose was swollen but the bleeding had stopped and there was really no pain. But my mother insisted that I was not going back to that club anymore. That was not the way I saw it. After all, I had boxed with a professional and had given as much as I received. And to some extent I regarded it as an honour that it had taken a champion to break my nose. However, I reckoned without my oldest brother, James. Him and Walter Scott, one of my cousins, went up to the boxing club and they warned Devlin that if he took a liberty with me again there would be a real confrontation, and no Marquis of Queensborough rules this time.

My broken nose did not alter my appearance. But I had to get an operation much much later (the 1990s) in the Glasgow Royal Infirmary when it became apparent the broken bone was obstructing my breathing. While I never went back to McGhee's club I retained my interest in boxing and managed to see some of Scotland's favourite boxers, and there were many during the 1930s. However, as you get older you witness many of the fighters you always admired once they are over the hill and in very poor circumstances – in boxing parlance, shuffling along. I remember Benny Lynch as a can-boy when they were building Hillington Estate. I mentioned earlier the great Jake Kilrain, British middleweight champion, but who was working as a toller at one of the biggest tossing-schools on the banks of the Clyde. I also met a retired boxer called Paddy Docherty who had beaten Benny Lynch three times as an amateur. He was working as a handyman and cleaner in Pollok library.

Later when I was working with the Gas Board I had a mate called Alex Ferries who had been a flyweight boxer during the Benny Lynch era. He actually fought Lynch for the Scottish flyweight championship and was beaten on points. His purse for that fight was 30 shillings for fifteen rounds and Benny Lynch had given him an extra £I.

Alex lived in a small room and kitchen in Fielden Street off London Road. He was one of the nicest men you could meet, despite his broken nose, cauliflower ears and marked eyebrows, his 'earnings' from over two hundred fights. He was so gentle and soft spoken it was hard to believe that he had been a professional boxer. When you contrast the Alex Ferries of this world with the people behind-the-scenes in professional boxing, like George Dingley for instance, a manager and promotor of the late 1930s, there is no contest. It is another indictment of a system that brutalises people, all in pursuit of profit at any cost.

RELIGION, GANGS AND A GANGBUSTER

THE ONLY real gang activity I ever witnessed was when one gang invaded another gang's street or territory. In many cases it was a reprisal for some earlier affray where a member of the invading gang had been set about. The gang fight consisted of one group of boys, some as young as 8 or 9 years old, chasing the other boys and shouting 'cha-orge', at the same time as they threw stones or sticks. If they managed to catch somebody then they punched or kicked him. When the other gang saw this happening they re-grouped and made a countercharge to rescue the victim. It never lasted more than 15 minutes or so. Then someone would shout, 'Here comes the polis' and it was all over. There may have been serious injuries suffered but I cannot recall any.

While I never was a member or went about with any gang I was a Catholic in a predominantly Protestant district and that meant you had to be prepared to defend yourself if you were attacked. As many of the boys I played with were Protestants, and my mother was one as well, I never had any hang-ups about religion. The one definite occasion I got involved in fights about religion was St Patrick's day. At my school it was a Holiday of Obligation and we went to the chapel with a sprig of shamrock pinned to our jerseys.

When we walked past John Street school in Hozier Street we were regularly challenged by the 'toffs'. We called them that because they wore a school uniform. They would surround us and shout, 'A Billy or a Dan?' Some of the smaller boys usually cried and ran away. I could never do that and no matter the odds most of us stood our ground and gave as much as we got.

In all the years I lived in Brigton these were the only times I can remember when it was my religion that caused the fight. But it unfortunately was true that I did seem to fight a lot, and regularly some boy would be saying to me, 'I'll see you after four.' And many a time I regretted turning up because I was not a big boy and those I seemed to challenge were older and bigger than me. And of course when my mother saw the torn jersey and bleeding nose there was no pictures for me on Saturday.

In the tough environment that was part and parcel of my upbringing I felt that you had no alternative but face the bully or there would be no end to it. I remember once I was fighting a big boy called Jackson round a backcourt off Dalmarnock Road. It was an old cobbled back. At one point he went to grab me after I hit him but he tripped and hit his nose on an iron clothes pole, just as a woman came down the backstairs and was shouting at him, 'Away you go and leave the wee boy alone, you should be ashamed of yourself.' I did not wait, I grabbed my school bag and left, looking back to see Jackson holding his nose.

But one of the most brutal things I ever remember seeing was a bare-knuckle fight at Emery's farm on the banks of the Clyde. It was between two men, both stripped to the waist. One was quite tall, about 19 or 20 years of age. The other was a small man, heavily built and older, probably in his late twenties or hitting thirty. Within a few minutes the body of the shorter man was covered in blood as the tall man had burst his nose with the first torrent of punches. It seemed so one-sided. But despite being put on the ground repeatedly the wee man kept getting up and rushing the younger man. This must have went on for at least twenty minutes or a half an hour and the crowd were calling for it to stop. But whenever somebody stepped in to try to end it the wee man punched him away and again kept rushing at his opponent.

Eventually he was back down on the ground once again and the tall young man stepped forward and, after helping him to his feet, he held out his hand and said, 'Alright you win Johnny'. The wee man wiped the blood from his body with his shirt. The next thing was a bunnet was put round the crowd and the cash proceeds were divided between the two protagonists. They smoked a Woodbine together then the crowd left the scene. I found out much later that the older guy was the notorious Johnny Phillips. He always stood at Bridgeton Cross and issued challenges at the drop of a hat. Regularly he got jailed for breach of the peace. He survived right into his late fifties when he died while in 'police custody'. But that bare-knuckle battle was a more common agenda than the headline-grabbing talk of gangs and gang fights.

Many observations have been made about the Glasgow street gangs of the 1930s and books both factual and fictional have been written about them. Speaking as a teenager in the late thirties I do not recognise the characters described in books like *No Mean City*. I never saw or even heard of any individual gang-member strutting about the street with two open razors sticking out of his waistcoat pocket. It makes you smile when you read about the exploits of the so-called 'Gangbuster' Chief Constable, Percy Sillitoe. Regarding his claims that he had smashed the Glasgow street gangs, as a young boy I once saw a single policeman appear in a street where two gangs were having a confrontation and both groups of so-called gangsters disappeared like snaw aff a dyke.

That Brigton and the east end were tough areas goes without saying but anyone who used a razor, a knife or an axe was ostracised. And if it was clear that a 'liberty' had been taken some of the local hard men who did not require weapons had a 'quiet word' with the culprits. The largest and best known gang was undoubtedly the Billy Boys who stood at Brigton Cross. Their praises still get sang about every Saturday at Ibrox Park. Nearly seventy years after I first heard it sung, as a person who had a Catholic upbringing, it still hurts when I hear the tens of thousands of Rangers' supporters singing, 'Up to the knees in Fenian blood surrender or you'll die'.

Of course in Brigton and the east end you had probably more gangs than anywhere else in Glasgow. There were the Sally Boys from Salamanca Street, Parkhead and then the Norman Conqs from Norman Street in Dalmarnock. Also you had the Chanty Boys from Fraser Street, off London Road and there were gatherings of older men at street corners in Bernard Street and they were known as the Stickit. The Baltic Fleet came from Baltic Street and the Nunny Boys came from Nuneaton Street, both in Dalmarnock. From the Calton you had the San Toy, The Tongs, the Tiny Tongs and the Calton Entry Boys. I heard about the Cumbie from Cumberland Street, and the Bee Hives also from the south side, and then there was the Cheeky Forty from Garngad. No doubt there were many more in all the other districts that I had never heard about. The above-mentioned were only street gangs and as far as I know many of them had a majority of Roman Catholics in their ranks.

The only time I did see weapons used was when an Orange Walk went through Bernard Street. Despite the fact that most of the residents were Protestants the majority were not sympathetic to the Orange Walk and resented them taking the march into Bernard Street. Some of the Stickit Boys were standing peacefully at the corner of Marquis Street on this occasion. When some of the Billy Boys who were in the Walk started to attack them the whole procession was brought to a halt. Hundreds of fights broke out all along the street and weapons were definitely used. This I do know as my sister Peggy went to the aid of a young man who had sought shelter in our close when chased by the Billy Boys. He was bleeding profusely from a head wound caused by an axe. We took him into our house and gave him a cup of tea after bandaging his head. To my knowledge that was the last time an Orange Walk ever went through Bernard Street.[26]

There is no doubt that Billy Fullerton was the best known gang member. He was regarded as the leader of the Billy Boys, particularly after Chief Constable Sillittoe was interviewed by many newspapers. I do not know where or when Billy Fullerton led anybody. I passed Brigton Cross nearly every day of the week and anytime I saw him he was standing at the corner of Orr Street and London Road, laughing and joking with a crowd of young men.

The only time I gave the Brigton Cross a miss was on a Saturday afternoon when the Celtic supporters were coming from Parkhead because you could be sure there would be a confrontation. There was also another gang at Brigton Cross called the Derry Boys. They were the youth section and were equally as vehement against Celtic supporters. The highlight of their year's activity was the 12th of July when they participated in the Orange Walk, even although the officials of the Orange order did not openly recognise them.

Despite the fact that his father was a Shop Steward in a factory in Dagenham, and apparently a left-wing one, Chief Constable Percy Sillitoe seemed to reserve his hatred for politically-motivated activists. He went onto become the head of the Secret Service.[27]

---

[26] But see McIvor and Paterson's essay 'Combating the Left: Victimisation and Anti-Labour Activities on Clydeside, 1900-1939' [from *Militant Workers*, edited by Duncan and McIvor] that during the earlier part of the twentieth century 'the delinquent wing of the Orange Order campaigned vigorously and violently against socialist meetings. . . Orange disruption of socialist gatherings continued into the 1920s and 1930s with, for example, the notorious Billy Boys especially in the Glasgow East End. . .'

[27] Sir Percy Sillitoe was appointed Director-General of MI5 1946-53, by the post-war Labour Government.

Prior to coming to Glasgow he spent some time as a trooper in the South African police force, a private organisation controlled by the British South African Company. He was stationed in Salisbury where much of the police activity was of a military nature, controlling the Matabeles. So his formative years were spent as a military policeman putting down rebellions by natives.

His first experience as a Chief Constable was in Chesterfield from 1923 then in 1926 he moved to Sheffield, and on to Glasgow in 1931. Sillitoe was regarded as a Chief Constable who could get results and his reputation extended far and wide. However, while there were similarities between Sheffield and Glasgow it was obvious from his attitude that he did not realise the extent to which the 1930s slump had affected the social conditions in Glasgow.

He dismissed the unemployed workers who had the courage to take to the streets and also dismissed the people who spoke on their behalf, men like John Maclean,[28] Peter Colin Blair McIntyre,[29] Harry McShane and Guy Aldred.[30] He referred to them all simply as 'Communist agitators'. To anybody who advocated left wing solutions to social issues like bad housing, unemployment and poverty, Sillitoe's attitude was totally authoritarian. He showed hostility towards any attempt to organise and educate politically the victims of the slump.

Most despicable was his treatment of a retired barber called Petrie, alias 'The Clincher', a well-known Glasgow character who was active in the Free Speech campaign. 'The Clincher' had spoken out for years at the Speakers' Corner, accusing Glasgow Councillors

---

[28] John Maclean [1879-1923]. More than a decade after his death, in his Introduction to Wal Hannington's *Unemployed Struggles 1919-1936*, Tom Mann still felt the urge to 'raise my hat in reverence – John Maclean of Glasgow – a splendid man and fearless fighter, who literally died for the cause. . .'

[29] Peter McIntyre was a member of the Scottish Workers' Republican Party which had been founded by John Maclean.

[30] Guy Aldred [1886-1963], like Maclean, a pivotal figure; London-born and bred; 'Boy Preacher, Social Democrat, Prisoner of Conscience (repeatedly), Conscientious Objector, Anarcho-Communist, orator, writer, publisher. . .' see John Taylor Caldwell's biography *Come Dungeons Dark*. A comprehensive selection of Aldred's own writings has been in the pipeline by AK Press for a while.

of corruption. In company with his comrade Peter McIntyre and alongside Guy Aldred he urged the unemployed workers to rise up against the system and take to the streets.[31]

Sillitoe eventually managed to get 'The Clincher' incarcerated illegally in Forest Hall, by saying that he was mentally retarded. Then he actually tried to have the man certified insane, using a method not unlike the kind operated in Russia to permanently intern critics and opponents of the system. 'The Clincher' was left having to prove his sanity. But the Court decided in his favour and afterwards he carried the certificate about with him, he became the only man in Glasgow who carried a certificate to prove he was sane.

Along with Guy Aldred, Peter McIntyre was one of the first of the early Socialists to call for rent strikes and for homeless people to occupy empty property. When the police found out he himself was occupying an empty house in one of the better parts of Govan without paying any rent they tried to evict him. Peter and his comrades cut down a large tree and rammed it from the back door right the way through the hall all the way to the front door, to thwart the police. It is true that in the 1950s, when he was an old man, Peter McIntyre came back as an elected councillor. Despite holding open-air meetings at Govan Cross he failed to make any impact in the council.

---

[31] See also J.T.Caldwell's informative essay, 'The Battle For The Green' for more on the Free Speech fights; Caldwell's writings are also recommended for a view of McShane and others from an anarchist perspective.

Hugh Savage – a studio picture aged 18

Part 2
Work and Growing up, Serving your Time

WHEN I approached my fourteenth birthday I had made up my mind to leave school. It was not a difficult decision to make as in no way could I be described as an intellectual. It seemed to be my misfortune to be stuck firmly in the middle of the class. In subjects like English, geography and history I was above average but on most other subjects, except physical training, I languished in the lower half. While in no way blaming any of the teachers for my failure, none of them ever impressed me, right through nine years of education.

And many of them I hated, particularly the priests I had when I first went to Sacred Heart. There were two of them, Father Francis and Father Bernard. When they reached into their robes and pulled out the black three-tonged strap it was really frightening. And when they made you double your hands and then gave sometimes six lashes, very few boys could hold back the tears. What worried me was the fact they seemed to feel so pleased, as if it was a job well done. As one who got his share of that belt I can say your hand was sore for days and on one occasion when my mother noticed how black and blue it was she said if it happened again she would take it up with the headmaster. Afraid of the retribution I kept my hands well out of sight from her in future.

The priests were not alone of course, most of the other teachers had no interest in their pupils. Either you kept up with the best in the class or you fell by the wayside. I could not get out of school fast enough.

The first week after my fourteenth birthday I started to work my way around the factories in Brigton looking for a job. It was my first experience of discrimination. I began at the Acme Wringer Company, then Templeton's Carpets, Tullis and Martin's leatherworks and so on. In all I must have gone to nearly twenty factories and all said the same, 'What school did you go to?' There was I with my new short trousers and shoes, my best woollen jersey and shirt and tie, a wee boy looking for his first job, and all these people could think about was what religion I was. Probably that was the first time I became angry. Not with the bigots that were denying me a job because of religion, but the whole stupidity that divided people in their way through life.

The next thing I did was attend the vacancy section at the Labour Exchange in Megan Street off Dalmarnock Road. The first day there I got a green-card to go and see about a job for a message boy at the bottom of Saltmarket. It was a golf shop based in one of the tenements that you had to approach by going upstairs right at the front of the building. It was owned by a professional golfer named J.T.Donaldson. He had won several tournaments and now gave golfing lessons. He also manufactured and repaired golf clubs.

He was a very nice man in his fifties with red hair and he always wore tweed plus-fours. My main job was to deliver clubs to warehouses like Rattray's in Candleriggs and French's off Argyle Street, and many more. I also carried clubs and golf bags along to a new shop opened by J. Letters in Main Street, Gorbals. He later became a very big name in the golfing world with many top players using his clubs.

My boss was a very unassuming man who had a liking for a good dram, and he seemed to thrive with plenty of people around him. He stayed in a small house in Oatlands and worked long hours, not only making golf clubs himself but travelling to many courses giving lessons. His favourite was the old Turnberry course where his long-time friend Jimmy McDowall was the Club professional. It was a regular journey once or twice a month to catch the first train from the old St Enoch Station to Girvan and then he took a taxi from there to Turnberry.

In those days Turnberry was owned by LMS railways along with top class hotels like Gleneagles, the Glasgow Central and many more. J.T.Donaldson assisted his friend on the Turnberry course giving golfing lessons. But I think my boss looked forward to it as a day away from what was for him a long and hard working shift in Glasgow. And of course he always carried his wee whisky flask, purely for medical purposes, for when they reached the 19th hole. He never spoke about the people he gave lessons to but once he did mention somebody. This was Lady Bird of the famous custard people. Apparently she got under his skin and he said it would be the last time he would go back to Turnberry if she was one of his pupils. In those days only the real *créme de la créme* could afford to stay there.

J.T.Donaldson liked golfing stories and one of his favourite was the one that Henry Longhurst wrote about when Walter Hagen and Gene Sarazen tied in the final of the British Open and the play-off was scheduled early the next morning. Longhurst was staying in the Turnberry Hotel with them. Passing the residents' lounge well past 12 midnight he was surprised to see Walter Hagen laughing and drinking with a number of very attractive lady friends. Hagen greeted Longhurst as he walked past and asked him if he wanted a refreshment. 'No thank you' said Longhurst 'but do you know that Gene Sarazen has been up in his bed since 7 o'clock?'

'Yes Henry, but he sure aint sleeping.'

J.T.Donaldson loved golf. He had a small practice room and nets in the back shop where he gave lessons most days. My time was taken up in the morning delivering clubs and bags, and generally going messages but I also started to fit grips onto the clubs and to sandpaper woods for the French polishers. And if there was nothing for me to do the boss did not object if I practiced at the nets. You used real golf balls and there was a reinforced canvas with a bulls-eye target that you aimed at. So with watching the many good golfers who came about the shop, and with some basic instructions from the boss, I developed as a good striker of the ball without ever setting eyes on a golf course. He eventually gave me an old secondhand set for myself but I was too self conscious to take them home. I would not be seen walking into Bernard Street carrying golf clubs. In those days golf was regarded as a toffs' game. At least that was what I thought.

Saltmarket was one of the busiest streets in Glasgow in those days, with hundreds of people passing your doors and before street-trading was licenced most of the street corners had a barrow selling some kind of food, from fruit and fish to hot chestnuts. My first job in the morning after the shop opened was to fix the two showcases atop with two large golf balls to the railings at the bottom of the stairs.

The boss was a good mixer and all sort of characters came about the shop. A regular was the well-known Mickey Casey. He had been quite a dandy in his day but drink and the good life – with a few fights and rough and tumbles thrown in – had left poor Mickey with a slight deficiency. He was completely harmless and for a few shillings some of the bookies and shopkeepers would give him some suit or costume or other to wear for a dare. Some days he would be dressed in full evening-wear, other days he would be done up as a kiltie in full highland regalia, or else he would be like Charlie Chaplin with a bowler hat. There was always crowds of children following him. While he sometimes carried a cane he never was violent and the police treated him with respect. Unless he had become intoxicated. Then he was given a bed for the night. Or if he was fined some of the local shopkeepers would pay his fine. Every morning the famous florist Mary Fox put a fresh flower in the buttonhole of whatever costume he was wearing. There were so many characters from that period, including the Clincher himself who I well remember seeing with his top hat and cane, selling his paper, *The Clincher*, at the corner of Argyle Street and St Enoch Square.

Some of the men who frequented the golf shop used to take the hickery tips that I cut off the top of the clubs and do practical jokes. They put a small bent nail through them, cut a cigarette packet into a windmill and attached it to the nail. They would stand next to our showcases at the bottom of the front door and one of them would ask a passerby for a light. In those days most men wore caps or bunnets. When the man held up his fag to give a light, a windmill with a nail would be attached to the back of his bunnet and the poor unsuspecting fellow would stroll up the Saltmarket with his windmill belting away, wondering why he was being stared at. I can never recall anyone getting annoyed, we seemed to be more tolerant in those days.

One of the men who regularly gave us a visit was a very nice grey-haired man who lived round the corner in Steele Street. He was badly deformed and had very bad legs that must have reduced his height by more than 18 inches. His name was Mr McFarlane and his son was the famous Willie McFarlane who won the Powderhall Sprint[32] a record number of times and in his own day was the fastest man in the world. The boss told me that young Willie

[32] The Powderhall Sprint took place annually in Edinburgh at the Powderhall Stadium. The 'sprint' was a handicap race for professional athletes and a great betting event.

and his pals played football in Steele Street in the evenings or Sundays. The Central Police station was just round the corner and the boys were regularly chased by the polis, but they could never manage to confiscate the ball. Every time they came Willie seized it and ran right into the Glasgow Green. None of the cops could ever catch him. This really annoyed them. Eventually they got one of their beat-police who was an amateur athlete, so he could get after Willie, but he was not successful either. After making enquiries he approached the family and at the end of it all I think it was him got Willie Mcfarlane to take the running up seriously,.

In many respects the job with J.T.Donaldson was probably the most interesting and satisfying I ever had. But fate played me a dirty trick. The man who did the French polishing of the wooden clubs lived in a house above the shop and my last job before I left at night was to take him all the clubs that were required to be polished urgently. He lived two stairs up and I used to dive up the stairs and down again, unfortunately I had a habit of leaving the back door of the shop open for the few minutes necessary. One morning when I came in the boss confronted me. A very expensive leather golf-bag was missing and the only explanation was that someone had taken advantage of me leaving the door open the night before and had come in and stolen it.

I could not believe it as I was a very fit wee boy and fast, I could jump the stairs four at a time. I had never seen anyone near the door. The boss said he had warned me before about this happening, which was true. By that time I was crying and I told him I would just leave and get another job and I would try to pay for the bag. The boss said there was no need for that and I could carry on. However, I put on my jacket and walked away. I did not wait for the wages I was due. I went greeting along through the Glasgow Green then I reached Megan Street and the employment exchange. I wiped my tears away, walked into the vacancy section and asked if they had any jobs. They gave me a green-card for a paperworks in Moncur Street, Calton. I went right up immediately and got a start for the very next day. By the time I got home my mother was frantic. 'Where have you been?'

'Away gettin a job.'

'But you've got a job.'

I told her what had happened about the golf bag and everything.

Then she floored me. 'Mr Donaldson has been up to the house. There was no bag stolen. He just wanted to learn you a lesson.'

I started to cry again. 'You mean to say he told me a lie?'

That destroyed my wee world, I would never work for him again, no matter what he offered me. My mother tried to coax me but there was no way I could ever trust a person who could hurt a wee boy that had looked up to him like I did. I never saw J.T.Donaldson in my life again. I never took the secondhand set of clubs he gave me either and do not know what happened to the business.

Pulling the Barrow

S O I started with the firm of Dunlop & Jack at their premises in Moncur Street and it was my first experience of pulling a barrow. My job was to deliver toilet rolls to hardware shops and uplift paper and deliver it to printers all over Glasgow. It was a very light barrow but when you carried several reams of brown paper inside it became quite a pull going up places like the High Street. Fortunately there were plenty of horse-drawn carts in those days and the carter let you hook the barrow onto the back of his cart if your load was really heavy. I suppose my eight shillings a week wage was much less expensive than it took to keep a horse.

I did spend some time in the factory with the other few boys making up toilet rolls and parcelling orders. It was close to the Moncur Street barrows and on a Saturday morning while waiting on the factory opening I used to give some of the stall-holders a hand to set up their wares. I was intrigued by their methods and activity, the speed with which they set up the stalls with row after row of blooming apples interspersed with oranges, bananas and other fruits. I had never seen anything like it before.

The most famous stall was Mary Ann's. At first I thought Mary Ann was the small woman with the loud voice who wore men's boots all the time. I soon found out that it was the other, older woman who wore expensive cardigans and very expensive rings and brooches. The highlight of their operation was the sale of bags of fruit. The small woman with the loud voice would shout, 'Number one and number two' and so on down the rows until the bag was full of assorted fruit. Then she would shout 'Who'll gie me two bob. Never mind two bob, who'll gie me wan and a tanner!'

Then the hands started to go up and dozens of people walked away with bags of fruit. For years after I left the Calton job I still saw the wee woman, pulling a big barrow filled with fruit and vegetables into the city centre where they had a corner barrow stall. I never knew her name but Mary Ann was a very fortunate fruit hawker to have had such a faithful and dedicated grafter.

My job at Dunlop & Jacks was not very interesting and the

131

pulling of the barrow through the Glasgow streets was beginning to get me down. I had begun to take an interest in clothes and I found the few bob I got for pocket money did not go very far. I started looking for another job. I heard that a firm in Rutherglen was looking for boys and the starting wage was 14/- per week compared to the 8/- I was getting. The firm was the well-known British Wire Rope Works at Farm Cross. I just asked for an hour off my work and went for an interview with them and the foreman asked me to start on Monday, so I handed in my notice and left Dunlop & Jacks on Saturday.

As I rode on my bike along Dalmarnock Road to my new job I kept thinking what I would do with the extra pocket money that would come my way. I was not prepared for the noise in the factory when I stepped through the doors to clock in. It was really deafening and the different types of machines confused me. Once the gaffer took me to the machine that I was to operate it was much better. There were quite a few new-starts like me and they seemed to master it quite well. The machine was a winder, not unlike the operation that took place in my mother's cotton mills, although this time it was wire we were winding, not thread.

The foreman was a nice pleasant man and very patient. After an hour or so of basic instruction he told the boy next to me to keep his eye on me. It all seemed quite simple. I was in control of a machine that took the wire off a large wooden reel and rolled it onto a small bobbin. When full it was ready to be placed in the large machines along with many other bobbins. Depending on the diameter it would be spliced through the machine to make wire-rope, sometimes over 2" thick. After a couple of days it seemed easy enough. Most of the workers in this section were boys of my own age and they were all very helpful.

The days seemed to pass quite fast. The British Wire Rope Works sent their products not only throughout the United Kingdom but to the far east and to Australia and Canada, so there was always plenty of orders to fulfil and there must have been about a hundred workers. That was excluding those in the offices who worked in a very distinctive building right on Farm Cross which, after decades of demolition and closures, is the only part of the works still standing.

I struck up a friendship with a wee boy called Bertie, my nearest workmate on the winding section. After we had our pieces at dinnertime he took me to the football game at the back of the works. This was the highlight of the day. Bertie was a good wee player, very tricky. He told me he had been in his school team and they had reached the schoolboys' championship semi-final. I could believe that, I could tell it by the way he played.

There was no betting took place in those wee games but it was still quite competitive, and there was about seven or eight a-side. I did not expect to get playing that first time but they were short and asked me on. While I did not set the heather on fire I must have done alright as it became a regular event. Wee Bertie was pleased. His big pal Doddie ran the game and took care of the ball. I became a regular player and we formed a friendly group.

Doddie was mad about football as well. Although he was overweight he really must have played the game to a good level because when he got the ball he was dominant. He was also well-built. He always picked Bertie and me in his team if he could and he came and took his tea with us. If we had any trouble with our machines he helped to get them working again. Doddie seemed to look after wee Bertie. They both came from Cambuslang and they went on the same tram home together.

There was another man about twenty five years of age who operated the nearest large machine to our wee section. I was sure I knew him from somewhere, he was always very tidy in his appearance. It turned out he stayed in my part of Brigton and his name was Crawford. I passed him morning and evening, when he was walking home and I was cycling. I never paid him much attention. He seemed a bit of a loner, always taking his piece by the machine on his own, never coming to watch the football. For no reason he started to throw bits of waste at me and Bertie when we were bending over our machines. We tried to ignore him. Then one day Bertie let out a cry and started shouting at the man. I went down to see what had happened and he told me that when he bent over his machine Crawford had stuck a pin into his backside. Crawford denied it. There was a piece of metal bar I used to tighten up my bobbin. After that, if I saw Crawford coming I kept it in my hand until he passed. I told him if he came near me I would belt him with it.

Apparently this had been going on for a long time and he

seemed to get pleasure out of it. It is a fact that you cannot be vigilant all of the time and the following week, one afternoon we had come back in from the football, I was leaning over my machine and I did not see Crawford at my back, he stuck me with a pin. I let out a yell. I turned roundabout and saw him moving sharply back to his machine. I threw the metal bar at him, it just missed his shoulder. But just as I walked towards him the gaffer came into the passage and I had to go back to my work. Crawford had pushed the pin in so far it drew blood.

I told wee Bertie what had happened and he said something must be done about it. Things were quiet for a few days then one afternoon I saw Doddie approaching Crawford. He told him in no uncertain manner if he did not stop annoying and bullying the boys he would be sorted out. The very next day me and Bertie were round reloading the large reels into position and I left him to get a drink of water. As I made my way back I could see Crawford walking to the back of our machines and I hurried faster, then I heard Bert crying. Crawford had a hold of his arm and was twisting it up his back. I took a few more strides and as hard as I could I sunk my boot into his arse. He made an attempt to come at me but I grabbed the iron bar and I said to him, 'This time I willni miss.'

I gave Bertie a lift up and he was in pain, but we decided not to tell the gaffer. Our pal Doddie sorted Crawford out when he was leaving the works that night, and that was the end of his days as a bully. He approached me the next morning and said he was sorry and he did not mean any harm. Later I discovered he was in the Salvation Army, so was his mother and father, and his young brother played in their band. I saw him on many occasions marching in the ranks, long after I had left the British Wire Rope Works.

SHOCKS FOR A CELTIC SUPPORTER

W HEN I reached my sixteenth birthday the time had come to start my apprenticeship as a plumber with the firm that employed my big brother Walter. I gave my notice into the Wire Rope Works and on the first working day after the Christmas and New Year holidays I began serving my time. The firm of plumbers and electricians I worked for was called John Irving and Sons and was based at Victoria Road, across from Larkfield bus depot. It was the farthest I had ever worked away from home.

When I set off with my big brother I assumed I would start with menial tasks in and around the workshop, which was what Walter had told me. So with a brand new pair of bib-overalls and my piece and my new tea-can, and my 3 ft. wooden Rabone rule, I stepped into the workshop. To my surprise, between the apprentices of various ages and journeymen there were over twenty other guys about to start work. One of them was a plumber called Willie Hunter. I was told by the foreman this was my mate and we were going to work at a new church being built at Cardonald.

When I walked out of John Irving's premises that morning with my new overalls on and carrying the tools I felt quite proud, particularly since it was my mother's wish being fulfilled. She always said that all of us would learn a trade. My entry into plumbing meant there were now two plumbers and a joiner in the family.

On the journey to Cardonald I discovered that my mate stayed in Mathieson Street in the south side. Willie Hunter was a man in his late forties and had two daughters. We arrived at the church building site and while he was talking to the site foreman I was told to put the tools in one of the huts and wait. In a short time we started to take the cast iron U.G. gutters from the back of the hut to the side of the newly-erected church. Our first job was to fit the gutters to allow the roof to be slated. After an hour or so Willie told me to get the can on for both of us. I boiled up at the joiners' fire then shouted on him, and we sat on the joiners' wood pile up outside the huts and enjoyed our lunch.

Sitting in the yellow tramcar taking me home I really felt quite content, and fortunate that my mate was a nice man. It had been hard work carrying these cast-iron gutters onto the roof but when you looked up and saw the brand new gutters on the new church building you felt satisfied.

Within a few days the next operation started. This was taking the rainwater down-pipes down to meet the fireclay drains, and fitting in the soil-pipes to take in connections for the wash-hand basins, sinks and w.c.s. I found out the hard way that when you are dooking holes in the outside walls to take the holdfasts that hold the cast-iron pipes, you have to keep your eye on the head of the dooking iron. The first day on that work my left hand was badly bruised after several hours of chiselling holes in the wall. When I got home my mother bandaged my hand and gave me a left handed glove to save me further damage.

We were on the church job for quite a few weeks. We got so far ahead Mr Jim Irving, one of the sons, told us to come back into the shop on Monday morning to do repairs till the job was ready for the next stage. My mate Willie Hunter was given the repairs, the burst pipes, choked drains, washers etc. while I was given the job of melting down old lead into a big cast-iron pot which was placed on the charcoal fire in the backshop. The hot lead was then poured into steel ingot pots which when cold weighed a quarter of a cwt. These were built up in the workshop to await the arrival of the lead manufacturer. Apparently ingots sold in this way were twice as valuable. It was quite boring work but it allowed me to speak to the other apperentices and get to know them and the rest of the plumbers working there.

It was around this time I was introduced to my number one enemy, the Irving barrow. It was a huge thing with large heavy wheels and a rope between the shafts so that it could be pulled up hills. It made the small barrow I had had at Dunlop & Jacks look and feel like a scooter. My first job with the barrow was when Willie and myself had to load it up for a job at the old Halfway House in Paisley Road.

The most direct road to our destination was to head for Mosspark Boulevard. As it was a climb all the way I consoled myself that it would be downhill on the way back. Willie was kind of slight in build and really did not assist me much. The first time I saw a horse and cart going in our direction I asked the carter if it would be alright if I hooked onto the back of his cart. There was no trouble and we got to the Halfway pub just in time for our piece. After dinner we started to strip out what I took to be the old lead pipe in the attic. As I started to put it alongside the old lead waterpipe Willie said, 'No son, this is block tin and it has to be kept separate.'

He explained that it had about the same value as silver. At three o'clock the boss appeared with bags. I had to put all the block tin in them, then hide it all under the lead and take it back to the shop, and I was not to let the guy in charge of the pub see me doing it. I never gave the boss' remarks much consideration. That afternoon I did not get back to the shop until after 5 pm. The workshop was closed but the girl in the office let me take the barrow in. It did not seem right to me that there were at least three cars amongst the three Irving sons but they still could not afford a van to transport all the waste-pipes and soil-pipes, putty for fitting taps, gratings to the sanitary fittings, slate nails for fitting lead aprons around the chimney stocks on the roof, boss-white for sealing joints on the brass fittings, and all the other essential material that was needed for the work. It was my first experience with the barrow but most certainly not my last. I had spent five hours pushing and pulling the thing. I made several more trips to Halfway taking a load of block tin and lead away every time.

We eventually finished the job there and we were sent to another one, the State Bar in Holland Street. A new 'Spanish' lounge had to be fitted into the old beer cellar without interfering with the pub's normal functioning, and it was always very busy. The job was very complicated. This put a lot of strain on Willie Hunter and when he got excited he had a bad stammer. I had to calm him down and reassure him that he was doing okay. Then we had to re-line a lead storage system above the staircase entry to a billiard and snooker hall. Willie was not agile and the only way inside the cistern was to step up a 10 ft. ladder and squeeze through a 12 inch space. I had to do it. Once inside there was plenty of room, it was least 6ft. x 4ft.

I stripped the old lead out and lowered it with a rope to the ground. Willie tied on the new lead which had been cut to size. I pulled it up and fitted on the bottom and sides. He then gave me in the solder and the blow lamp and I started to solder the joints and draw off points. Willie had the tea-cans going by this time.

The job was half finished when he shouted that my can was boiled. I was really glad as it had been extremely warm inside the cistern. But then as I tried to come out head first I found I could not get out through the space. I tried doing it leg first but that was worse. At last I sat down. Willie came up the ladder and I was glad to see him but he said, 'What are we going to do?'

I looked at him in astonishment. He was beginning to panic probably because if anybody found out I was in here it would not look right, I was only into my second year and should not have been undertaking such a job. I said, 'Bring me up my can and my piece and I'll take my dinner. I'll cool down and the space'll get cooler as well, and then I'll try again.' That was what we did and sure enough, with me taking off my dungarees, eventually I managed to squeeze out through the 12 inch space onto the ladder.

While we were working at the State Bar we were sent to put in a water supply to the garden of Mr Don Grant, the boss of the firm. The State Bar was just one of many pubs owned by the Grant family, including the Rogano.[33] They also had the Royal licensed restaurant in West Nile Street, a famous gathering point for professional football players.

Mr Don Grant lived in an old style villa along the road from Victoria Hospital. It was a beautiful house, kept in good condition and seemed to be very exclusively furnished. They had a gardener who told us where to dig the track for the new water supply. We started to clear away the red chips and map the route. When I turned to use the pick-axe I saw a boy about five or six years of age, he was pulling the pick across the lawn. I shouted on him and he moved faster but the pick was too big for him to lift and he tripped and fell. I ran over and picked him up but he ran away into the house crying I had hit him. I lifted the pick and an angry lady came out of the house and said, 'Did you hit the wee boy?' Just as I

---

[33] The Rogano is a famous Glasgow restaurant. Scott Savage writes: 'One Friday lunchtime Ted Heath, later a Prime Minister, entered with three colleagues and walked towards an empty table. Don Grant who used to wear 'plus fours', was present at the time and he yelled, 'Have you booked?' One of Ted's colleagues replied, 'D'you know who you're talking to! That 's Ted Heath!' 'I don't care who he is, if he hasn't booked he's not getting a table.' So Ted Heath and his party ended up in a wee corner at the bar with a plate of sandwiches.

was about to deny it the gardener came and told the lady what had happened, she turned and went back into the house We finished that job in record time and I was glad to get back to the State Bar.

Eventually my mate Willie Hunter and myself were split up. He went on to some other job and I was kept in the shop to run errands and help out wee Davie Neilson the jobbing plumber. Davie did all the maintenance and repairs in the tenements on the south side of the city. He was a very conscientious man and an Elder in his kirk. He had worked with the firm all his life, going back to the days when its founder, old John Irving, had started the business.

One of the first jobs we had to attend to was a choked drain in a backcourt in the Gorbals, at Florence Street. It was a typical choked drain in the backcourt with the whole close and some of the low-down houses awash with filthy water. We had to locate the draincover which was at least 8 inches under water. Davie told me to gather up some of the bricks that lay strewn about the place and make some stepping stones in through the water towards the grating. We did this and then Davie stepped his way towards the centre but just as he reached it the last brick slid away beneath his feet and he did a swan-dive right into the puddle. I ran into the water splashing through without using the bricks and helped Davie to his feet.

When he got up he took his dungaree jacket off. It was covered in shite. He just shrugged his shoulders and took the draincover off the grating, and using the drain-rods he cleared the water away. Then while one of the woman in the close was cleaning Davie's jacket and dungarees I washed the surface dirt away and brushed his back clean, and then we made our way back to the workshop. Waiting at the stop for the tramcar Davie said to me, 'Are you sure I don't smell?'

'No.'

When we boarded the tram we went upstairs. We handed over our tuppence fares to the woman conductor. She looked at us and said, 'I've heard of shite-bags but this is ridiculous. I should take yous two straight to Calder Street baths.'

We got off as soon as we could. Davie's main concern was the loss of his clay pipe which had been smashed when he fell in the water. It was a 'jaw-warmer'. He soon got himself a new one.

The next mishap we had was when we were repairing an underground waterpipe in a back court in Shawlands. It was a high back with steps up from the close. And it was covered in grass. Where the route of the pipe was the digging was very soft and mainly sand. In no time at all we were down nearly three feet and our prodding to where the water was coming indicated that we still had a bit to go. Davie told me to get back to the workshop for a ladder and support boards.

I was away nearly forty five minutes because I had to bring it all on the barrow. When I got into the backcourt I could not see Davie. When I asked one of the women who lived up the close she said he had never left the back. I went across to the trench which by this time was over six feet in length. When I looked down the hole it was nearly five feet in depth and Davie was sitting there smoking his new clay pipe. I said, 'What are you sitting down there for?'

'Well I just kept digging and then when I tried to get out the sides didn't seem secure so I waited till you came.'

We got the sides of the trench supported by our boards and completed the job then Davie treated me to one of his favourite things, a big London bun bought out of the City Bakeries, and then we made our way back to the workshop with the barrow.

The next day we got a job to renew a broken w.c. in a tenement in Pollokshaws Road. We never stocked sanitary-ware in the workshop so it was usually necessary for me to collect whatever it was from Smith & Holroyds at Bath Lane off Renfield Street.

Davie had to alter the pipework and get prepared for my return. I went round to the workshop to get an order and my tramcar fare. They only gave me thruppence for this so it just took me to Argyle Street both ways. It had been my practice to walk down to Cook Street. This then allowed me get a tram to Argyle Street and walk empty handed up to Bath Lane. I was then left with tuppence and could get another tram outside the door of Smith & Holroyds right to Eglinton Toll.

In those days Renfield Street was one of the busiest streets in Glasgow and it was no joke balancing a w.c. on your shoulders as you squeezed through the crowds. Then too of course there was always the possibility that you could bump into some of the lassies that went to the dancing at the Calton Masonic. It would not have done any good for my image, at that time I was trying to kid on I was a fully-fledged plumber.

However, after all that, when I got into the workshop the next morning Jessie the clerkess told me that Mr Jim Irving wanted to see me in the office. When I went into his room you could imagine my surprise when the first question he asked me was, 'How much did you receive for your tram fare yesterday when you were going to Smith & Holroyds?'

'Thruppence.'

'And what were you doing walking into town?'

I tried to explain my reasons but it was obvious he did not believe me and thought I was cheating on the money. Then I said to him if I could see if I still had the tram tickets in my jacket pocket. And I went to where my jacket was hung up and lo and behold both the tickets, the one penny and the two penny, were still there. I took them into the office and showed them to him. Then I could see the real disappointment in his face. He gruffly told me to go back to my work. I began to think to myself what kind of man was it that wanted to humiliate a young apprentice.

A few weeks later I went into the workshop in the morning quite early and Davie was sitting puffing his pipe. It was part of his job that he opened the shop up in the morning. He seemed to be quite sad. I said, 'What's wrong Davie, is your wife no well?'

'I'll tell you when we get to the job.'

As we were walking up to Pearson's hardware stores where we were working, he told me that Jim Irving had said he could no longer keep him working for the full week. If there was no work for him he would just have to go back home after he had opened up.

This more or less confirmed my belief that Mr Jim Irving was not a nice guy. How could Davie Nielson be treated in that manner, he had given his whole working life to the Irving family.

I told Davie to raise the issue with Sanny McIntyre who was the union man, in fact I think he was an official in the trade union lodge. But Davie was afraid to say anything. So without a word I went away myself and I told Sanny McIntyre the situation. Sanny went straight into the office and told the Irvings there would be no part-time plumbers working with this firm. Neither Sanny McIntyre nor myself ever mentioned it to anybody.

After a short spell in the workshop I was actually sent to the next job with Sanny. It was to fit a cocktail bar in the main stand adjacent to the directors' box at Ibrox Park. To more than half of all the boys in Glasgow this would have been a dream come true.

But I had always regarded myself as a Celtic supporter so my feelings were somewhat mixed. Nevertheless, when entering the empty stadium, the home of Glasgow Rangers, you could not be anything but impressed by the atmosphere.

It was much larger than I expected. The stand was built to provide space and the red terracotta brick gave it a strength to match its size. The main entrance was most impressive with its marble floor and columns, and its marble staircase with blue carpets to the fore. What took me by surprise was the friendly atmosphere. Everybody from the wee women who worked in the kitchen and the squad of cleaners who came into clean the whole stadium, right the way up to Mr Cameron the assistant coach, they were all genuinely obliging and helpful.

No one objected when me and Sanny took our tea-can and piece and sat on the steps of the stand watching the players train. Of course the highlight was the trial games they played at least once a week with the reserves playing the first team. It was no stroll either. All the players put their maximum effort into the game and when they left the field they were sweating heavily. I used to smile to myself and wonder what all the fanatic Rangers' supporters would say if they knew a 'tim'[34] was watching players like Davie Meiklejohn, Jerry Dawson, George Brown, Jimmy Simpson, Dougie Gray, Bob McPhail out training. All the above-named were automatic choices for any Scottish team, with Meiklejohn regular captain.

The job took much longer than was envisaged and additional work cropped up. Many other tradesmen were working in the stadium. In those days we continued going till 12 noon on a Saturday. The second week there I was in the new cocktail bar with Sanny McIntyre when Mr Struth the manager approached and handed both of us an envelope. We did not know what it contained. When he held it out to me he said, 'Now don't you be giving it away.'

As soon as he disappeared I hurriedly opened the envelope. It was a complimentary ticket for the stand for the match with Aberdeen that same afternoon.

Apparently this had been a practice for a long time and Mr Bill

---

[34] 'tim' = a Celtic supporter and/or Roman Catholic, derived from the rhyming slang, Tim Malloy = bhoy, an Irish spelling variant of boy.

Struth always carried it out himself. The joiner who was there working with us had done some work at Celtic Park and I asked him if this practice prevailed there too. He said to me, 'Not on your life, I was there for over two months and not only did I not get a ticket but I never knew anyone who did.'

So for a 'tim' like me there were a few illusions dashed that Saturday morning when the great Rangers' manager handed me an envelope.

Mr Bill Struth was a genuine legend in his own time. He had never been a professional football player but he had been an athlete and the Rangers' Annual Sports Day was probably the most attractive athletic event in the entire sports' calendar. In those days there were no professionals in athletics but the quality of the prizes and the treatment of the participants ensured that most world-class athletes welcomed an invitation. I remember seeing the great Sidney Wooderson, slightly built with his straight hair parted in the middle and wearing glasses, leaving a world-class field in his wake as he smashed the mile record. The famous Finnish long-distance runner Pavvo Nurmi appeared at Ibrox Park and lapped the best in the world.

My most embarrassing experience at Ibrox was one weekday when taking material up to my mate working in the stand. A player – I think his name was Bobby Mains – asked me if I would close the door after he had put his car under the stand. I never gave it a thought and after closing it I ran up the stairs to the stand and virtually ran right into Mr Struth who was standing at the top of the steps. I apologised and made to pass him but he stopped me.

'Excuse me but who told you to close that door?'

'The driver.'

Mr Struth then said very firmly, 'Your job here is to fit pipes, not to close doors, so go back to your work.'

As far as I remember he told the player off for bringing his car to Ibrox on a training day because it was an unwritten law that all players had to walk from the rail or bus stations. But he never stopped giving me a complimentary ticket for games so he did not seem to regard my mistake as too serious.

Most informed opinion on Glasgow Rangers regards Bill Struth, if not the best, as one of the best managers they ever had. As an apprentice plumber I can only say that all the players and staff at

Ibrox respected him. Maybe his demeanour guaranteed that. He was a fit man despite his greying hair, and he was always well-dressed in a comfortable way, with a well-cut suit and a soft brown hat. In those days Ibrox seemed a well-run club with a very capable staff and I was very sorry to leave that particular job.

Eventually I was sent to work on the 'Giffnock job'. This was a full, new estate of red sandstone houses being built by Thomas Stewart of Lochleven Road, Battlefield. Stewart had a good reputation as a builder and you could see why from the quality of work itself. While there were always at least two plumbers and an apprentice on the job, the plumber in charge sometimes worked by himself. His name was Wilson and he was really mean with materials, not popular at all with the rest of the plumbers. They regarded him as a real creep. The apprentices called him Rat Wilson.

But it was more experience for me and because I cycled to the job I could save the few coins I got for travelling expenses. There was another plumber on the job from Busby and a number of apprentice joiners and bricklayers so we always had a good game of football at dinnertime. The only fly in the ointment was Wilson, he kept asking me to go to the shop for material and bring it all the way out to Giffnock on the barrow.

One morning I had to go into the workshop first thing. Jim Irving saw me and passed on a note from Wilson who urgently required two bundles of lead pipe out at the new estate. Of course I had to take it on the barrow. I left at 8.30 am, taking as many side streets as possible to avoid the hills on the way up to Shawlands Cross. I thought I was making good time but by 10 o'clock I had only reached Merrylee. It is quite a pull up to Giffnock from there so I waited for a horse-drawn cart to come along to ask the carter if it would be alright if I hooked my barrow on. One did come. It was a laundry firm's cart, either Bowie's or Richmond Park. The carter was a young man and I remember him saying to me, 'What kind of firm sends a wee boy like you out with a load like that?'

I got to the job about half past eleven and by the time I took the material off it was dinnertime. I did not play football that day. And despite the objections of Wilson I started with the barrow back to the shop about 2 o'clock. He was wanting me to take a whole load of scrap metal back to the workshop but I put as little as possible on the barrow.

Even although it was mostly downhill I did not get back to Victoria Road until 5 o'clock and at Shawlands Cross it had started to rain. I always left my bike at the workshop so I was soaking wet by the time I rode home at nearly 6 pm.

I told my big brother Walter what had happened and he 'claimed' Wilson in the shop the next morning. He told him I was not to pull that barrow loaded on my own ever again. But it did not stop. Many a day I had to boil my can at the Statute of Labour tarpaulin road-howfs, leaving the barrow at the side of the road while I had my tea.

One morning when I was in the workshop Jim Irving told me Wilson would be off for a while because he was ill and I would have to run the job myself. I felt quite good about this even although, on reflection, it was ridiculous that a third-year apprentice plumber should be in charge of a full housing estate. I made a note of all the basic items that Wilson never ordered and went in the following morning with my list, which included rope-yarn for making joints on the connections for the wash-hand basins, sinks and w.c.s.

Mr Irving listened when I told him about the plumbing materials listed above, then he told me I could get rope-yarn from the builders fitting the drains, and the glazier would give me all the putty I wanted, and as far as slate-nails went, the slater threw away more slate-nails than I would ever use, and I really did not need boss-white anyway because the oil-bound paint used by the painters is the best thing for fittings. In other words I was supposed to thieve the material off other tradesmen working on the site

It was all getting too much for me. As I cycled to the Giffnock job I made my mind up that I did not want to work for a guy like Mr Jim Irving, Elder in the church at Mount Florida, a pillar of society, while here he was depending on a third-year apprentice to steal for him so he could carry out his job contracts. It also occurred to me that not only did I despise the man but I felt superior to him.

When I went home that night I told my older brother Walter and I did not go into work on Saturday morning. Instead I went to the firm of R. S. Renfrew at North Street Lane, Charing Cross. I was seen by the foreman, a Mr Brown, who gave me a start for first thing on Monday. My brother told the clerkess in John Irving and Sons and picked up my cards. One point that convinced me that the firm of Renfrew's would suit me was the fact that they had a big lorry instead of a hand-barrow to shift material out to jobs.

I was put to work on the roofs at Gourock railway station, renewing gutters and lead work. It was very heavy going but I found it interesting plus you got a great view of the ferry service to Dunoon and other places. The plumber in charge was called Peter, he came from Maryhill and was an ardent member of the Territorial Army.[35] There was another apprentice and plumber on the job. We got the 7 am train to Gourock every morning but you got your full expenses plus an hour each way travelling time. This made my wages up to over 25 shillings a week, compared to what I took home from Irving's which was not much more than 14 shillings. The weather was great as well, so in no time at all I was looking quite tanned.

R.S. Renfrew carried quite a number of large contracts and the original owner had been a baillie in the Glasgow Corporation. His son was now the boss and while he made regular visits to the job at Gourock he never spoke to anybody except Peter the foreman. One Friday when Peter gave me my wages he told me not to come on Saturday, instead I was to go into the shop at North Street lane because they were stocktaking. The Gourock job had lasted all summer and I did not manage to see any of the other plumbers and apprentices employed by my new firm. Now when I turned up at 8 am. I discovered that one of the final-year apprentices was Eddie Murphy. Eddie had been at Sacred Heart with me although I had never spoken to him. At school I was always a rebel and continually fighting in and out of the playground, whereas Eddie was a quiet boy. He was a year or so older than me and there was not much contact between us until now. He was very self conscious about his lack of hair and never took off his cap, even when the boys were larking about during stocktaking. I already knew about

---

[35] The Territorial Army is still based in Maryhill which has been a military centre, both territorial and 'regular', since 1873. 'The original Maryhill Barracks was built. . . to replace the old and unsuitable Gallowgate barracks [as] requested by the city magistrates because they were worried about possible riot and disorder amongst the large, and mostly immigrant, industrial labouring population.' (see *Old Maryhill* by Guthrie Hutton, publ. Richard Stenlake 1994). The 'regular' army left in 1958 and the barracks closed although the surrounding walls are in great shape. A new police station now stands across the road and reputedly is designed for a capacity of 2000 prisoners. . .'

his lack of hair because by this time I was going to the Barrowland Ballroom regularly and I saw him there. Eddie became quite a good ballroom dancer. The girls he danced with were alright, but considering that he was only a year or two older than me, what with his lack of hair and the mature dress they wore, him and his partner always seemed ancient.

Saturday mornings in the shop were good fun while we still got our work done. We always bought in bottles of ginger, Irn Bru and Tizer, and left some for Monday mornings till we found it was being guzzled by a plumber with the nickname 'Joe the Bull'. He was built like one and ate like one. His real name was Joe Bates and he came from Brigton. His sister worked alongside my mother and sister at Wilson's cotton mill in Marquis Street.

Wee Sanny, another of the apprentices, was getting so fed up with the disappearing ginger that he put a double-strength laxative into the bottles and gave them a good shake, then left them in the usual place. It came Monday morning and as usual Joe the Bull emptied both bottles then left the workshop. He and his apprentice were making their way to a job out in Bishopbriggs. The apprentice told us about it later. For the rest of that day Joe kept going to the toilet wondering what was causing the problem because 'I'm never like this I'm always regular.' On the bus going home his apprentice said to him, 'Take my advice Joe, never drink people's leavings.' From that day on neither Joe nor any of the rest of the journeymen ever touched the apprentices' ginger.

Most of the plumbers were okay, they were all good tradesmen and could tackle any aspect of the trade, and most of them were in the union. But there was one plumber who stood out and even the boss was deferential to him. This was Willie Dick, an outstanding lead burner and copper brazer. Willie could plan the largest job with meticulous care. He was not a young man but never seemed to panic. When he spoke he did not like to waste his breath and was listened to with respect. He always wore dungarees and never tried to boss anybody. He was my next mate when we started the plumbing in the new school being built out in Clydebank.

It was at the top of Kilbowie Road, a brand new secondary school, and the builders were McDougals from Davaar Street, Brigton, next to Celtic Park. The site looked down on the famous, or infamous, housing scheme nicknamed The Holy City. This scheme was built by the present Lord McAlpine's forefathers back in the 1920s and was not regarded as a model for house design. It had a completely new method of construction with large concrete blocks built in sections, like a Meccano set. These buildings were to become coffins when Hitler's bombers visited Clydebank for two nights during the Second World War.

The job was the largest I had ever worked on and there did not seem to be any trouble. Willie Dick knew exactly what work the four or five plumbers and two apprentices had to do from day to day. I got to experience nearly every branch of the plumbing trade. Willie only showed you once, then he let you get on with it. I tried lead burning and even had a shot at brazing. And he usually asked me to help him when he was doing something complicated, so he could test me.

Apart from my progress in the work itself I met one of the best characters on the job. This was Mick who was in charge of the panmill cement-mixer for the builders. Mick was as strong as a horse and he had the fat to go with it. He was always pulling my leg and playing tricks on me but it was done in good spirit. I worked with Mick's father too. He was the main drainer on the job and he had to connect up to our pipework or vice versa. Unlike his son he was very quiet and also a devout Catholic. He was always giving Mick a row for using bad language and he would warn me not to be led astray by him.

They both stayed in Cedar Street, just next to the Round Toll. Mick organised events in the street and one time he invited me on a bus-run to Portobello. I asked along my pal Jimmy Brown and we made our way to the bus on Saturday morning at 10 o'clock. There were two buses and both were full, each had its crate of booze. But I was quite embarrassed with the crowd that was there. Mick had told me there was loads of birds going and they were all stoaters. And I had told Jimmy Brown that. Now I could see Jimmy's face fall. All the men and woman were older than us and there were plenty of weans. We felt over-dressed with our drape suits and suede shoes, although we made the best of it. Mick kidded the life out of me.

We were only halfway to Portobello when the driver in the front bus stopped to let his passengers relieve themselves, so both of the buses pulled into the small parking space on the old Edinburgh

Road. The men peed against the bus in the inside away from the road and the women went through a small break in the hedges at the side of the road. Me and Jimmy Brown never left the bus and lo and behold did the best-looking girl on the bus not relieve herself just facing us. In our elevated position we could see much more than her bare bottom. Jimmy took a new lease of life and put on his best and first smile of the day.

When we got to Portobello it was surprising to find that the buffet we sat down to was in the cafeteria of the new swimming pool. It was very pleasant but I regretted not bringing my trunks. Plenty of girls were there and apart from the noise of the weans all the Cedar Street crowd were really enjoying themselves, and not one fight in progress. Jimmy was talking ten-to-the-dozen with the Cedar Street Marlyn Monroe, or was it Lana Turner in those days. The meal was also good. Mick was there with us and I told him it was turning out alright after all. He said to me, 'Fine, but tell your pal to keep his eyes off my bird.'

On the way back to Glasgow after a nice day we managed to get a seat right behind the girl with the nice bottom and her pal but I saw Mick was wagging his finger at us and then a wee bit later I began to feel my seude shoes were wet and I looked down to find the whole floor was awash with pish, so that put the damper on any romantic bliss me and Jimmy might have felt.

Avoidable Accidents
and the Big World Outside

I WAS on the Clydebank High School job all that summer but
then one day the boss brought me into the workshop at North
Street Lane to prepare for an office development in Glasgow. I
was cutting sheet-lead outside in the yard when a new load of sheet-
lead rolls was delivered. It came on the horse-drawn cart belonging
to the lead manufacturer, Stevenson. The usual old carter was in
charge of the Clydesdale, his pride and joy.

Each roll of lead weighed one ton and there was no crane nor
mechanical means to unload them. The method we used was to
roll the lead to one side of the lorry then onto two ropes which
were attached to two hooks on the other side. The lead rolls were
then eased on to the skids which went from one side of the lorry
down onto the ground. I was holding a small two-wheeled barrow,
which we called a 'jeanie', between the two skids as the carter eased
the ropes. One of the plumbers giving us a hand with the unloading
noticed that the ropes were frayed and he drew attention to it. The
old carter said, 'Safe as the bank, I've taken off tons with these ropes.'

The plumber said, 'Aye but is that not the problem?'

Now the lead was eased onto the skids and I had taken my
place holding the jeanie at the appropriate height to meet the lead.
The rope had just began to take the strain when it snapped and the
ton of lead lunged towards me. I put my hand on the ground to
throw myself away and the roll of lead trapped it. I saw the blood
and knew my hand was badly damaged. The big plumber made a
dive towards the carter. 'You stupid old bastard, you've crippled
that boy for life.'

The amazing thing was that due to the fact that there was a
dent on the roll of lead precisely where it hit the ground only the
pinkie finger on my right hand was trapped. The foreman and
another man lifted one end of the roll of lead and I managed to
get my hand free. The boss, Mr Renfrew, came out and after
remonstrating with the old carter who did not seem much
concerned, he gave Tam the lorry driver the keys of his car and
told him to drive me to the Western Infirmary.

When we got there the feeling was beginning to come back into my finger and it was quite sore. Tam did not make things better when he said to me, 'No doubt about it son they'll have to take your finger off.'

But I was quite determined there was no way that would happen, even if the finger was badly damaged, come what may it would remain joined to my hand. The surgeon seemed to agree. The small bone was broken and protruding through the skin but he told me they could reset it and stitch the wound up, put a small splint on it. I could come back in three weeks and they would see how it was. He also told me my finger would never truly straighten or get back to normal. But I did not care, just as long as my finger was saved.

After that I was taken into the office by the boss and got put to work on some menial tasks, things I could do with my arm in a sling. In the office a framed plaque took up a prominent place on the wall and it consisted of about fifteen names of employees that had died in the 1914-1918 War. I also discovered that Mr Renfrew junior was a reserve captain in the Territorials. At the same time the boss kept asking about my age and he had the habit of saying, 'It will not be long now till you get called up.' I had always been too busy with my after-work pursuits to pay much attention to what was happening in the outside world. The only papers I read were the *Daily Express* and the *Evening Citizen*, and even then it was only the sport pages. Now I faced this new fact, that what was happening in the outside world might affect me personally. Probably for the first time I had to think about serious issues.

I went about the menial work of running errands and so on but I missed my real work. Even although I was getting my wages it was not the same as being on the job with your mates, also I missed the feeling that you were achieving something by helping to build things.

One point I should make, there was never the slightest hint made to me about compensation for an industrial injury. Most of the plumbers were in the union but nobody volunteered information, nobody suggested that I was entitled to anything.

After three or four weeks I got all the dressing off my hand and was hoping to go back to the Clydebank High School job, but it was not to be, so I never saw my pal big Mick and old Pat his dad, to say cheerio. I later heard Mick went back to his job as a lorry driver and then one time I met him in Helensburgh, unloading goods in a housing scheme. I was sorry when he told me old Pat had died. The two of them were the salt of the earth.

The boss put me to work on a contract job at Evanton Airport north of Inverness. My mother was very worried as I had never been away from home. But I was looking forward to it, it was a new adventure. The guy in charge, George McCormack, was one of the best plumbers I ever worked with. He did most of what we called 'the country jobs'. The two of us caught the Inverness train from the old Buchanan Street Station and travelled for nearly six hours. We got a good lunch on the train which George paid for. At Inverness we changed trains for one taking us on to Evanton, beyond Dingwall. We did not arrive till mid afternoon and were told we would get digs in a small scheme on the outside of the village, not far from the airport.

The landlady was Mrs Corbett, she was quite a nice woman, not as old as her husband who I think was a farm labourer, a friendly old guy. She was a great cook and baker and her house while plain was very clean. I had a small room of my own next to the bathroom for which I was glad. The Corbetts had a Collie dog which in next to no time became my pal. After we had a cup of tea that first afternoon it was decided to visit the site and see the general foreman.

The airport was a base for the RAF and our job was to carry out the plumbing on several houses for the officer staff, including the commandant of the air base. It was a marvellous site, looking right out to the Cromarty Firth. The place was abound with wild life and apparently most of the many streams had good fishing for salmon.

The first week or so we were busy taking delivery of material and carrying out all the outside work, fitting waste-pipes, connecting up to the drains. We fitted the gutters on the houses that stood ready, the lead around the chimneys, preparing the way for the slaters. When we got time to look around the air base we found it large, with a hundred or more personnel, and planes always coming and going.

The job was quite interesting and the local workers were a good squad, very obliging. During the week the days went quickly, it was the week-ends dragged a bit. If you were not working the only pastime was long walks, so I discovered all the beauty spots in and around Evanton.

Soon after we had managed to get ahead with the work big George started going away on Friday afternoons, staying over with somebody in Carrbridge, and I was left on my own.

We usually got our wages at the local post office in Evanton but occasionally the boss came up by car to bring some items of material and he brought the wages along with him. I was getting subsistence allowance for working away from home and Mrs Corbett did not take the full money off me, and on top of that I was getting a lot of overtime. For the first time in my working life I felt quite prosperous. I began sending my mother extra money home. But she sent me a swift return letter, ordering me to spend what money I had on buying new clothes. So on the next Saturday afternoon train I went straight into Inverness and spent the whole afternoon shopping. Then I bought myself a fish-tea, and went on to the Caledonia Hotel for the dancing. I had become quite reasonable at it due to my joiner pal so it was no problem getting girls to dance with me. I thought there would be a difficulty understanding the Highland accent but to my surprise that did not happen. I found out it was common knowledge that the people of Inverness spoke the best English in Britain.

Another plumber sent up from Glasgow was Alex McConnell who came from Ayrshire. He was a good guy and a good tradesman and during the dinnertime kickabout we soon discovered how good at football he was. In fact he played for a Junior team.[36] One of the big joiners was quite good as well and not only played for Muir of Ord Rovers he was the club secretary. He kept on at Alex to turn out for them till he finally agreed. He played with them a couple of times and was doing quite well. One Saturday they were playing a team from the Seaforth regiment at Fort George barracks. I was going into Inverness so Alex asked me to come along and support them. When we got off the Muir of Ord team bus and went into the dressing room in the barracks the big joiner discovered they were a man short and he asked me to play. I was wary but Alex told me not to worry, he would look after me.

The football-strip was so big I had to use my trouser-belt to hold up the shorts. What a massacre it was, we got beat by six goals,

---

[36] Players in Junior football are paid expenses and a nominal sum. Attendances for the larger Junior teams can be more than those in the lower reaches of the Senior leagues.

it could have been twenty six. The Seaforths kicked us off the park and Alex, the best player, was put up in the air every time he went near the ball. All in though it was good. The regiment laid on a very nice high-tea for the Muir of Ord Rovers team and officials. We left Fort George bruised and battered, but happy.

One of the slaters on the job came from Glasgow. He had a big Norton motorbike and went home on alternate week-ends. I asked him if he would give me a lift and I would share the petrol. He was quite glad to do so. I asked George if it would be alright if I left on Friday at dinnertime. I had been on the job two months without being home and as the work now neared completion he gladly gave permission. We left Evanton at 12 noon and by going straight down the old A82 road we were in Glasgow at 6.30 pm. The slater dropped me right at my close, he lived in Sunnybank Street so it did not take him much out of his way.

After a home-cooked meal from my mother and a good wash I went up to Garngad and picked up my pal Jimmy Brown. We arrived at the Barrowland Ballroom about 8.30 pm. I felt great, wearing the new sports jacket I had bought out a good quality shop in Inverness, and on the Saturday and Sunday I was back out socialising again. When I hopped onto the pillion of the big Norton at 5 o'clock on Monday morning the road back up to Evanton flew by. I managed to get one more weekend home before the job finished.

George McCormack's absences were becoming more frequent and I had to cover up for him whenever the boss phoned, but soon it did not matter. Alex McConnell returned home first and then a few weeks later George and myself followed.

When I started back in the Glasgow workshop a few things happened that made me think about my future. Mr Renfrew kept on asking me if I had got my call-up papers and not to worry because it would not be long till I did. It was beginning to get me down. I also started reading more about what was happening in the world. I was not clear about the role of the Tory government and its attitude towards Germany. Neither was I clear about its failure to support the Spanish people and their government, when they had been attacked by Franco and the Fascists of Italy and Germany. I was beginning to question what I read in the newspapers. Around this time an old plumber we called 'Chummy' got paid off. I cannot remember his real name but a more decent man you could not work with. He may have reached retirement age, I cannot remember. But I could not understand the decision because I knew the firm had plenty of work on. The old guy lived out in Milngavie and I gave him a hand to carry his kit of tools up the road to the bus-stop. He was practically in tears. It seemed to me that there must be something wrong with any set-up that allowed people like old Chummy to be treated in such a way.

Then a couple of days later Eddie Murphy told me that his time was out, he was now a journeyman, but Mr Renfrew had told him he would need to work another year as an 'improver'. This was just so the firm could avoid paying him the proper rate for the job. So that was Eddie, he said he was leaving. On top of what else had happened in the last few weeks I decided to leave with him, and the two of us left that Friday even although I had still not completed my own apprenticeship.

First thing Monday morning we were down Brigton Labour Exchange and were given 'green-cards' for the firm of Laidlaw's. We started on a building site at Glen Mavis, north of Coatbridge, working on prefabricated houses. Our job was to complete the plumbing. It was not a bad job although the organisation left a lot to be desired, we were always running out of material. It was just a small housing scheme, with the first 'prefabs' ever built in that area. We got our travelling expenses and were put on the full pumbers' rate which was three times what I had got at Renfrew's. But the job ended three months later and the foreman paid us off, and told us it would be few weeks before another site was ready. We had no intention of hanging around, we went back to the broo. Immediately we were given two green-cards for John Brown's shipyard, told to go there at 8 o'clock on Monday morning and be prepared to start straightaway. We were a bit apprehensive but my apprenticeship was now finished and I was a time-served plumber, so that was that. On the following Monday in May 1939 Eddie and myself caught the 7 am train from Bridgeton Cross Station to Clydebank. Little did I know that this change in employment would radically change my whole attitude to life itself.

Hugh Savage seated with son Brian on a float
for a May Day demonstration in Glasgow 1957

Part 3

WORK AND EDUCATION, ACTIVISM

I REMEMBER it was a fresh morning in late spring when Eddie and myself stepped through the doors of John Brown's. We had never been inside a shipyard in our lives yet here we were employed as ships' plumbers. It was quite a daunting experience, even alighting from the train at Clydebank Station, we were amazed to see the mass stampede to John Brown's gate. Apparently if you did not get through before 8 am they closed it and you could not get admission until 12 noon. There were no allowances. A minute late and it cost you four hours' wages. Later on they set up a Yard Committee under the EWO (Essential Working Orders), and if you were a habitual latecomer or an absentee without a reasonable excuse, it could lead to an appearance at the Sheriff Court and even some form of imprisonment.

After we were interviewed by Mr Barnes, the plumbers' foreman, we were allocated a job on *The Vanguard*, alongside an experienced ship's plumber. Another shock awaited us, a Shop Steward approached and asked us for our union card. We had come from a building site and had never been asked for a union card at any time before so it was a new experience. However, neither of us objected to being a member. We were told that the Glasgow East Lodge of the Plumbing Trades Union (PTU) met every Monday night in the Independent Labour Party (ILP) rooms in London Road. We duly went along and joined that evening. For the first time in my life I was a trade unionist.

First impressions of the shipyard were the noise, the dust and the fumes. The plumber we worked alongside was called Willie Fernie, quite an old man who travelled in from Rutherglen every day. He took me under his wing. It was all completely different from the building trade. Our job was to link up pipes running between decks and fit deck-blocks that came made-up from the plumbers' shop. We fitted them after the hole-borers had done their work. Old Willie was a great character and I really enjoyed working with him. He carried his wee quarter bottle of whisky every day and could tell of the old days when he went dancing at a hall in Bridgeton which later became Tobago Street police station.

There was no canteen in those days, only hot water was provided. At dinnertime me and Eddie boiled our cans at the bending-fires and we sat and ate our piece in the plumbers' shop.

One thing that struck me was not only the vast number of men employed in John Brown's but the wide and varied trades in the yard. There were plumbers, electricians, coppersmiths, sheet-metal workers, french-polishers, then there were riveters, holder-ons, hole-borers, rivet-heaters and catchers, and joiners, platers, shipwrights, welders, painters, red-leaders, laggers and pipe-coverers, caulkers, riggers, and cranedrivers. In all my time in the yard I do not recall one demarcation dispute. There was a multitude of sweeper-ups as well. Then too you had the white-collar staff, office-workers, draughtsmen and the tally-men who counted the work done by the piece-workers. Finally there were the private detectives who patrolled the yard and the ships under construction, making sure you did not steal anything. Not only that, the private detectives could fine you 2/6d for drinking tea between hours, they could even kick over your full tea-can if they wanted.

So it was into this industrial jungle as a young greenhorn plumber that I found myself. Yet strangely enough I discovered it was not a hostile atmosphere at all. The main trait you had to acquire was the ability to wait. At most stages of your work as a plumber it became necessary to get a hole-borer to allow you to take a pipe through a deck or a bulkhead. On other occasions it could be a welder or a sheet-metal worker you needed. As you were only one of several hundred plumbers on the ship you had to learn to be patient. When you had completed your part of a particular job, again you had to wait until your gaffer gave you another job, so a great part of your time was spent on waiting.

Another aspect of shipbuilding that intrigued me was the management-structure. You had your immediate gaffer who was answerable to the foreman and he in turn was responsible to the plumbing-manager. It went from him to the ship's manager who was in charge of the whole ship. He in turn was responsible to the yard manager who in those days was the famous Donald Skivington, a legend in his time. Above him was Sir Stephen Piggot, the managing director. The final supremo was Lord Abercormbie himself, he owned John Brown's, lock, stock and barrel.

Yet despite all the superstructure, to a novice like me it seemed antediluvian beyond belief. There was no provision of any nature to have your dinner.[37] In the summer you boiled your can and sat somewhere in the open, eating your piece. In the winter you went into the platers' shed or the plumbers' shop which was quite warm due to the fires used for bending big pipes. If you could afford it you used some of the restaurants in Clydebank that served a reasonable cheap lunch.

The most important thing, and it really shocked me, was the fact that there seemed a complete disregard for safety. Everyday, summer and winter, when the ships were on the stocks or in the fitting-out basins, large plate-sections were being lifted aboard by huge cranes, right over the heads of dozens of workers. These cranes lifted thousands of tons of equipment aboard. Yet there seemed to be nobody responsible for safety. Every solitary day there were accidents. It was a miracle that most of them were minor. There was only one person handling accidents, a nurse, operating from a small ambulance room. This in a yard that employed approximately 10,000 people. To me it was an obscenity.

The infamous John Brown's toilets came as another shock. They were beyond belief. Many people have written about them before but you really had to experience it for yourself. These tiny wee cubicles, so wee that your knees were jammed against the door, even if you were quite small. You sat on a wooden board that overhung a metal trough and you had to do your business into the water along with forty or so other workers. The shout 'Timberrr!' went up everytime the trough was flushed by the attendant and you risked getting soaked by a cascade of water, pish and shite.

You had to give the attendant your metal-check with your department number when you went in. You were allowed seven minutes. If you went over that by the slightest margin you were docked half an hour. But I would have been looking for the Victoria Cross medal if I had stayed in one of them for longer than seven minutes.

---

[37] 'Churchill had to write to John Brown's to try to persuade them to open a canteen for their workers. See 'Clyde Apprentices' Strikes' by Sandy Hobbs, in the anthology *Workers City*, edited by Farquhar McLay (Clydeside Press 1988).

In all the years I worked in Brown's I managed to use their carsies very seldom indeed. The real abomination was the rows of metal spikes fitted along the back of the trough, this was just so nobody could lean or rest against the partition. It was maybe the first time I became aware that we definitely live in a class-divided society. The fine Victorian, Christian industrialist who designed them really must have hated the working class.

However, the new breed of workers coming into Brown's shipyard were not the same as the employees of the past and they were unwilling just to accept things. The carsies became a target for many workers. They devised methods to make them a menace, eventually to make them unusuable.They were desperate to get them closed down and force the management to instal a more modern type, ones that would allow some privacy as well.

One thing they did was put together small boats made out of seagull feathers and when the troughs were flushed they launched them. Many an unsuspecting worker got the fright of his life when he felt a feather caressing his bum. Some of the more daring apprentices started to use oily waste and as the attendant flushed the troughs they threw a lighted bit into them and then got off their mark. While it no doubt gave some of the older men a warm glow the only real hurt they received was to their dignity. But it worked, soon nobody would use the toilets at all and at long last the Shop Stewards were successful in getting new ones installed.

After a few days being bewildered by all this strangeness we became very conscious of the fact that we were locked in. You could not get out without a pass from the foreman for which time was docked from your wage. As a building-trade plumber I was used to the freedom to go off the site to a shop at dinnertime, or even just go out for a walk, so this confinement was a particularly bitter pill to swallow. But it was also around these early days that I heard my first street meeting. The speaker was putting a case for the anti-Fascist fight, he spoke on behalf of the Communist Party. I was not particularly interested, my own concerns lay elsewhere, mainly in dancing and buying clothes from the Co-operative.

Things changed for me when I was transferred to Pollock's engineers' shop as a dilution engineer, it was here my political education began to develop. During the war the employers had introduced dilution of labour. It meant that all tradesmen, no matter your qualifications, could be put to another trade. They were fitting air-lines to the machinery which was in abundance aboard the modern warships and I was put on the gun-turret squad under a nice chap called Tommy McGee. There was only six of us and our job was to face deck-blocks by hand to a very accurate degree. It was quite boring but the lads were cheery and the days passed quickly.

Because he knew I was a Celtic supporter Tommy confided in me. He was a devout Catholic which was a great surprise, that because he was a gaffer at all. It was common knowledge that the path to a supervisory position lay through the Masonic Lodge. Yet here was Tommy McGee. He felt we had a lot in common through religion and invited me up to his house in Yoker one night for my tea. I went and I met his wife, they had only been married a few months and their wee house was spotless. To crown it all she was a great baker and I was always a sucker for home-baking.

Unfortunately for Tommy, by this time I was already starting to read some of the Socialist pamphlets that were being circulated in the department. Before going to work at John Brown's I had no knowledge of politics and hardly any knowledge of the world at all outside my immediate environment. In fact I was still a practising Catholic and I was considered quite devout. My family seemed to have too much to do without looking beyond. While I was a prolific reader there were never any really serious books in the house, it was either 'true romances' or westerns. Very seldom did anybody ever buy a newspaper except my father who studied the *Noon Record* for hours, and occasionally my mother bought the *Weekly News*. Although my father was of Irish stock I never ever heard him take any political points of view.

Now I began to realise how politically ignorant I was. Most of the apprentices in the department were political and many were in the Young Communist League (YCL), and I was enjoying their paper *Challenge*. Also I had begun reading the *Free Thinker* which was readily available inside John Brown's. These were points of vew I never knew existed and it was beginning to throw doubts on my Catholic upbringing, much to the annoyance of Tommy McGee. For the first time I realised there was more to life than sport, dancing and wearing good clothes. I saw a new role that workers should play.

In John Brown's the 'black-squads' – the riveters, platers, rackers, hole-borers or welders – all were employed to a piece-work rate and counters measured their output. But there was no production bonus operating in departments like the engineers or plumbers. So although you always had to look busy time was not that important. I began watching the activities of the Young Communist League (YCL) and the Communist Party who dominated political discussion and led the struggle for better conditions in all departments. The steps I took were faltering but were based on the attitude I had grown to admire among the leading Communists.

I became friendly and supportive of the YCL members in my own department. This despite Tommy McGee who was always telling me that as a Catholic I had nothing in common with the Communists. But I could see for myself the growing battles they were putting up against the management's attempts to use the war as an excuse not to pay better wages. Meanwhile their contracts were based on the notorious 'cost plus 20%'. It was a licence to print money. All their obsolete machinery and equipment were being renewed as quickly as possible and money was no object. Yet some last-year apprentices were lucky to get a wage of £1/10/- a week. Trouble was definitely looming.

The political scene in John Brown's was a million miles away from any of my previous experiences. As I said, before coming to work there my knowledge of politics could have been put on the back of a postage stamp. I do remember seeing Jimmy Maxton[38]

---

[38] James Maxton (1885-1946) ILP MP for Bridgeton from 1922 until his death; 'converted to socialism by John Maclean, who introduced him to the writings of Blatchford and Karl Marx. . . [p117] When the Labour Party won the General Election of 1945 so decisively, the leaders of the ILP felt that that was the organisation they should be in. The question of re-affiliation arose. . . and Maxton was willing to merge the two parties but hesitated to make a move. . . [but after] he died on 26th June 1946, there was a scramble out of the ILP into the Labour Party.' [see p242 of *Come Dungeons Dark; the life and times of Guy Aldred, Glasgow Anarchist* J.T.Caldwell; Luath Press 1988). In *No Mean Fighter* by Joan Smith and Harry McShane (Pluto Press 1975) McShane tells us that 'the unscrupulous' John McGovern 'became dominant' but Maxton continued to be the figurehead [which] left the ILP in a very difficult position. It

speaking in the Booly to over a thousand people and I know my father voted for him. I can also recall his Unionist opponent, McCracken. The ILP used to sing:

Vote vote vote for Jimmy Maxton
vote vote vote for all his men
then we'll buy a tommy gun
and we'll make McCracken run

Instead of counting Maxton's votes they use to weigh them. I think it is true to say that the Catholics voted for him but the bulk of the Protestants must have voted for him as well to gain the high majority he enjoyed, until his death in 1946.

While I had been brought up in ILP territory there did not seem to be any real activity between elections. What action there was at a local level and some of the ILP and Labour Party councillors did not speak the same language as the people on the streets. Then too of course there were the housing bribery scandals of the 1930s which resulted in a few councillors being jailed, so that did nothing to enhance the role of of the working class political parties of the time. But it should be said that one of the most successful touring-cycle clubs around at that time was the Socialist Cycle Club and it was mainly the ILP that ran it. On a good day there would be at least eighty girls and boys on bicycles leaving from Brigton Cross.

---

had been formed to get Labour represented in parliament and had always worked in the Labour Party; the split took away its foundations. The members were torn in all directions. In Scotland McGovern came on NUWM marches, but in England the ILP couldn't be seen to be identified with the Communist Party. They had to find an existence as a separate party. They even formed their own unemployed organisation, which had a few branches in England but got nowhere in Scotland. The more right wing members finished with the ILP, and the rump moved to the left. They made revolutionary statements, and even applied to the Communist International for affiliation.' [p198] But there remained 'enmity' between the ILP and the CPGB 'particularly over the former's support of the POUM in the Spanish conflict and its condemnation of the Moscow show-trials of the mid-1930s.' [Knox p208]

But now for the first time in my life I was grappling with books on philosophy and economics. I was a Catholic who was interested in the materialist conception of history and ultimately, after reading Darwin and Ingersoll's lectures, and Brother Joseph McCabe's *Twelve Years in a Monastery,* I was looking at an atheist explanation of society. My new way of thinking was not a real problem as far as my family was concerned, I had really been the only practising Catholic in the house and my father was dead by this time.

One day I was helping in handing out Communist leaflets outside the engineering shop and I gave one to a good-looking, dark curly-haired boy that I had never seen before. When I asked him to buy a *Daily Worker* he just laughed and walked past me. One of the other apprentices told me his name was Johnnie Moore. He was the outstanding apprentices' leader in John Brown's and was on the National Committee of the YCL. He was also Secretary of the Clyde Apprentices Committee who were leading the campaign to improve apprentices' wages and conditions, which had remained stagnant for years. Johnnie Moore had an easy-going attitude and was quite unassuming.[39]

Another of my fellow workers was a plumber from Helensburgh called Alistair McKillop. He was a smashing football player, a centre-forward. He was tall and fast and had a great shot with either foot. He played for a junior team from Rhu. We were both attached to the gun-squad and became good friends. He soon became famous by signing for Rangers but he was never big-headed. Like myself he was attracted by what the Young Communists were saying and how they were trying to defend against a really authoritarian management team led by Lord Abercrombie, Sir Stephen Piggot and, last but not least, the general manager, Donald Skivington.

I eventually joined the Communist Party several months after starting work at John Brown's and I became very enthusiastic about it. I was surprised to find out the workers who were Party members and the extent of their support. I discovered that every department

---

[39] In a late letter to Hugh, Johnnie Moore wrote: 'It is 46 years since I first met you standing at the engineering store window and you had the audacity to hand me a *Daily Worker*, not realising that I was a wee high heid yin of the Young Communist League. Then you invited me to meet Jim McLaren and you in the Pop In pub in Glasgow. . . I thought you were just another dilettante.

in the yard had a group of members and a representative on the executive. Most of the Shop Stewards were either members or supporters of the Party. It is not surprising that should have been the case when you examine the calibre of the Shop Stewards, they were some of the most talented in the trade union movement. And the Shop Stewards' Convenor was Bob McLennan who was employed as a dilution electrician. Bob had been to the Lenin school in Moscow and was on the Scottish Committee of the Party. I always found him very approachable, never aloof and never dictatorial, he was a modest man and very intelligent.

Bob McLennan had a long record of activity in the working class movement and when I got to know Harry McShane later he always spoke highly of him. He told me how Bob had played a leading role in the National Unemployed Workers Movement (NUWM[40]) and took part on all the Hunger Marches. Bob was a member of the ETU (Electricians Trade Union). After he left John Brown's he became Assistant General Secretary at national level, until later still he was expelled during the ballot-rigging exposure of the 1960s. Bob McLennan was the best Shop Steward I ever met and I really liked him.[41]

---

[40] The history of the NUWM in Scotland is inextricably linked with the social, political and economic issues that affected the working class throughout the second quarter of the twentieth century. The organisation was formed out of the demobilised sailors' and soldiers' associations of 1918. It campaigned on a bewildering array of issues; supporting the struggles of the employed against wage cuts, speed-ups and under-employment; it was active in rent strikes, campaigns against eviction, task work and labour camps, the transference of labour, and discrimination against women workers; it agitated against the means test; defended the Spanish Republic; opposed intervention in the Soviet Union in the early 1920s; fought for peace in the 1930s. From its inception the basis of support for the NUWM lay within working-class communities and its history epitomises the concept of independent working-class action enshrined in the words of the Internationale. . . [Harry McShane in *No Mean Fighter*]

[41] TUC President Vic Feather was prepared to use the informal channels of Common Cause and Industrial Research and Information Services to reach into union branches [and] played a crucial role in unseating the communists from the Electrical

At John Brown's he was ably assisted by Davie Burke who recruited me into the Party. Davie was one of the best-read guys I knew and as well as being on the the the Scottish Committee of the CP he was Shop Steward in the electrical department. He was quite a good speaker and always easy-going, instantly recognisable with his glasses and pipe. He went on to be the National President of the Tobacco Workers Union when he left the shipyards. Then there was Arnold Henderson, recruited into the Party by Bob McLennan. Arnold served on the Clydebank District Council as a Communist Party member for a number of years after the war.[42] The plumbers' Shop Steward was Joe Brown of the YCL who later became regional officer of the Plumbers Trade Union.

One of the outstanding theoreticians in the Party at that time was Hamish Fraser who worked in the foundry, the dirtiest job in the yard. When I used to call on him you could hardly see him for soot and dust. Yet behind that dirty exterior Hamish spoke the flawless English that could have belonged to any teacher of the language. Hamish was well thought of in the yard but as far as playing any part in the activity, he only took his allocation of Party literature and did not get involved. I found that disappointing because in the course of time, as well as being put in charge of literature and propaganda I had the dinnertime gate-meetings, which were run by the CP, and a speaker of the calibre of Hamish

Trades Union [ETU] which climaxed with the famous 1961 court case over ballot rigging. His role was to sustain the leader of the anti-communist campaign, Les Cannon. One of Feather's associates outside the Labour Movement was David James. . . a director of Common Cause. James agreed to help and arranged for a group of Catholic businessmen to pay Cannon a weekly subsistence allowance. . .

In the decade following World War Two. . . the international anti-communist scare was. . . enthusiastically adopted by the TUC and applied at home. On the TUC General Council of 1954. . . there was not a single member who could be called a socialist. There were, however, two members of Common Cause's Advisory Council, Tom O'Brien and Florence Hancock . . . both past TUC presidents. See 'In a Common Cause: the Anti-Communist Crusade in Britain 1945-60' by Stephen Dorril and Robin Ramsay. *Lobster Magazine 19*.

[42] But his brother, H.W., was editor of the far right *Common Cause* magazine.

Fraser would have been a real asset. But despite repeated approaches I could never get him to speak at any of our regular meetings. We held them outside Brown's engine-shop gate nearly every day. I heard many years later that Hamish was living in Ayrshire and was writing and speaking for the Catholic church.

In the sheet metal department there was a strong group led by Charlie Gormley, a hard working Shop Steward and Party member. His son became known for his involvement in Scottish film-making. And a mention must be made of Ian Clark who worked with me in the yard as a plumber. Although he had joined the Party Ian was not very active in the yard but after the war he got totally involved in the union and became a Scottish Executive Officer. Ian Clark was a really intense person and also a dedicated body-builder, he reached fourth place in the British section of the Mr Universe championship. His experience in the union led him to resign from the Party in the 1950s and then unfortunately at an early age he took a brain tumour and died, leaving a young wife and family.

But the most dominant member of the Party in John Brown's was big Tommy Stewart. He took his responsibilities very seriously and never shirked any fight on behalf of the workers. He was a riveter with the black squad, a giant of a man with the rugged strong features of a Slav or a Pole. He was also a very simple sort of man and when he spoke he was gentle and persuasive, never raised his voice in anger. His knowledge was extensive and even outside of the CP he was always regarded as an honest man. I got to know him quite well because after a short term of membership, like I said, I was put in charge of literature and propaganda in the group.

For years the 'black squad' – the platers, riveters, caulkers and hole-borers – had dominated the official trade union structure within the yard. It was no secret that most trade union represent-atives and Shop Stewards had to be Free Masons. As this was also the case on the management side it made for a very cosy relationship, and it led to a conflict of interest when it came to defending and improving working conditions. Tommy Stewart told me he had joined the Masonic Order when he was a young man and no doubt would die as one. When I attended Tommy's funeral many years later the only tribute paid to him came from the Communist Party. I found it sad, prominent people in the Labour Movement were conspicuous by their absence, it only seemed to be the remaining stalwarts of the local branch that were in attendance.

At the factory-gate meetings in those days we could get nearly a hundred workers to listen to our speakers, particularly if we had somebody that was a well-known figure in the working class movement. But most of our speakers came from inside the yard and we were fortunate in having people like big Tommy Stewart, Bob McLennan and Arnold Henderson. I was in charge of meetings so I had to chalk the streets, help out with the platform, collect the literature from the Party shop. We also distributed pamphlets, sold the *Daily Worker* and the *Challenge*, and then we gave out forms to possible recruits to the Party.

We always managed to get some leading figures from the Party, like John Gollan who was the Scottish Secretary at that time.[43] We had Alex Moffat of the Scottish miners, brother of Abe Moffat, the Chairman.[44] I very nearly got the famous Arthur Horner[45] who became the General Secretary of the National Union of Mineworkers to speak at the factory gate. I heard him speak one Sunday at the St

---

[43] 'I had a suspicion that [John] Gollan wanted me out of the Glasgow secretaryship. . . ' [McShane 236]

[44] Alex Moffat (1904-67), brother of Abe Moffat who was Leader of the NUM. Alex was involved in the Hunger Marches. On the famous one to Edinburgh in June 1933 he was a member of the deputation that met with government officials. See Harry McShane's *Three Days that shook Edinburgh* (1933, reprinted AK Press 1994).

[45] Arthur Horner (1894-1968) a founder member of the CPGB was also involved in the 1930s Hunger Marches.

'On the 24th February at Cardiff Assizes. . . well-known miners' militant leader Arthur Horner was sentenced to fifteen months' hard labour. . . Horner was negotiating with the authorities [to prevent the eviction of a miner's family when] later, to the astonishment of the Rhondda workers, Horner and twenty-eight well-known militant unemployed miners of Mardy were arrested [and] charged with riotous behaviour. . . The police evidence. . . was of the most astounding nature. . .' [see Wal Hannington's *Unemployed Struggles*]

'On one occasion someone remarked how strange it was that the comrades who did the mass work were always being awkward on the party's leading committees. The reference was to Wal Hannington, Arthur Horner and myself, and it was true – we were all heretics. . .' [p215 McShane].

Andrew's Hall in Glasgow and he was the best I ever heard. With his Welsh lilt he could bring tears to your eyes when he spoke about the conditions miners had to endure, and bring anger in your heart when this was compared to the absent pit-owners who lived in splendour on the backs of the miners.

I chaired most of these meetings, one reason being that I was usually the only guy there on time. Of course the fact that I had quite a loud voice did help and on a few occasions it came in very handy because we could not afford a public address system. I remember one time we had just started a meeting when a crowd of Salvation Army supporters, complete with their band, marched into the street and stood across the road from us. They started to sing hymns and play their drums. My loud voice proved invaluable as the speaker was a wee Asian member and his voice was quite soft and high-pitched. When the band stopped playing and he started speaking it was no contest. We got our meeting finished and as I was folding up the platfrom he and the Salvation Army captain, who was a woman, came up to me and apologised for interrupting our meeting. She then said to me, 'You are a very clear and loud speaker, have you ever considered joining the Salvation Army?'

At first I thought genuinely she was joking, then I saw they were both quite serious. She gave me a card to contact them, although I never saw them back again at Brown's gate. On another occasion as I was putting the collection and literature cash in my tin a wee guy I knew from the Calton came up to me and said, 'I enjoyed your speech.' Then he looked at the money in the tin and said, 'Aye you must be doing alright.' The usual proceeds never exceeded fifteen shillings or at the most a £1. I just smiled and walked away.

COMMUNIST PARTY

GRAND DANCE
will be held in
Bridgeton Public Hall (lesser
Friday, 6th December, 1946
7.30 to 10.30 p.m.
D. BILSLAND'S BAND

Ticket 2/-

4 DRUMFORK CT.
HELENSBURGH
THE S.

Dear Hugh,

So nice to hear.
I would have ~~~~~~~~~.

As for your friend who wants to write about the early Clydeside industrial struggles obviously it must be from the beginning of the war, because it has all been well written and documented by numerous writings including your old pal McShane. But on the other hand not much has been written about the youth struggle. Of course I can go back to the 1936 apprentices strike and have some material on that, also the failed 1938 apprentices strike against conscription.

This is not the first time that I have been asked for this information. I have helped pupils doing projects at colleges and students doing papers at University, and allways gave them old clippings from the newspapers and party documents, but allways never got them all back, untill now I have ~~practically~~ practically nothing left. The most valuable is the complete record of the statement that I made at the Court of Inquiry, and it is in a very tattered state, and is now in the hands of my daughter who lives in Kilcreggan.

Letter from Johnnie Moore, a leading member of the of the 1941 Apprentices Strike in reponse to contact from Hugh Savatge in the 1980s

170

THROUGHOUT the world the fight against fascism had been led by the Communist Party. They had watched the world powers re-arming Germany and Italy, and had seen them retreat from Fascist aggression in Spain, Abysinnia and China. They were foremost in forming the International Brigade that fought in Spain and called for collective action to oppose German, Italian and Japanese aggression. So when Britain declared war in September 1939 people assumed that this at long last was a fight against fascism.

But things were not as simple as that. During the early years the CP was opposed to it, they called it 'a capitalist war'. Yet some of the leadership were in favour, like Harry Pollitt[46] and Peter Kerrigan,[47] also Willie Gallacher the Communist MP[48] who had come out and hailed Chamberlain's declaration. But the actual

---

[46] Harry Pollitt (1890-1960); 'entered a cotton mill at 12 and joined the ILP at 16, shop steward at 21, Secretary of the Naional Minority Movement 1924-1929. . . imprisoned for seditious libel 1925. . . deported from Belfast 1933.' McShane 'found [Pollitt] a very likeable decent human being'. It was Pollitt who wrote the article at the centre of the 'Campbell Case' [see note below]. He remained General Secretary of the CPGB from 1929 right through until 1956 and Chairman from then until the year he died [see his autobiography, *Serving My Time* 1940]. At the turn of the 21st century the Labour Government revealed that Pollitt's secretary of ten years had been working against him on behalf of British Intelligence.

[47] Peter Kerrigan (1899-1977) member of the CPGB executive 1927-29 and then from 1931 to 1965, held the posts of Scottish Secretary, National Organiser and Industrial Organiser.

[48] Willie Gallacher (1881-1965), first and only elected Communist MP. See his autobiography. Even as a young man his reputation extended beyond the Paisley and Glasgow boundaries. His name is still capable of producing violent reactions in some quarters. 'Yes,' said Trotsky in 1938, in a letter to Emrys Hughes, Labour MP for South Ayrshire. 'I remember that Mr Gallacher was made immortal in 'Infantile Sickness of the Left'. Times have changed, however, and now he should be

policy of the Communist Party of this period was not to offer
support. The Soviet Union's Foreign Minister, Molotov, signed a
non-aggression pact with Germany. Pollitt was then General
Secretary of the Party but he resigned and went back to industry as
a boilermaker. J. R. Cambell returned as the Scottish organiser, he
had been involved with the infamous Zinoviev letter during the
1924 election.[49] Eventually Molotov was to sign the Treaty of Alliance
with Britain in 1942. Much later Kruschev called him 'a saboteur
of peace' and in 1957 sent him as ambassador to Outer Mongolia.

After Harry Pollitt had gone the Party line was espoused by
Palme Dutt, editor of the *Labour Monthly,* and the new General
Secretary.[50] At a by-election being held in the Vale of Leven the
Party put up a Peace Candidate, a journalist called Malcolm McEwan
who spoke at John Brown's gate. I was to meet him a few years later
at a by-election in the Gorbals. There were over three hundred
Party members in John Brown's yard at this time and our policy
was guarded opposition to the war. So my first political activity as a

---

mentioned in the 'Senile Sickness of the Right'. See Raymond
Ross 'Trotsky Among the Scots'. In this essay Ross 'explores
Leon Trotsky's connections with Scotland through his
unpublished correspondence with Emrys Hughes. The essay
was published in *Cencrastus 28* and the unpublished
correspondence between Hughes and Trotsky lies in the
National Library of Scotland.

[49] The 'Zinoviev Letter' of 1924. The counterfeit letter was
addressed to J.R. Campbell, secretary of the CPGB. The other
two whose signatures had been forged were Harry Pollitt and
Arthur McManus. 'One of the most notorious intelligence
scandals of the twentieth century. . . appeared on the eve of the
1924 general election. . . purportedly from Grigori Zinoviev,
the head of the Soviet Union's international propaganda
section, Comintern. . .' *Independent* 23/6/2000. 'Papers released
to the Public Records Office at Kew show how the head of MI6
in the 1950s. . . authorised the destruction of important files
relating to the scandal.' Although the Zinoviev Letter was
blamed for bringing down the first Labour Government the
Labour Government of 2000 agreed with the permanent British
State that some of these papers are still too sensitive to be
revealed to the British public.

[50] Palme Dutt 'became the new secretary of the Party [after]
Pollitt and Campbell had been removed from the leadership
[following] a complete turn-about in the Communist Party's
policy. . .' [McShane p232]

new Communist was advancing the call for a People's Peace for negotiations with Germany and Hitler.

During the course of my activities in the yard I would get involved in heated arguments about countries I knew very little about. However I was an avid reader and spent every night expanding my knowledge. I was attending lectures on Marxism and getting through two or three books a week, starting to build up my own library.

But it was a difficult time for a novice like me, having to defend policies like the Soviet Union's invasion of Finland, a small country that scarcely seemed capable of threatening such a mighty power. Then the invasion of Poland had also to be justified. I remember working down the bottom of a gun-turret and spending over two hours arguing with a Catholic worker. It was only stopped when I caught a glancing blow from a rivet, thrown by somebody who disagreed in particular with me. I needed four stitches from the Western Infirmary. That was my first real baptism into the fight to defend the Party line.

On the industrial front, with the growth of the Clyde Shop Stewards and the Clyde Apprentices Committee, it was felt that the time had come to tackle long-standing grievances. We had no hesitation in downing tools to defend working conditions, even although we were accused of stabbing our soliders in the back. We were building up the Party membership and strengthening the Shop Stewards' committee in the six departments. I remember the management under the EWO set up so-called workers' councils in the yard, comprising six representatives from the workforce and six from the management, all chosen by themselves. Then they posted up the names of the workers' delegates still without any consultation with the workers. The official Shop Stewards demanded an election and nominated six names against the management's selection. When the vote was taken it was a wipe-out for the names put forward by the employers and an overwhelming endorsement for the Shop Stewards. Every one of the six they put forward was elected by an overwhelming majority.

This meant we could now get the management to discuss items they used to insist were the sole function of management. For the first time we got a say in absenteeism and could prevent cases of that and bad-timekeeping from finishing up at Dumbarton Sheriff

Court. Despite the government's war-time measure of freezing wages, but not profits, we could raise the question of extra payments. We could insist that every safety measure was examined and improved, and no change in working conditions could be introduced without union approval.

It also meant a larger number of apprentices in the welding department and the need to allow dilution, with a crash course on welding being carried out in the platers' shed. But despite the efforts of the management and the Boilermakers' Shop Stewards, not many riveters, hole-borers or caulkers crossed over. As a matter of fact most of the dilutees seemed to be plumbers like myself. Then of course most plumbers had some experience as welders even if it had been with acetylene.

The biggest strike that took place at that time was the apprentices' strike (1941) and it was the best organised I ever saw.[51] The Clyde Apprentices Committee was a rank and file organisation that had been campaigning on the scandal of apprentices' wage rates for a long time. Everybody knew that for years the apprentices were regarded as a source of cheap labour. Now for the first time many of them had joined the union and could raise the issue in their branches.

Apart from the scandalous wages virtually no training was given to them by the employers, it really depended on the tradesman the boy got as a mate and in most cases they were left to their own devices. If the apprentices wished technical qualifications they had to enrol in an evening school and attend for the full term, although during the war most classes were suspended. And then if they worked in John Brown's the average week was a full seven days plus overtime, so it was next to impossible anyway. Even in the last year of their apprenticeships some young guys were lucky if they got 30/-

[51] The anthology *Workers City* has the essay 'Clyde Apprentices' Strikes' by Sandy Hobbs, who tells us that 'In some ways, the 1941 strike was the most dramatic one of [the apprentices' strikes on the Clyde]. Not only did it coincide with the Clydebank Blitz, but it was the biggest dispute to affect the munitions' industry in the whole of the Second World War. . . ' In another essay from *Workers City* Robert Lynn discusses another apprentices' strike, that of 1943-44, when he was serving his time as an apprentice engineer in Yarrows. On this occasion 'the Communist Party opposed the strike because Russia was by that time into the war on the side of the Allies.

(£1.50) a week. The average wage for a journeyman not on piece-work at that time would have been about £5. Overtime was an absolute necessity. Nobody worked less than 52 hours and the normal working week was seven days long including Tuesday and Thursday nights late till 8 pm, while the Sunday shift was 9 till 5 pm.

The Clyde Apprentices Committee had delegates from all the leading shipyards, from John Brown's to Fairfields in the upper reaches on the Clyde to Denny's at Dumbarton, right down to Lithgow's at Port Glasgow. They unanimously recommended that all apprentices down tools and take strike action in pursuance of a long overdue increase in wages and improvement in conditions. Within a short time every yard, factory and engineering establishment that employed apprentices was strike-bound. Then it was extended throughout Scotland. Within days it had spread to the north of England. There were at least 15,000 apprentices on strike and a few weeks later the employers were powerless. While the strike only involved apprentices it had unanimous support within the whole trade union movement. In John Brown's yard the Shop Stewards' committee launched a mass campaign of solidarity and neither journeyman nor labourer would do any job previously done by an apprentice. The strike was solid.

The Young Communist League were the main leaders of the strike. The Chairman was Harry Sheriff, later an AEU official. Johnnie Moore was Secretary and worked night and day to gain support for the cause. He addressed meetings all over the country, sometimes four or five meetings a day. He could not have coped without the assistance of the Scottish YCL organiser. This was Murdie Taylor who was John Gollan's brother-in-law and ever present in the Plasterers' Hall in Gallowgate which was where the strike headquarters were. He played an important role in helping to organise the strike. I did what I could as a Communist group-leader to see that all departments collected funds every week to support the lads. And that support was 100%. I also helped organise gate-meetings and made sure leaflets and statements published by the apprentices were distributed throughout all the shipyards, so nobody was ignorant of the justice of the apprentices' cause and the men made sure none of them did any work formerly done by the apprentices. The Shop Stewards' committee and the three hundred-odd CP members were fully organised to black such work and all activity was concentrated on supporting the apprentices.

After two weeks the Government set up an enquiry committee under the chairmanship of Sir John Forster and the terms of reference were 'to enquire into the reasons for the industrial dispute'. It was held in the Central Hotel, Glasgow. No contact was made with representatives of the apprentices until the first meeting took place. The only problem was that when the committee met that first day in the Central Hotel, with all the captains of industry and all the state representatives firmly in their seats, it occurred to them that the main people involved – the actual 15,000 apprentices – had not been invited, so the whole thing was a mockery.

A car was sent along to the strike-centre at the Plasterers' Hall. But instead of sending any of their leading spokesmen the strike-leaders sent two of the youngest delegates. They asked for two weeks' postponement to allow the apprentices to prepare their case, and it proved a master stroke. The two delegates reported back that evening. The request for two weeks had been rejected but the apprentices could have two days. The two boys told us that when they were at the hotel they were offered as much food and drink as they wished. For most of that night Johnnie Moore, Murdie Taylor and Harry Sheriff prepared the apprentices' case.

When the real strike-leaders, led by Johnnie Moore and Harry Sheriff, did attend the Central Hotel you could feel the excitement stirring from the journalists, and the surprise from Sir John Foster and his committee when they saw the age and calibre of the apprentices' representatives. Once again he rejected the apprentices' demand for a proper postponement. Then he asked Johnnie Moore if he could inform the enquiry when the apprentices would be resuming work. Johnnie said, 'As I understand it this committee was set up by the government to enquire into the reasons for the stoppage, so your question is out of order.' When Sir John Foster persisted with the question Johnnie raised his voice, but he kept the tone quite measured. 'Even if your question was in order, it isn't one I could answer, it would be up to the thousands of apprentices themselves, only they can decide when they'll return to work.'

By the time the enquiry resumed the next day the strike-leaders had a dossier on all the major firms in shipbuilding and engineering, on the working conditions and the wages they paid, and the result was devastating. Among other things it showed that some final-year apprentices were lucky to take home a £1 per week, training was non-existent, and in most cases the boys had to buy their own tools.

The committee became very uncomfortable with the way the enquiry was going. Sir John Foster introduced Major Mavor of Mavor and Coulson and proceeded to ask him questions of a very mild nature about the working conditions of the apprentices in his employment but when he was finished and about to dismiss him Johnnie Moore got to his feet, he told the Chairman he would like to ask Major Mavor some of his own questions. There was an uncomfortable silence, but he was allowed to put his questions. Johnnie had all the details listed on the wages and conditions operating within Mavor's firm, and under cross-examination he destroyed him. He showed the committee that 16 year old boys were having to work over 60 hours a week if they wanted to earn a decent wage. After Major Mavor sat down Johnnie and Harry Sheriff spent most of the day outlining the apprentices' case and answering further questions. The unions did not emerge with clean hands either because it was they who had accepted these conditions for the apprentices in the first place and nor did they organise the apprentices' strike, it was completely unofficial.

After that decisive stand by the apprentices and the wide support they got from the workers the Foster Enquiry was wound up. They could only make recommendations to the government but as a result of their findings the largest wage amount ever was won by the apprentices, and most of their demands were granted. So one of the best advances in trade union history was achieved by its youngest members. For the very first time their importance was recognised and never again would they be regarded as slave labour.

The atmosphere in the yards was great after this victory. The status of the Party had also grown because everybody knew the leaders of the apprentices were Young Communists. However, as one battle is won another appears. A few weeks later I got a pass out at dinnertime to go into town for a meeting that afternoon. I went home to get washed and changed out of my working clothes. As I entered the house my mother said, 'There's a letter from the government for you.'

I immediately assumed it was a tax rebate but when I picked it up I could see it was from the War Department. It enclosed a travel-warrant and instructed me to report to the Royal Marines stationed at Seaham Barracks, Portsmouth within fourteen days. I knew quite a lot of guys who had been called up, including some of my pals, so I never really gave it much consideration. I decided I would go into work the next morning and tell the gaffer I was leaving, then collect my cards and wages and maybe have a break before going down to Portsmouth.

The next day I made my way into Brown's with my best suit on my back to lift my cards. But when I got into Pollock's engineering department the first person I met was Johnnie Moore. Before I could tell him anything he said, 'What do you think, the bastards have called me up. I'm joining the Marines.' Then I told him I was too and showed him my papers from the War Office. We agreed it was more than a coincidence. Our ages did not match and alphabetically our names did not match either. Johnnie said, 'They're not on, we'll fight the bastards all the way.'

We went to see Bob McLennan, the Convenor of Shop Stewards, who was with his deputy Davie Burke and showed them the call-up papers. Right away Bob McLennan said, 'You're not going.' He told us to disregard it and go home, and then to carry on back at work as normal.

I was still slightly confused. I could understand the victimisation of Johnnie Moore for his leading role in the strike but I had held no official position on the Clyde Apprentices Committee. All I had done was ensure that the strike was supported within the yard.

The next few days was a period of intense activity. Bob McLennan held an emergency meeting of all the yard's Shop Stewards. Including the engineers' shop there were probably about sixty of them. Then he delivered an ultimatum to Donald Skivington the general manager. It was blatant and obvious victimisation following the success of the apprentices' strike. He told him if the two call-ups were not cancelled the whole yard would be on strike and he also told him that he had assurances through the Clyde Shop Stewards Committee that the whole of the Clyde were prepared to take supportive strike-action if the call-ups went ahead. The Clyde Apprentices Committee made a similar decision. But the management started blustering and said it was nothing to do with them, they could not do a thing about it.

The apprentices started holding meetings regularly to reinforce their determination to down tools if the call-ups were not cancelled. They took a strike-ballot and gave the management seven days' notice. Both Johnnie Moore and I carried on working, and I still went on with the street-corner meetings. The call-up date was drawing nearer. It seemed as we went into the second week that the management were determined to sit it out. About three days before the day in question, after a dinnertime meeting unknown to Johnnie and myself, John Brown's apprentices started to walk out. They were being led by a young engineer's apprentice called Jimmy Gallacher. It was quite funny because when they got halfway, out came Sir Stephen Piggot the managing director, and he pursued them across the yard to tell them the call-ups had been cancelled. Nevertheless the apprentices still walked out.

Mass meetings were arranged for Friday at dinnertime and the apprentices contacted all the other shipyards. At 3 pm that afternoon Sir Stephen Piggot and Donald Skivington made their way up the gangway of the *Vanguard*, an aircraft carrier then being fitted out, and they had in their hands two telegrams. Then they sent for Johnnie Moore and myself and showed us them. The telegrams were from Ernest Bevin the Minister of Labour, cancelling both our call-ups to the Marines because 'we were in a reserved occupation'. These were the exact words that appeared. When I got home that night there was another telegram waiting for me saying the same thing.

Fifty odd years have passed since that incident but I can still recall that at that period in the war the Royal Marines were going through a particularly bad spell with land assaults being launched from places like Crete and they were having very heavy casualities. Now I knew how vicious and mean the capitalist class could be and quickly learned what governments and the establishment have in store for anyone who dares to challenge their authority. But really the authorities had been very stupid, they could just have staggered the call-ups and made sure we went to different regiments. In my own case I would not have known, being politically quite immature. I really did not suspect a thing if it had not been for the others, maybe especially when I saw the determination on Bob McLennan's face that morning and then when he said to us, 'The bastards are not going to murder any workers from John Brown's.'

Once again I resumed my activity, and with additional urgency although I started getting shifted about the place. Eventually, within a month or so, I landed in the welders' department, this because as a plumber I had some knowledge of welding. I did not object because the welders were on piece-work. This meant you did not have to work overtime to get a decent wage. It would also allow me to attend more meetings in the evening.

It was quite a new section and was rapidly taking over the role of the departments that had been the backbone of the 'black-squad' for over a generation. With the introduction of welded bulkheads on all ships being constructed the management at a stroke had eliminated the need for caulkers and hole-borers and drastically reduced the riveting squads. There was a push on for more efficiency and more cost-effective operations and the ship owners realised that one welder on a plate could eliminate a hole-borer and his mate, a caulker, a riveter and a holder-on, a rivet-heater and a catcher, all in one operation. A total of six men. And that not counting the cost of material, so the welders were in demand.

On the type of people that made up the welding department it would be a mistake just to take a quick look at their job description or previous occupation. Most of them, like myself, were there by accident rather than design. For instance two of the most intelligent, Peter O'Neil and a guy called McLean, made a book at the Albion greyhound track. Peter had a sardonic sense of humour that baffled even his best mates. He was well-read and could not be fooled politically. While he was no doubt a Socialist and in the main supported the Shop Stewards I am sure he shook his head many a time at the zeal which I showed when pursuing an issue or an argument.

One of the welders that I got to know very well was Archie Duncan, apart from the fact that he was a Communist supporter he was in Unity Theatre and so was I, I attended it regularly. Although he held a Party card I do not think Archie was suited to the strong discipline that was required of Party members. He was a dedicated actor and an active member of Unity and I feel maybe it was only that that kept him in the Party. He was one of Unity's main actors and played leading roles in most of their productions. He was over six feet tall, a very gentle person and very modest, and he never raised his voice. I remember I felt sorry for him when he produced some of the homemade scones baked by his mother. Straightaway he would be surrounded by the hungry waifs from the welders' department.

When he was playing the part of Lennie in Steinbeck's *Of Mice and Men,* which is a very demanding role, he brought the script into our howf on the *Vanguard* and at the dinner break some of us read out the dialogue to help him with his part. Eventually a welcome relief from Brown's came for him when he got an offer to turn professional from the famous Wilson Barrett touring company. He told us about Sir Stephen Piggot's reluctantance to give him permission to accept, and the derisive tone he used just in talking about it. And then about Donald Skivington, Archie gave us a laugh when he told us how the general manager had said the same sort of thing as Goering, only instead of 'guns before butter' his words were 'culture came behind battleships'.

Archie Duncan went onto greater things as an actor after he went to stay in London. He became well known in the part of Little John when the *Robin Hood* series (starring Richard Greene) ran for such a long time on television. The last time I saw him was when he paid one of his rare visits to the Citizens Theatre to play the lead in Arthur Miller's new play *A View From The Bridge*. It caused something of a stir in Glasgow in those days as it was the first play to show a homosexual scene. And as far as I know Archie was the first actor in Glasgow ever to do such a scene. The other actor involved was Fulton Mackay, who worked as a welder in John Brown's as well and went on to become very famous alongside Ronnie Barker in another television series, *Porridge*.

I never saw Archie Duncan again after that although I knew he was based in London. He appeared in many different parts but some of them I felt did not develop the ability that many of us felt he was capable of. A few years after I had left John Brown's it came through the grapevine that he had some illness and was confined to a wheelchair. Later on I was shocked to hear he had died.

Also in Unity Theatre, apart from Archie, there was Johnnie

Trotter, and Russell Hunter who became famous as the television character 'Lonely' and was still going strong into the 1990s. After the war Unity continued to make a major contribution to the cultural scene in Glasgow even when they lost their leading director, Bob Mitchell, who joined the Co-operative. But the loss of Abie Greenbaum and most of the Jewish members, no doubt hastened by the signs of blatant anti-Semitism emanating from the Soviet Union, was obviously a major loss for Unity Theatre. The Jewish Institute players went on to win the Scottish Amateur Dramatic Festival award several years in succesion. They dominated the Scottish scene for many years, long after the old Jewish Institute in South Portugal Street was demolished.

One of the leading young welders was Bartholomew (Bartley) Dick. He participated in all the debates and was one of the most influential welders in the department, possibly in the whole yard. He was very well-informed on most subjects, but particularly football and Irish history. Also he was funny, smart and with a brash, friendly manner, he could talk himself out of any situation. He had the habit of starting arguments then walking away leaving other folk involved. But not only was he all of that, he was an exceptional tenor-singer. We became friends, and the friendship between us lasted 45 years, in fact the rest of our lives. He was born in the Calton and had worked as an apprentice hairdresser, a 'soap-boy', at Barneys in Abercrombie Street. His father, Reddy Dick, was an angle-iron blacksmith who also worked in John Brown's. Bartley was to become better known under the name 'Glen Daly'.[52]

Contrary to the opinion of those who did not know him well he was not only very articulate but he was well-read and could debate with the best. He was the first person to give me lessons in Irish history and it was he who made me aware of figures like Wolfe Tone and James Connolly. I was so occupied by the Party line and the

---

[52] It was Alex Frutin, owner of the Metropole, who 'changed my name to Glen Daly.' He writes that when he landed his first full professional contract, which was at the old Metropole Theatre in Stockwell Street, there was a sketch calling for his use of a genuine welding kit: 'One night the gaffer from Brown's was in the house and he came round to see me afterwards. He told me, 'I was your gaffer for eleven years in Brown's, and that's the first time I saw you welding.'

defence of the Soviet Union that I never had time to realise that Ireland was the first English colony.

Bartley was the best seller of literature the CP had. I remember a welder called Eddie McCarron, a polite-spoken chap and very good artist, but he had ambitions to be an intellectual. So he was a sitting duck for Bartley who sold him most of Lenin's *Selected Works* and with all sorts of pamphlets thrown in. Nobody could resist Bartley's charm, he could have sold ice-cream to the Eskimoes. But he was never at his job when he should have been and Bobby Adams, the welders' gaffer, was always out looking for him. However, the gaffer liked Junior football and Bartley would always get him talking about it and so his anger would vanish.

His own knowledge and love of football, particularly Celtic, was legendary. He also had a talent for spotting good players and that was apparent when he and a few other welders formed a Secondary Juvenile team they called Kerrydale Celtic. In a short time it was just about the best team in Glasgow, undefeated for 42 games. Considering the lack of resources they were remarkably successful, winning several competitions. Unfortunately, like numerous teams of the day, they were found guilty of playing 'ringers' – unqualified players – and that led to their suspension. I remember a welder coming up to me and telling me he had seen my younger brother Andrew playing for the Kerrydale and that he was some player. It was news to me because Andrew never played football. But as he was under 21 years of age he was eligible to play Secondary football, so a very good Junior player who had been roped into the 'Celtic' played under his name. I did not think this was a serious matter (and I still don't) but Kerrydale Celtic had won the Maryhill Junior Shield twice and reached the final of the Scottish Cup. Bartley always cocked a snook at the authorities but this time they took action and the entire committee of Kerrydale was suspended *sine die*, including him, and that was the end of the team.

His good tenor voice came to be noticed when he sang in the BBC *Workers' Playtime* series on the wireless, when the programme was produced from Brown's canteen. It was the beginning of a career that saw him sing all over the world, besides making Glasgow's Ashfield Club one of the best known in Britain (after he left it barely survived). For a time he was Lex McLean's 'straight man' at the

Pavilion Theatre, and McLean was known as a red hot Rangers' supporter. Bartley was one of the top recording stars in Scotland with gold discs to his credit and his recording of *The Celtic Song* is perhaps the best known football club song in Britain. It is still played at Celtic Park to this day. Yet despite his strong attachment to Celtic he managed to bridge the religous gap, and as a Rangers' supporter once said of him, 'He might be a tim but he's not a bigot.'

It is to be hoped that the story of 'Glen Daly' will be told properly some day soon. He was a remarkable man, a giant in comparison to the pygmies who held him back.

Our howf was a really lively place to be. Sometimes it resembled the reading room in the Mitchell Library. The most prominent newspaper was the *Daily Worker* but most other ones could be seen, the *Bulletin,* the *Glasgow Herald,* even the *Financial Times*. Magazines and books were also available and it was not just the girlie or western type. Dickens, Burns and Jack London's books could be bought or borrowed. With the CP so active in the yard Marx, Lenin and Stalin obviously could be seen but the two most-read books were Upton Sinclair's *The Jungle* and Robert Tressell's *The Ragged Trousered Philanthropists*. It is not surprising to find that while the main topic of conversation of course was football other discussions went on to do with religion, nationality, philosophy and politics – Marxism and Anarchism mainly. They were real debates and could last over a period of several days. Some fellows were very well-read and could quote not only from Burns or Scott but also from Adam Smith, Wolf Tone, James Connolly and John Maclean.

Most of the older welders were ILP or Labour Party supporters but one of them had fought with the International Brigade in Spain. His first name I remember was Hector, he used to get very impatient with some of the young welders. They were Catholics and quite hesitant about some things. But they were definitely receptive to Socialist ideas and most would have supported the actions of the Communist Party. The religous and political mix of the workers in that part of the ship saw that no subject was taboo.

It was quite a young department, most of the welders were just the right side of twenty and having been involved in the apprentices' strike they had little respect for some of the out-moded traditions of the 'black squad'. Most of them were on a type of piece-work so every job had its price. Even the most hazardous and unhealthy, as long as you got extra cash it was acceptable. While my activity with the Communist Party had restrained me from accepting any union nomination within the yard, at one of the welding departmental meetings my name was put forward as a Shop Steward and was unopposed. So I decided to take it on and raise the issue of health and safety.

I had some personal experience, particularly with welding galvanised steel and it had long been accepted that extra payments were paid when doing this type of work. One time I had been welding some galvanised deck-blocks in a confined space aboard a ship for a full day and when I was sitting on the train going home that night I felt quite ill, sweating profusely and feeling chilly at the same time. I went that night to Dr Whiteford, our family doctor. He examined me thoroughly and then said, 'The only thing wrong with you is you've got a chill and it seems to have developed into influenza.' Despite all my protests about the galvanised fumes and gas I had been inhaling that day Dr Whiteford gave me a prescription for some medicine, and a panel-line certificate stating I was suffering from influenza.

After I recovered, and a few months later, I was going home on the train and met a welder called Davie Harewood, he stayed in Bernard Street the same as myself. Davie was also a member of the Glasgow East Lodge of the Plumbing Trade Union where I was by now on the committee. But he looked unwell and when I asked him where he was working he told me he was welding galvanised deck blocks. Some weeks later his wife came down to the union branch and said Davie was off work, he was ill. We told her to keep us informed about it but before I could get to see him he died.

The Glasgow East Lodge of the Plumbing Trade Union took up the tragic case of Davie's death and Tommy McMenemy, the Scottish E.C. delegate, was successful in winning compensation but the amount awarded was a derisory figure of six hundred pounds, an insult to Davie Harewood's wife and family.

But about this same time an article in the *Daily Worker* by Professor Haldane dealt extensively with the question of industrial diseases and the need for the proper ventilation of compartments where the welding of certain metals created toxic fumes. I wrote to the professor and asked him if I could publish his letter as a leaflet for distribution amongst our members. The reply giving his consent came by return. He emphasised that fresh air should be distributed by a fan throughout the compartment. Not only that, but an extractor fan must also be placed as near as possible to the source of the toxic fumes.

We distributed the leaflet everywhere. Never did I see such confusion as in the welding department. Welders who had previously been only concerned with an extra cash payment were now demanding a sucker and a blower fan.

It was only a start. Welders in John Brown's, unlike in many other shipyards, were never provided with protective clothing. Everybody knew a welder because the sleeves of your overalls were riddled with burns. Many a time they went on fire and you had regular burn marks on your arms and chest. Even the welding helmets that John Brown's provided were 'hand-knitted', sealed with black bitumen which would just fall off if the helmet fell on the deck. This resulted in the flash from the weld striking your eye, something which you were not aware of. And most days welders had to go over to the ambulance room to have pieces of slag removed from their eyes. These pieces flew off the weld very hot and either went into your eye or else down the front of your shirt.

There must be plenty of old welders who have had a piece of slag in their eyes for years without even being aware of it, just like myself, a large piece of slag has been lodged in my eye for more than forty years.[53]

---

[53] This became aggravated in the early 1990s and Hugh had to have an operation on his eye.

THE ASHFIELD CLUB

404 HAWTHORN STREET · GLASGOW, N.2

TELEPHONES: OFFICE — 336 - 7578   RECEPTION — 336 - 7579

JIMMY DONALD AND GLEN
The most successful team in Clubland.
" The Old Firm," says Glen—" He's old and I'm firm."

Handbill for Glen Daly, a friend of Hugh Savage for 45 years and one of the best sellers of literature the Communist Party ever had!

The gates at John Brown's 1930s

Leaving John Brown's, Blacklisted

A S THE END of the war drew near, despite being transferred
for periods to Elderslie dry-dock and Fairfields, I had a
strong desire to try for pastures new. Some of the leading
activists in the yard had left to take up other jobs. There had been
an improvement in our working conditions but there is no doubt
that shipyard welding is a dirty, unhealthy occupation and I felt I
needed a change of scenery.

One of my last battles was with the new shipyard manager, Mr
John Rannie. While he was new to most of us personally it was
common knowledge he had been employed by John Brown's for
years and was being groomed for the management job. He had
been all over the world studying shipbuilding techniques, from
Scandinavia to the Far East and the USA and it showed as well, for
example in the growing development of prefabrication in the
platers' department.

Rannie was like the exact opposite of Donald Skivington, the
previous shipyard manager. While Skivington growled or shouted
at people Rannie gave the impression that he was approachable
and was even capable of listening to the men. However, there is no
substitute for the practicalities when it comes to most jobs and
managment is no different. The new man shocked us all at a meeting
by presenting us, the four welders' Shop Stewards, with a full new
price-list then asking us to discuss it.

It was a four page typewritten document. After we had looked
at it I told him there was no way negotiations would take place until
our members had discussed the management's proposals. We held
our own meeting where we set up a committee of six welders. I
surprised them by saying we should not discuss Rannie's paper at
all. Instead we should draw up a list of our own demands, including
a more detailed price-list. We added in points to do with working
conditions, covering safety and the need for protective clothing,
improved first-aid facilities. And from now on there would be no
welding in closed spaces, all working compartments would have to
be fully ventilated.

Immediately after this meeting the welders' manager, Sanny Greer, sent for me and said, 'I'm disappointed that you didn't come to inform me of the result of the meeting.' I was taken aback by this but his next remark was worse. 'All the previous Shop Stewards always came and told me what took place at their meetings.'

I was so angry. But I had to control myself, bear in mind he was many years my senior. But how naive he was to tell me such things. I told him it was not my role or purpose to inform him what took place among the welders or the Shop Stewards, and I said, 'Mr Greer, as you are part of the management of John Brown's there will be no Shop Stewards reporting to you ever again.'

It took the new welders' committee on prices a few weeks to finalise proposals and after we had got agreement with most of the welders we informed the area representatives of the union. While they thought our demands were perhaps ambitious, they had no objections and endorsed them.

All this time Mr Rannie was pressing us to meet again and draw up a new price-list. We notified him and met him within a week. He was quite surprised, to say the least, when I gave him our type-written proposals and introduced the welders' pricing committee. In fact he started laughing. We told him that was how we reacted when we first saw his proposals. Then he said, 'Who ever heard of workers having a pricing committee?'

We told him was it not about time that the workers at the point of production had a genuine say in determining their own wages and conditions.

The negotiations with management went on over a few weeks and while we did not get our full demands, we did get more than Rannie had put on the table. And too what was very important, although they were not implemented immediately, most of our proposals on safety were accepted.

While we had had a partial victory I was still not happy with my own situation. I was a member and branch official of the Plumbing Trade Union yet I was also a Shop Steward for the welders who were represented by the Boilermakers Union, but I did not wish to follow Finlay Hart's example of becoming a member.[54]

---

[54] Finlay Hart (1901–198?); founder member of the Clydebank Branch of the CPGB and Harry McShane's deputy during the 1934 hunger march. 'If anything happened to Harry I was to

The Boilermakers' Union had been a product of the industrial revolution and as many of their members were on piece-work rates so they had a cash mentality. Basic questions to do with safety could always be solved by an extra few quid in the pay packet. The two district officials that came into John Brown's were called Forgie and Neilson, I think. Although some of the welders called them 'Laurel and Hardy' they were quite decent men. I could never complain about them as they were always straight with me and actually it was they who suggested that I should join their union. While some plumbers in the welding department did join the Boilermakers I did not. But the National President at that time was Ted Hill[55] who was not the worst when you compared him to Ernest Bevin[56] or Arthur Deakin.[57]

It is not without irony that a plater who was in the local Labour Party called Chalmers[58] became the President of the Boilermakers after the war.

---

take over. As the Party man – if anything happened to Peter Kerrigan – I had to take over. So I was Peter's deputy and I was Harry's deputy.' Scottish Secretary of the CP 1935-37, then based in London as National Industrial Secretary. See p192 of his informative contribution to *Voices from the Hunger Marches* Volume 1. Ian MacDougall compiled the book and mentions that Finlay Hart was one of the veterans who died between the time when he gave the interview and publication. However, in discussing how 'any criticism of Stalin was intolerable to the party leadership' McShane also recounts that 'Finlay Hart. . . supported everything. When I criticised. . . the *Economic Problems of Socialism in the USSR*. . . the very last book Stalin wrote. . . he jumped to his feet and said that this was the turn that the party had been waiting for. He always said that, no matter what the turn was, and the other sycophants followed.'

[55] Ted Hill, President of the Boilermakers' Union. In his *A Matter of Trust: MI5 1945–72* Nigel West refers to the Czech defector Joseph Frolik who 'was anxious to expose the Soviet and Czech agents who had been recruited from the British trades union movement. However steps were taken to ensure that the names of several senior figures in the British trades union movement were deleted from the final manuscript of his memoirs. Among them was Ted Hill. . .' [p166] West is here discussing the 'built-in disadvantage in accepting defectors [because it can] neutralize friendly double agents.'

It was a dilemma for me altogether and like I said I had a strong desire to move on. I got a great deal of satisfaction being involved in the industrial and political struggle within John Brown's but the closed-in nature of a shipyard, as a welder having to operate in small confined spaces, it was all creating a longing within me for a

---

[56] Ernest Bevin (1881-1951) A central figure in founding the TGWU from more than thirty trade unions; General Secretary from 1921-40; became '. . . minister of labour and national service in Churchill's coalition government [and] a significant member of the war cabinet. . . successfully attained complete mobilization of Britain's manpower by 1943. See *Chambers Biographical Dictionary* 1961. While Foreign Secretary in 1948 Bevin approved Foreign Office proposals for anti-communist propaganda operations.

'It is for us as Europeans and a Social Democratic Government, not the Americans, to give a lead in the spiritual, moral and political sphere to all democratic elements in Western Europe which are anti-communist and, at the same time, genuinely progressive and reformist, believing in freedom, planning and social justice – what one might call the Third Force. . .'

During this 1947-48 period the propaganda unit, the Information Research Department, was formed by Bevin and Labour MP Christopher Mayhew. . . '[whose] brainchild it was [and] who recognised that "since anti-communist propaganda would be anathema to much of the Labour Party, it would have to be organsied secretly." In a minute to Bevin he commented that, "One of the problems that constantly faces us in anti-communist publicity work is to discover publicity media which are definitely non-official so as to avoid undesirable diplomatic and political repercussions when certain issues are raised." ' See *Lobster 19* essay by Stephen Dorrill and Robin Ramsay.

During the affair of Colonel Tasoev questions were being asked of Bevin in the House of Commons (see p34 Nigel West); the exchanges were relatively light-humoured until the veteran communist MP for West Fife, William Gallacher, suggested that Bevin evidently 'knew as much about MI5 as he did, and that was damn all'. The Foreign Secretary . . . retorted that since Gallacher was a communist he probably had more dealings with MI5 that the Minister did.'

[57] Arthur Deakin (1890-1955) 'assistant to Bevin from 1935, General Secretary of TGWU 1945-49. . . President of World

job on the outside. And when I was collecting trade union dues at the branch meetings I could not fail to compare my pale complexion with some of the guys that were working out on building sites. They all seemed to exude fitness and good health with their tanned faces.

As well as that some of the leading figures had left to take on full-time jobs. Davie Burke was one, he had left to become an organiser in the Tobacco Workers Union. Bob McLennan had also gone and was now a full-time official in the Electricians Union, and quite a few others were away as well. So I felt that my future lay somewhere else. Despite pleas from some of my friends I handed in my notice and so it was *bon voyage* from among others John Rannie the manager who met me as I made my way to the main gate.

I was surprised when I went to the vacancy section at the old broo, the only job on offer was one as a jobbing plumber with a wage well below what I had been getting in John Brown's. I was now married with a family and it was a bit of a daunting prospect so instead I took the offer of a welding job in Fairfield's shipyard. As I had been transferred there when working for Brown's I knew my way around. I also knew the Shop Stewards' Convenor, Nutty Jamieson, who worked in the engine shop, and one or two others. I started working in a welding bay in the plumbers' shop.

At this period on the Clyde there was a campaign on for a five-day week, eliminating all Saturday work. The fight was organised by the Clyde Shop Stewards' Committee, an unofficial body. To most workers it was a long overdue demand, and to many employers it was a sensible proposal as they knew that bringing the workers in for only four hours on a Saturday and having to get all the plant set up for that short time was wasteful. Especially with it being the morning following pay-day and for many guys filling in the coupon or picking a winner was a more important occupation. In any case

---

Federation of Trade Unions, [and] led the British withdrawal. . . because of its Communist domination. . . a founder of the International Confederation of Free Trade Unions [which] received considerable financial assistance from the CIA and, often through the Trade Secretariats associated with it, was also heavily infiltrated and thereby controlled by the Agency.' (See *Lobster 31*, the essay by Peter E. Newell.)

[58] John Chalmers was secretary of the Boilermakers Union.

the growing absenteeism showed that on the subject of Saturday working a great deal of workers were voting with their feet.

Having been voted in as a Shop Steward I embraced the campaign and set about working for a voluntary ban on all Saturday working. But I could detect a growing opposition. It was true that it meant a loss of four hours' wages. While I had sympathy for the loss of wages I felt establishing a five-day week was long overdue. It was also true and became clear to me there was a much more Masonic influence in the workshops in Fairfield's than in John Brown's. Then I came into work one Monday and was told that at least fifteen workers, excluding the staff, had disregarded the ban that previous Saturday morning. However, being an unofficial action there was no way the overtime ban could be enforced, the members who had broken it could not be dealt with by the official union, so the Shop Stewards decided to convene a meeting that dinnertime.

There was quite a good turn out but there seemed to be faces present who normally never attended meetings. And these people who had always opposed the ban and carried on working the Saturday were well to the fore. It was only a half hour meeting so we quickly decided to take a vote. The Shop Stewards were substantially defeated. As the decision was more or less a vote of no-confidence I asked for another vote on that actual point, and once again it was defeated.

I discovered that an unholy alliance had been formed between two men, one of them was called Kerrigan, a Catholic who was very anti-Communist and who went on to become a full-time official with the EEPTU which emerged after amalgamation. The other guy was a true-blue Orangeman, a rabid Rangers' supporter, who might have known I was a Celtic supporter but what he definitely did know was that he wanted to work as many hours in the day as he could get, and I was against it. So the old Orange and Green hostility had not only left off. It united to oust what they felt was a common enemy, me, a Communist who wanted a shorter working week without loss of earnings.

Within three weeks of me being removed as Shop Steward there was a pay-off made of about ten plumbers. Needless to say I was on the list. I am proud to say that it was not the last time this kind of thing happened to me either. The one redeeming feature is the fact that the fight for the five-day working week was carried on and eventually succeeded not only in shipbuilding but throughout the whole of industry.

When I went to the broo I was told they were looking for plumbers with welding experience in Stephen's shipyard, next door to Fairfield's, so I went along and met the plunbers' foreman. I gave in my details and experience and told him the name of my former employers. He told me to start right away. But when I turned up next morning I was told to wait at the gatehouse. Ten minutes later a man wearing a bowler hat came up to me and said, 'Is your name Savage?'

'Yes.'

'I'm afraid there has been some mistake, we've got our full quota, but you can try again in a few weeks.'

It was obvious the establishment had closed ranks.[59] I did not even bother replying to him. I knew as well, bowler hat or not, he was only a message boy. So the next morning saw me back in Meighan Street at the good old Brigton Broo. I was told there was a job for a plumbers' welder in Munroe & Millars (the workers used to call it 'Murder and Manslaughter'). The workshop was next to Ibrox Park, home to Glasgow Rangers.

It was the middle of winter and I was glad it was an inside job working in a welding bay. However, I was not prepared for the sight when I stepped into the factory that Monday morning. There was at least ten coke-braziers going full blast and it was like Dante's Inferno. The braziers were distributed around the place because there was no heating system. The whole place was the size of an aircraft hangar and very draughty so it was reasonably well ventilated but the smell of burning charcoal caught in your throat and combined with the welding fumes it made John Brown's seem like working in a park.

I stayed for about three months. The wages were quite good and the travelling was easy, a yellow tramcar took me right to the door. My workmates were good and I already knew the Shop

---

[59] Clydeside employers were amongst the most autocratic and anti-union of British capitalists. Selective re-employment – weeding out activists – after a dispute was common practice, as was the blacklisting of workers. . . ' see 'Victimisation and Anti-Labour Activities, 1900-1939' by McIvor and Paterson in *Militant Workers: Labour and Class Conflict on the Clyde 1900 –1950*.

Stewards. Apart from the braziers, which were really quite toxic and affected the breathing, there was no problem working in the place. There was a collective bonus-system in operation. It seemed to be more or less controlled by the head timekeeper, and not necessarily to the workers' advantage. However, I did not intend to stay very long in the job and was not getting involved. But it was really tempting, the timekeeper was a creep and too closely aligned with the management. Instead I handed in my notice and started at a firm called Shaw & Petrie, based in Hillington Estate.

It was a 'head-down' sort of place with very little time for conversation. They did the same type of work as Munroe & Millar but their set-up was more modern, more so than I ever imagined, as I found out much later. The young welder who was the Shop Steward knew me and when he asked me to assist him I could hardly refuse.

I was there for several months, the workshop was the usual type of building with adequate heating without coke-braziers. The welding bays were quite well-equipped and the quality of work was quite high. One morning I was welding a flanged pipe in my bay when I became conscious that somebody else was there, then I saw the reflection in my welding-helmet glass, a guy was standing right behind me. I immediately stopped welding and was confronted with a well dressed young man with a writing-board and a stop-watch in his hand. I said to him, 'What are you up to?'

'It's alright, this doesn't mean anything.'

'Well if it doesn't mean anything what's the point of doing it?'

'Just you carry on.'

I took off my gloves. 'There's no way I'm going to work to a stop-watch. As long as you're standing there I'm not welding.'

I went to the manager straight away and he withdrew the time-and-motion man. But when I spoke to the Shop Steward he told me it had been agreed. I pointed out that the union had not agreed and as it was a departure from accepted practice it had to be negotiated and would have to win the approval of the majority of the workforce. The Shop Steward would not call a meeting. But the matter was raised during the dinnertime. Most workers saw nothing wrong with the procedure and were quite convinced by the management's promise that wages would rise considerably with the introduction of time-and-motion studies. So I just told the manager to make up my pay and I walked away from Shaw and Petrie ('Shaw and Totties' as they were known).

It was not long before I started with a firm called Tannahill who carried on the same type of work and were also based at Hillington Estate. After a few weeks, when I had got my bearings, I discovered that although most of the workforce were PTU members they were not organised at shopfloor level. I called a meeting and myself and another young fellow became the Shop Stewards.

It was quite a good job, no one bothered you and the wee gaffer was a decent type of person. However, one morning when I came in he told me I better have a look at the notice-board. I went along and studied it. The management had changed the working hours.

The notice had been signed by a Mr Swan who was the manager. But I knew he had been a foreman with Munroe & Millar before that and I suspected that this was his first managerial attempt, and that he was feeling the need to flex his muscles, especially now me and the other guy had got the workforce organised.

So we called a meeting at dinnertime and after a full discussion with the members it was agreed that as there had been no negotiations on a change of the working hours it was 'as you were', we would just carry on like before. In the meantime I checked up on the matter of changes to working hours. I found out that we were all still under the EWO (Essential Works Order) which controlled the power requirements of any industrial or commercial business. So any change in the working hours that might alter the time-periods when power was required could not be implemented without the notification and permission of the Chief Administrator. Once we had this information we notified the manager whom my fellow Shop Steward now referred to as 'Quack Quack'.

We conveyed to him the fact that we intended to carry on with the existing hours because his proposals meant an extension of the working day and no such change could take place without both our consent and the permission of the Chief Administrator who was in charge of power. Mr Swan jumped up with rage and shouted, 'You will do what I tell you or else I'll clear the shop.'

I said, 'We'll work the hours that we have always worked and you can do what you want.'

So we went back to work and carried on with our usual working hours. It meant that we started at 8 am instead of the manager's proposal of 8.30 am and we stopped at 12 noon for lunch as against 12.30 pm, then at the end of the day we left the work at 5 pm instead of 5.30 pm. The tactics we employed were when I checked in or out every one else followed. The only problem was, we always started work when the wee gaffer blew his whistle, and we stopped when he blew it again. Like I say, he was a decent wee man. After two weeks he came up and said to me, 'Hughie, can we not get this thing settled. I'm going about the factory blowing my whistle and nobody's paying any attention. When I blow the whistle for you to start work in the morning you're all already working, and when I blow the whistle at dinnertime you've already stopped. Then when I blow for you to start you've started. But the final stupidity is the fact that I've got to stay behind after you've all left, and I've got to blow a whistle in an empty factory. For Christ's sake get the thing settled, I feel as if I'm blowing the bloody thing in my sleep.'

A few weeks after the work-to-rule had begun he came rushing in to tell me that our union's District Secretary had just gone up the stairs and into the manager's office. But none of us, neither the Shop Stewards nor the men, had decided to involve the union officials in this dispute. So we went right up to the office and chapped the door, and we walked right in. The official was called Paterson, the full-time District Secretary, he was also a member of the CP. He was sitting drinking tea with Mr Swan. When we walked in he said to me, 'Hello Hughie, sit down and have a cup.'

I said to him quite firmly, 'We would like to see you outside.'

He saw I was angry. When he came out I asked him what he was doing here and he said, 'Swan sent for me, he's a member of the union, I had to come.'

I told him management did not have a case and we neither needed nor wanted any official involvement. I explained the legal position regarding E.W.O. and changing the hours and told him that he was not required so he should back off. Comparatively speaking he did not have the same industrial experience as myself and he knew that, so he did not argue with me but left the factory immediately. At dinnertime we held a meeting and the men endorsed my action. When we came in the following Monday morning the notice had been taken down, so that was that, and the wee gaffer went back to blowing his whistle at the right times.

Then later the factory was very short of work and the gaffer asked me if I would like to do some welding at Stern's refridgeration factory at North Woodside Road. I did not hesitate as I was getting fed up with travelling to Hillington Estate every day, and the shifts were very long if you were not busy. The job at Stern's was supposed to last only a few days but I was there for three weeks. Normally the lorry driver brought my wages on the Friday morning. But one Friday he never arrived until 4 o'clock in the afternoon, then he said, 'I've got bad news for you Hughie, I've got your cards.'

I was still the Shop Steward so my first reaction was to challenge the pay-off. However, when I saw I had been given a week's notice and wages in lieu, I just walked away. I never saw Swan again in my life. But from time to time on union business I did meet up with Paterson, the District Secretary. Then it happened I had not seen him for quite a long while and somebody told me he had electrocuted himself. I did not hear anything more about it but it was very sad considering by that time he was quite an old man.

ONCE AGAIN I had joined the ranks of the unemployed. There seemed to be very little work around in Glasgow, particularly with my industrial record.[60] I heard there was plenty of work in London and decided to try it as an experience. So did my pal Jimmy Brown, he could not get a job either. I went to see Bob McLennan who was now the Assistant General Secretary of the Electricians Trade Union and he gave me the address of Tommy Sullivan, Secretary of the PTU down in London.

So me and Jimmy Brown set off. Our first task down in London was to contact Tommy. I found to my surprise that down there most plumbers contacted the union office whenever they were unemployed and that there was always a list of the work available, and you could rest assured it would be the trade union rate of pay for the job.

Tommy Sullivan was also a member of the Communist Party. He was a typical Cockney with a wicked sense of humour. You could never tell if he was serious or not. The first thing he did was show us a long list of vacancies. I said, 'But we've got to get digs first.'

He laughed and said, 'That'll be alright, I know the guy who runs the model around the corner from where I stay, he'll fix you up.'

Tommy stayed in Finsbury Park and the union office was just off Tottenham Court Road, not far from Euston Station. When we got off the tube at Finsbury Park station we had to walk about two hundred yards up Seven Sisters Road and turn the first corner into

---

[60] Bob Horne, CP organiser in the Glasgow District Office in the 1940s and early 1950s, recalled how agents of Special Branch MI5 penetrated the CPGB in Scotland, through phone-tapping, interference with the post, break-ins (to see files) and information passed by *agents provocateurs*. Horne worked for the builders George Wimpey and 'discovered [they] operated not one but two blacklists. One was of their own devising. . . The other was supplied by the Economic League.' See 'Victimisation and Anti-Labour Activities, 1900-1939' in *Militant Workers* by McIvor and Paterson.

Adolphus Road. This was where Tommy lived with his wife Anne and his two teenage daughters. It was a typical mid-terrace house with three floors. He had the flat on the ground floor and his younger brother lived on the first floor. Another plumber and his family lived on the top.

I felt at home right away, despite the gales of laughter from everybody when he said to us, 'We hope you like the model.'

I got a single room on the ground floor and Jimmy Brown got a room upstairs. The living room-cum-dining room was very large and all the family activity took place in it. There was never a dull moment. Members of the family and their friends came in and out all the time, along with political friends who were mainly from the CP. There were all kinds of discussions on the go, as well as the typical family banter. It was a really invigorating place to stay. The next day both of us got fixed up with a job. I got started with a firm in Roman Road and Jimmy got a start as a plumbers' mate with one of the London Boroughs.

While my firm did a lot of maintenance work in and around the West End it was usually just small repairs and not exactly fulfilling. We were working in the top class luxury apartments of Mayfair and here at all times tradesmen had to use the back entrance, and spread sheets down wherever we walked. It was a very educational experience. I thought I knew how the other half lived, having worked in Glasgow areas like Newton Mearns and Kelvin Court. But really, the luxurious flats and homes I saw and worked in throughout the West End of London made some of the so-called better-class districts back home in Glasgow look like slums. Another fact was brought home to me very clearly, London was indeed the financial centre of the United Kingdom and many of the people who owned and controlled it were residents in the West End.

There was one job that I was sent to that I will never forget. It was to fit a new toilet and cistern at a flat in South Audley Street, just along from the Dorchester and round the corner from Park Lane. The flat was above a gunmaker's shop and was occupied by Mr Tom Purdie. Little did I know that it was probably the best-known shop in the world amongst the landed gentry and the sporting fraternity who were its best customers. I found out that theirs was the most expensive gun you could buy and not only had you to be recommended but you had to wait nearly a year after you had got interviewed and measured for one.

When my wee Cockney mate and I went up the stairs to the flat and rang the doorbell it was answered by an elderly man dressed like a butler. I told him who we were and he showed me to the bathroom. I was immediately struck by the way the flat was furnished. While it was not spacious every available space was utilised with alcoves and tasteful paintings and antiques. Eventually we started the job. It was to refit the old mahoganay-lined cistern and renew the down-pipe. I was up the steps disconnecting the water supply when I heard a real posh voice saying, 'And what are you doing here?'

I looked down and there was this man smiling up at me, probably in his 50s, wearing a dark blue, polka-dot dressing gown and smoking a cigar. I started to explain what I was doing but as soon as I did he began laughing and shouted, 'By God you're a Scot.' Then he called on his valet, 'Give Scotty a drink.'

But it was only about midday and my mate and myself did not drink. I tried to explain but he said 'I never met a Scot yet that did not drink.'

And the next thing a tray with two large whiskies was laid on the window sill and the gentleman with the dressing gown left the room. I pulled up the valet and said to him, 'You better take your tray away, we're going out for our lunch.'

When we came back the tray and the drinks were not to be seen, we spent the afternoon stripping out the old pipe and we left about 4.30 pm. As we were going out the main door I heard the voice from the living room shout, 'Goodnight Scotty.'

The job took much longer than I anticipated mainly due to the continual intervention of Mr Purdie which I found very interesting but it did not allow me to get on with the work. The valet drew my attention to one of the dozens of mahogany-framed pictures that adorned the walls of the flat. It was a school photograph of Winchester public school and one of the pupils sitting next to the young Purdie was Winston Churchill. When we were leaving the job at the end of the day Mr Purdie handed us two tickets for a movie premier being held in the Empire, Leicester Square. My wee Cockney mate was not interested so when I went home to my digs I asked Jimmy Brown if he wanted to go instead.

Tommy Sullivan said, 'You must be in with the toffs to get an invitation to a premier at the Empire.' When I told him where I was working he said, 'I'm not surprised, the Purdies are the *crème de la crème* of the establishment.'

So that decided us, we wanted to see how the other half lived. When we got to the Empire it was cordoned off by the police and we could not get through. But when we showed the police our tickets we got right up to the entrance. Here we had to line up outside until the main guests arrived. I have never seen so many Rolls Royces in my life. As we stood there watching, seeing the style of the guests, their evening suits, and the women with their mink-stoles, we made up our minds, it was not for us. We headed down to Piccadilly Circus for a walk and then got the tube home.

The next afternoon as we were finishing off the job Mr Purdie came in and asked us how we enjoyed the movie premier. I told him what had happened and he bellowed at me, 'You mean to say you were afraid to mix with all those snobs. You were more entitled to be there than most of them. I give very generously to their charity and I never go to their functions.'

When we were packing up our tools to leave the job he came in and handed me and my wee Cockney mate an envelope each. He said, 'There you are Scotty if you ever want a job call me.' Outside on South Audley Street we discovered that he had given us a £5 note each. My mate said, 'I think that old boy fancies you.' I laughed. In those days homosexuality was still an issue that was not taken seriously although when I thought about it it was true that like my wee mate said to me, 'You never see a bird in the flat, only these three old crones on their own.'

I continued to work with the firm for another month or so. I liked the activity in and around my digs. I went to the Unity Theatre as well and enjoyed that very much. Of course there were some outstanding rallies in Trafalgar Square, calling for an end to nuclear re-armament and for the banning of the bomb, with such speakers as Nye Bevan[61] and Frank Cousins of the TGWU.[62]

---

[61] Aneurin [Nye] Bevan (1897-1960) 'led the Welsh miners in the 1926 General Strike. . . brilliant, irreverent, often tempestuous orator. . . left the ILP to join the Labour Party in 1931. . . Minister of Labour in 1951. . . resigned over proposed National Health charges. . . From [when] dated

Another fact to impress me about London was the facilities provided in most districts by the local authorities. Apart from the local public halls and libraries similar to those in Glasgow there were also leisure parks complete with big open-air swimming pools and sun bathing spaces, and in some cases there were sand-pits for the toddlers. In many ways it was more advanced than Glasgow, and their local authority housing was of a better standard and with no sign of the slum-clearance type of house like you got back home.

After three months or so I felt it was time to head off back to Glasgow. I was not involved in any personal way with the different actions or campaigns then on the go and while the wages were alright, when you had two homes to run things were quite tight. As I sat on the train I decided it was necessary to get a job with some guaranteed permanence. I approached Glasgow Corporation Direct Labour Department and got a start on the new housing scheme being built at Pollok.

It was a really big scheme reaching out near to Barrhead. Also it was reasonably well organised, there was a good Shop Stewards' committee and they had a Convenor. More plumbers started when the scheme fanned out to include Penilee and additional Shop Stewards were elected to look after their sections. They were recognised by the heads of the department and all in it was quite a good atmosphere. A campaign was on the go at that time for a substantial increase in the basic rate. While the unions did not like overtime being worked they did not make an official ruling on it. Most workers depended on overtime or a bonus scheme to augment their pay packet. But it was a fact that certain workers could get overtime while others got none. A meeting was called and it was decided unanimously that either the whole of the workforce would be on overtime or else none at all.

This ban operated for several weeks, then I was approached by

---

'Bevanism', the left-wing nagging movement to make the Labour Party more Socialist and less 'reformist'. . . [but] he ceased to be a 'Bevanite' [in] 1957 when he opposed a one-sided renunciation of the hydrogen bomb in Britain.'
(*Chambers Biographical Dictionary*)

[62] Frank Cousins (1904-86) general secretary of the TGWU from 1955 into the 1960s when he became Labour MP but he eventually resigned and went back into the TGWU.

some of the men who had been in the department for a long time. They felt I should ask the management to give overtime to those who wanted it. I told them I had never asked an employer for overtime in my life and I was not starting now.

The next day we had the usual monthly meeting of all the sites. It was held in the canteen at the south part of the housing scheme. It was my intention to move an emergency resolution at the end of the agenda on the issue of the strike that was then taking place in Paris. It was intended as a statement of solidarity with the French workers. I was quite surprised when the Shop Stewards' Convenor, who was a plasterer, came into the meeting accompanied with his full-time official, a man called Nesbitt. There were four other people with him whom he introduced as the Glasgow Corporation Housing Convenor, the General Manager and two other officials.

The Chairman of the meeting asked the Shop Stewards if it was alright for the people to sit in and listen to the business without in any way participating. We discussed wages and conditions and most of the Stewards felt it was time they got to know the depth of feeling regarding these matters.

It was a heated discussion and there were calls for further action on our demands. Afterwards the Convenor said, 'Brother Savage has a resolution he wishes the committee to support.' I outlined the background to the strike in Paris and the demands of the Paris workers. I caught a glimpse of Nesbitt the full-time official and got the impression that he was embarrassed. The resolution was passed unanimously, nothing was said by any of the officials present.

The area of the Pollok site that I was working on came near to completion and the plumbers' general foreman who travelled round all the sites learned that I was a welder. He asked me if I was prepared to work in the new Foam Slab prefabrication unit at Tollcross. As it was nearer home and an extra rate would be paid, I agreed. It seemed quite an exciting experience to begin with. The idea was that large sections of reinforced concrete slabs were created with windows and door spaces set in. Some of these sections weighed several tons. It all meant that with no more than five or six of them a house could be assembled in a few hours on site and ready for the roof and internal finishing. Of course it was not a new idea really, I had worked with the Blackburn in Dumbarton. They erected the whole house in sections and built thousands of them all over

Scotland. They can still be seen, for instance in Carntyne in the east end of Glasgow.

Glasgow Corporation pushed ahead with its plan to solve the city's housing problem by building thousands of these Foam Slab houses. The number of areas it was happening kept growing. As far as we understood it several sites were ready, including one at Wellshot Road in Tollcross. Unfortunately the sections of reinforced concrete slabs they used here were not only ten times heavier but some were at least 15 feet x 22 feet. It was a big day as the first extended lorry with ribbons got ready to carry in the first sections. The Lady Provost made a speech saying how important this development was for Glasgow's housing problem and she cut the ribbon. All the councillors and dignitaries cheered as the lorry went on its way to the site. Then the whole company, except the workers, retired to the factory office at Amulree Street for drinks and a buffet, and did not leave the place until mid-afternoon. But if the dignitaries had waited they would have seen the lorries returning to the factory with all the prefabricated sections. It had been discovered that no mobile crane with appropriate lifting power and required span was available not only in the city but throughout Scotland. Glasgow Corporation now had to open negotiations with a firm in England to hire a crane that could do the job.

That is not the end of the saga. When at last all these houses were completed and then occupied they were found to be structurally unsound. Large gaps had appeared at their joint sections. After a short time the tenants were rehoused and the Foam Slab houses were demolished. As a result of the failure the Amulree Street factory became a plant for manufacturing reinforced concrete lintels and slabs, and my services were no longer required.

In John Brown's shipyard most of my time had been spent in political propaganda and industrial matters. Now I was back working on building sites I was usually Shop Steward and I got more active in my union branch. I was elected onto the Glasgow East Lodge of the Plumbing Trade Union (PTU). The committee met in the ILP rooms in Bridgeton. Within a year I was the branch Vice President and a delegate to the Glasgow Trades Council, which was where I received my finest education. Glasgow Trades Council used to meet in the old Central Halls and the hall where we met was really large, it could hold about 200 people. At our monthly meetings it was unusual for it not to be nearly full. The Chairman at that time was John Johnston.[63]

I was still only in my twenties and when I look back it seems ridiculous that somebody as young could be involved in such an active role. Also because I started to get involved in Brigton and became Secretary of the local branch of the Party. It made a change though, that and getting more active in the union. I was now in touch with the officials quite often. A few of them had never worked in industry and it did not take too long for me to become disillusioned. I saw the methods the Party used to extend its influence on the membership. It was well-organised with a full-time industrial organiser responsible for trade union activity but it can be said that the main function was to get as many members or sympathisers elected to influential positions. You were always being pushed to recruit new members along with new readers of the *Daily Worker*. Nearly every night of the week you had to be at a meeting of one sort or another.

We began organising open-air propaganda meetings on Sundays in backcourts and at street-corners. The Brigton branch had always been lively, it had an old established membership going back to the 1930s. There was also an enthusiastic section of the Young Communist League and they held a social and dance every Saturday night. Their premises were central, quite near Brigton Cross. I was fortunate that James McLaren, one of my closest friends, had also joined the CP and his political understanding was invaluable in extending the work we were doing.[64] We did our fair share of fly-posting and most Friday nights we went out daubing slogans, so for the first time since the 1930s Brigton was regularly whitewashed. We started a local housing association and had good attendances at the meetings in Rumford Street School. Some of our members, including myself and James McLaren, were put onto the Calton Ward committee. We changed the nature of that cosy wee organisation, raising social issues and winding up its role as an

---

[63] John Johnstone 'a Labour man and far from revolutionary, but he was a very honest fellow and did much more effective work of a mass character than the Communist Party members who have more recently been in charge. . . ' See McShane and Smith p256-7.

[64] See the appendix for more on James McLaren.

Glasgow Trades Council Centenary Brochure 1858 – 1958, A Hundred Years of Progress (compiled by Harry McShane)

Hugh Savage (front row 2nd right) standing for local elections 1950. Also in this photo is Peter Kerrigan (2nd left back) and Harry McShane(2nd right back)

admiration society for the local councillor, an old ILP member who had a tendency to talk down to her constituents. We got the committee behind the fight for better housing.[65]

In 1948 there was a by-election in the Gorbals, brought about by the fact that the sitting MP had been made the Minister of Pensions by the Attlee Government. The sitting MP was Geordie Buchanan, one of the ILP group of original Red Clydesiders. When the date of the by-election was announced it was necessary for me to give up my job in Fairfield's shipyard where I worked as a plumbers' welder. I was also a Shop Steward there so I knew I would never return. The Glasgow City Committee of the CP appointed me to be the full-time election agent for Peter Kerrigan for the duration of the campaign.

It was a responsible role I had for somebody so young and was to be the first time I had any personal contact with Harry McShane. I have no doubt I was given the job because as well as being so active in Brigton I had that long experience as a group leader in the factory branch in John Brown's and also had formed a Housing Association in Bridgeton. With one thing and another it gave me the tough pedigree that was needed to face up to McShane and the rebellious members of the Gorbals' branch. As a good little Stalinist I was to do what I was told.

All the Gorbals' members viewed me with suspicion. After the first meeting of the election committee I left the premises with Bob Saunders who was the district organiser of the PTU. Harry McShane had a room in the Gorbals' branch premises and I remember when he was closing the door after us he was quite cheery and asked us

---

[65] As Hugh points out housing was a real concern to James McLaren and himself. In the immediate post-war years living conditions were horrendous in working class Glasgow and municipal housing was a necessary area of engagment for any prospective MP or Councillor, as an election promise if nothing more. Hugh and James McLaren had formed housing associations in Brigton and Calton districts before getting to know McShane; see Harry McShane's essay in *Militant Workers* for a background to the housing crisis in Glasgow at this period and also Les Forster and Ned Donaldson, *Sell and be Damned, The Glasgow Merrylee Housing Scandal of 1951* (Clydeside Press 1992).

JOINT COMMUNIST PARTY &
YOUNG COMMUNIST LEAGUE
===== MEETING =====
'A Future for Scotland'
in Unity Hall, 37 Dalmarnock Rd.
on Sunday, 25th May, at 7 p.m.

Speakers—
LES FULTON, Scottish Organiser Y.C.L.
JAMES McLAREN, Secy. Bridgeton C.P.

James McLaren, an inspirational
political activist who died
prematurely of tuberculosis.

JAMES McLAREN

It is with very deep regret that we announce the death of James McLaren.

Jimmy's premature death — he was only 28 years of age—has robbed the Party in Scotland and particularly in Glasgow, of an excellent Comrade indeed.

In whatever sphere he worked, whether in the Bishopton Factory, or as a Party Branch Secretary, member of the Glasgow Committee, Treasurer of the Party in the City, or as Lecturer and Propagandist, nothing but the best was good enough for Jimmy.

Coming from an ordinary working class home in the Calton district of Glasgow, he assiduously applied himself to learning and to education and became a splendid spokesman for and representative of Communism.

A victim of the scourge of tuberculosis, his courage never weakened nor his loyalty waver.

When I visited him on the eve of his death, he repeated to me his complete confidence in the Party and the working class.

His only regret was that he had not met the Party sooner than he did.

We are indeed poorer by the loss of Jimmy McLaren, but stronger for having known him and for having him in our ranks.

WM. McLAUCHLAN.

where we stayed. I said 'Oh we go east.' His reply was 'That's quite appropriate, all the wise men come from the east.'

However, as I started organising and working alongside Harry and the other Gorbals' comrades the cynicism with which they greeted some of the decisions of the Glasgow Committee were not entirely misplaced and I found to my surprise some of their political differences seemed to be sound.

Harry McShane's conversion to Marxism had taken its own route and he must have been one of the best-read people in the Socialist movement. He always returned to Marxism, never tired of explaining to young people its importance. One of his favourite stories was how Marx took Pierre Proudhon's *The Philosophy of Poverty* and wrote *The Poverty of Philosophy*. By turning Proudhon on his head Marx showed how it was the emerging working class, with their labour power for sale, who were the real 'gravediggers of capitalism' and not the petty bourgeois. McShane had a great deal of respect for Scottish philosophers like Adam Ferguson and Adam Smith and relished the fact that while Karl Marx rejected some of their conclusions he paid tribute to the contribution they made to the development of philosophical theory.[66]

It should be remembered that he started out in life as a Catholic and in his teens was ardent in defending his faith. His first contact with Socialists came through attending their public meetings, and challenging their beliefs. He was well versed in the scripture and had some knowledge of the 'Papal Bulls', the encyclicals that were proclaimed from Rome. The Socialists, he discovered, were tough nuts to crack who were promising some sort of heaven here on

---

[66] see Ronald L.Meek's essay 'The Scottish Contribution to Marxist Sociology' reprinted as a pamphlet from *Democracy and the Labour Movement* Lawrence & Wishart 1955, in which he sets out to show of the 'so-called Scottish historical school' that Marx can properly be said to be the heir of [their] basic ideas. . . [He] saw the connections which had been forgotten, and restored the unity which had been destroyed.' Meek argues that 'in the latter half of the eighteenth century the Scottish Historical School developed. . . Classical sociology to a stage where it was becoming remarkably similar, at least in its broad outlines, to Marxist sociology.' The four main figures were all professors: Adam Smith, Adam Ferguson, William Robertson and John Millar.

earth. Organised religion, they argued, was useless in halting the ravages of capitalism. Harry would go home and think again. His conversion to Socialism was as dramatic as it was deep. Now on the other side his former fellow Catholics were to suffer the whiplash of his tongue for being false prophets.

After joining the Communist Party in 1922 he had two visits to Russia,[67] but was not impressed when visiting an atheist museum. He thought the 'Anti-God' propaganda was crude and would have an adverse effect in dispelling religious superstition. Christian Socialists like Conrad Noel, George McLeod and Geoff Shaw had his admiration. In his later years he was to win the respect of his religious opponents like Archbishop Winning. His approach to churchgoing men and women was quite open, if they or the clerics

---

[67] Harry McShane mentions being in Russia in 1932 following 'the NUWM Conference of 1931 [when] elections were held for a delegate to be sent to Russia. Sid Elias, the chairman, topped the poll and I came second. . . The National Administrative Council of the NUWM decided national policy. People from various districts went to it as delegates: Len Yule was on it from Sheffield. I was on it from Scotland etc. The national organiser was Wal Hannington. . . Emrys Llewellyn was national secretary and Maud Brown was women's organiser. . . [but] the party used certain people to report back to it. Sid Elias used to watch and report back every little thing we did, and later Pat Devine. . . [both] used to insist on following the party line.' Sid Elias was eventually jailed for two years 'on a charge of inciting Wal Hannington and Emrys Llewellyn to sedition'. This was in 1932, following the Hunger March, and Hannington gives a detailed account of it in his *Unemployed Struggles 1919-1936*. Days after Sid Elias was jailed Llewellyn and Tom Mann were 'arrested under a six-hundred-year-old Act of Edward III.' At 76 years of age Mann, the NUWM treasurer, was already a legend yet alongside Emrys Llewellyn he was imprisoned for two months 'on the grounds that if they were allowed to remain at liberty they might incite to a disturbance of the peace.' Later on, during the 1936 March, Harry Pollitt 'called Wal Hannington to a meeting and showed him a photostat copy of a letter written by Sid Elias to the Economic League, offering to work for them while remaining a member of the Communist Party. Hannington identified the writing as that of Elias and we had to report back to the NAC of the NUWM that our ex-chairman was no longer trustworthy.' [McShane 219]. Wal

wanted to throw in their lot with the Socialist Movement they were more than welcome.

Free-thought literature he took to like a magnet, becoming an avid reader of Ingersoll and Chapman Cohen. I remember him telling me about a meeting of the Comintern in Moscow during the 1920s where he was one of the two Scottish delegates. The British delegation took a particular decision on the role of the CPGB within Britain and the two Scottish delegates supported it. The meeting then adjourned for lunch. When the delegates returned, to Harry's surprise the previous decision was dropped and the exact opposite was put forward. Finlay Hart was the other Scottish delegate. He went along with the change but Harry did not. He was always suspicious of unanimous decisions and was not afraid of discussion and disagreements, provided they led to action. I feel that was one of the main reasons he was respected within the Labour Movement. Finlay Hart, incidentally, was the only prominent Communist Party member to be present at Harry's funeral.

When I was made full-time election agent I was by now married with a young family and I assumed I would receive the normal wages of a party organiser, but to my surprise the Glasgow Secretary Bob McIlhone gave me at least 50 shillings more. I felt uncomfortable about it and I remember I mentioned it to Harry and he said 'Don't take any handouts, get the rate for the job,' so I just returned the cash.[68]

There were several disquieting features of the election campaign that were not apparent to most comrades involved. Peter Kerrigan

---

Hannington makes no mention of this affair in his *Unemployed Struggles 1919-1936* but as an opening paragraph to his Chapter VIII he writes: 'There is a pernicious toad-like species which occasionally reveals itself in the working class movement. It is the person who sells his birth-right to manhood for a mess of pottage. It is the type that, although belonging to the working class, is ready to stoop to the practice of betraying the workers who are striving to improve working class conditions. I am referring to persons commonly called police informers, spies and *agents provocateurs*.'

[68] 'I respected McIlhone because he had always made great personal sacrifices for the party, but he was also very bitter against anyone else who didn't hold the same views as he did.' [McShane 248]

was an imposing-looking candidate, standing over 6 feet tall, grey
haired and quite distinguished and as an ex-Junior football player
with Yoker Athletic he had the stature of a very fit man. In reality
he was quite an aloof person who tended to lecture people rather
than talk to them. I never got on friendly terms with him in the
eight or so weeks of the campaign. He never strayed from the Party
line and at the committee meetings his contributions were
completely unimaginative and quite predictable whereas Harry's
proposals and suggestions were mostly always different and original.
No doubt that was to be expected because of his wide experience
and long-time record of activity in the Labour Movement.

Harry was the Scottish correspondent for the *Daily Worker* during
the Second World War and then Scottish editor, and he remained
in the post till 1952. His reports covered the gamut, ranging from
the crofters' land seizure at Knoydart to the unmasking of the
'kangaroo courts' inside Polish army camps in Scotland. It was Harry
gave Alice Cullen, the Labour candidate, the nickname 'Silent Alice'.
He knew that although she had been a Councillor for eleven years
she had never spoken once at a meeting of Glasgow Corporation.
Over the years he built up a wide circle of contacts inside the Labour
Movement and was a kenspeckle figure on the conference circuit,
he became a doyen among industrial reporters. Being privy to inside
information helped him pull off a few scoops but he was never
selfish with knowledge, he shared it, and he assisted many a
gentleman of the press over a difficult stile. Apart from his job with
the *Daily Worker* he was Chairman of the Glasgow Branch of the
NUJ and all in all he had access to most newspapers and the media
in general. This was how Peter Kerrigan could get involved in issues
that none of the other candidates knew anything about.

So I was flabbergasted two weeks into the campaign when I got
a telephone call from John Gollan through to the Gorbals' rooms
telling me that he was sending up Malcolm McEwan to relieve Harry
McShane from the job as Press Secretary for the election. John
Gollan told me to tell Peter Kerrigan the situation but not to tell
Harry. This I could not do. I immediately told Harry and then told
Kerrigan. It should be said that I had absolutely no quarrel with
Malcolm McEwan who was a very capable journalist and had been
a feature writer with the *Daily Worker*.

That was my first but not my last experience of double-dealing within the Party. It was also the beginning of my close relationship with Harry McShane, it lasted for over forty years. The next battles took place in the Glasgow Committee where we were both regarded as 'deviationists'. All we wanted was the Party to get actively involved in all struggles, whether official or unofficial. But the election campaign in Gorbals was really outstanding. The Labour candidate was not at the races. With over a thousand activists from the Party and the YCL we really set the Gorbals alight. For a while it looked like Kerrigan could break the mould and be successful but we reckoned without the 'silent majority', including the Catholic vote. Even against that he got over 8000 votes, the best vote for a Communist candidate in Scotland.

Another issue that created divisions was housing. There was a waiting-list of nearly 100,000 for council housing. In order to spotlight the shortage people in unsanitary houses had started to withold their rents. While the Party full-time officials did not openly condemn the comrades who were assisting these people their support was lukewarm. Also at this period there were many thousands of empty houses and premises in private hands. These were seen by their owners as assets whereas those of us involved in the struggle saw them as places to rehouse the homeless. This led to the squatters' movement which to begin with was entirely spontaneous but a few comrades like Les Forster and John Gold were to the fore. It is significant that the only leading Communist to get involved in helping with publicity and legal aid where necessary was Harry McShane.

During this period there was another small issue, a question of misrepresentation, when two leading officials of the Communist Party got posters printed saying they were Housing Candidates in the municipal election, but no mention was made of their Party membership, nor that they were full-time officials. Harry regarded this as deception and the posters were destroyed but the malaise, in his opinion, had not been eradicated. Instead it was part of the growing desire for respectability within the Movement. Harry believed strongly in declaring your Communist principles and joining the workers in struggle.

Harry was well-kent in the Scottish Offices through in Edinburgh, municipal affairs were his abiding interest and the housing question high on his agenda. His lust for a big story about

MUNICIPAL ELECTION - TUESDAY, MAY 2nd, 1950

DALMARNOCK (3rd) WARD

Candidature of
HUGH
SAVAGE
(Communist Candidate)

To the Electors of Dalmarnock Ward

Dear Friend,

The Bridgeton Branch of the Communist Party has nominated me as candidate for the Dalmarnock Ward in the forthcoming Municipal Election.

I have been pleased to accept this nomination, because, as secretary of the Bridgeton Housing Association, I have long felt the need for a real active councillor prepared to fight on the problems affecting the people, especially housing.

At my meetings I will deal more extensively with the policy outlined in this address, and will be pleased during the course of the campaign to meet any electors to discuss with them the problems as they affect the Ward.

I have a record of consistent activity in the working class movement, having been shop steward in numerous building sites, and shipyards, including John Brown's.

I was born in the Ward and I know the nature of the problems confronting the workers in Dalmarnock. Apart from my responsibilities in the Housing Association, I am a member of Calton Ward Committee, Vice-President of the East Branch of the Plumbing Trades Union, delegate from my Union to the Glasgow Trades Council, and had the pleasure of serving on the Executive of that body for a number of years.

As a building trade worker, I confidently ask for your support, as I feel that more industrial workers are needed in the Council.

Yours sincerely,

HUGH SAVAGE

housing came off in the year 1951 when he reported the agitation and strikes against the sale of council houses at Merrylee in Glasgow. By this time he had become completely disillusioned with the Communist Party and behind the scenes was having a running battle with its leaders. Even although he was still a Party member they removed him from his position at the *Daily Worker.* The same tactic was to be used much later against Peter Fryer when he was asked to leave the *Daily Worker* because of editorial suppression of his despatches from the Hungarian Revolution of 1956.[69]

In his book *No Mean Fighter* Harry mentions a few events that led to him leaving the Communist Party. He was set against paid officials who only liked discussion within the Party on the line that had been laid down from the Central Committee. They tended to dictate policy and direct any action through official channels and more and more they frowned on small unofficial strikes. In contrast, those Party members who left for purely selfish motives, either to join the Labour Party or become a full-time official in a trade union still seemed to be acceptable to the Party leaders. Some went on to become MPs, even peers in the House of Lords but were still regarded as CP allies despite the fact that in thought and action they were real right-wingers who sold out and took the money.

The events leading up to my own resignation took place over a number of years but I think it really began with seeing the attitudes being adopted by the full-time officials on issues like housing, public activities and industrial policy. At first I believed it was local officials such as Bob McIlhone who formed campaigning activities like squatting, rent strikes and other strikes, and only later did I find

---

[69] Peter Fryer: *Worker* correspondent inside Hungary, sent truthful dispatches to London, blowing sky-high the Party line. His articles were suppressed or edited out of existence. . .
Hundreds of members of the Communist Party left. Peter Fryer joined the exodus. . . ' [Forster p63-4]
'At least 20,000 Hungarians dead; at least 3,500 Russians dead; tens of thousands wounded; the devastation of large areas of Budapest; mass deportations of Hungararian patriots; hunger verging on starvation, widespread despair and the virtual breakdown of ecomomic life; a burning hatred in the hearts of the people against Russia and all things Russian that will last a generation. . .' See Peter Fryer's Introduction to his *Hungarian Tragedy* (Dobson Books Ltd, 1956)

out different. In actual fact what we wanted was the Party to get involved in all struggles whether official or unofficial. On one occasion we were accused of being 'adventurers' because Les Forster suggested during a campaign that we should throw a few thousand leaflets out the top windows of Lewis's Store in Argyle Street.

Harry was indeed the last of the Red Clydesiders. He never lost his belief in the Socialist cause and while he had offers to join other parties, from the Labour Party to most of the left-wing parties, he remained suspicious of their rigidity and after his experiences in the Communist Party he had doubts about a 'vanguard'. He was no armchair philosopher either and it always gladdened his heart when the workers won a victory as a result of strike-action. In his time he had access to many establishment figures but he never used it for personal advantage, but he did use it to ensure that they listened to what the workers had to say, or else to arrange release or bail for somebody wrongly imprisoned. He was completely and utterly incorruptible. After leaving the Communist Party at sixty two years of age he returned to his trade as an engineer in Harland & Wolfe and he was really quite content working with his hands.

His autobiography, *No Mean Fighter*, covered a period from his birth on May 1891 up to 1953, the year he left the Communist Party.[70] Some mention was made of the years afterwards but it was only cursory. The Scottish Socialist weekly, *Forward*, asked him to do a series of articles in 1953. Harry was to write one of his best stories when Billy Graham, the American evangelist, arrived at

---

[70] Peter Hudis quotes Harry McShane's letters of 1974 and 1978, deposited in the National Museum of Labour History, Manchester, in which McShane said of *No Mean Fighter* that:

1] I am not writing an autobiography. Over a long period Joan Smith brought a tape-recorder every Tuesday afternoon. I took it that the purpose was to get a record of events. I refuse no one. It was later that I discovered that the material was to be used by Pluto Press for an autobiography. I have opposed this but have suggested that Joan Smith use it as a biography under her own name. I have not written a word.
2] I did not even see the proofs of the book before it was finished. Joan Smith sent me some chapters for revision. . . when it was recorded, five years ago, I did not think it would ever come out. . . The decision to put it out in its present form and with my name as joint author was not mine.

Glasgow's Kelvin Hall and his piece was headed 'There's no business like show business.' The time from 1953 to 1988, the year that he died, were perhaps the best years of his life and into his late eighties he was much in demand as a platform speaker, rousing audiences at the Free Trade Hall in Manchester, and the Albert Hall in London.

Party diehards were always at his meetings with very little to say except 'Why did you leave the party?' His answer was straight-forward, because the CP was no longer a revolutionary Party, and the Soviet Union was not, nor ever had been, a Socialist country. Year in year out they kept asking the same question. It was ludicrous. When he was over 90 years of age and speaking to a packed meeting a fellow stood up and asked him the same old thing. It was a meeting in Strathclyde University organised by the Glasgow Labour History Society and the theme was the Russian revolution. This was thirty four years after he had left the Party. 'Why did you leave the Party?' Harry's reply was instant, 'Why did you stay in it?' The questioner was dumfounded.

His newspaper training never left him and he was just as metic-ulous preparing a duplicated news-sheet for the Socialist Workers Federation as for anything else. There was one called *New Commune* and under Harry's guidance stories were published that others had not got and, for instance, a big splash was made with Lenin's last will and testament. Another issue was devoted to lengthy extracts from Kruschev's disclosures of life under Stalin. *New Commune* was restricted in size and out of it was born a new and bigger and better paper, *Socialist Revolt*. Harry here was in his element, writing, editing and encouraging others to put pen to paper.

Writing for the press was so different in those days. Word-processors, discs, tape recorders were not the tools of the trade, instead it was the pen, the pencil and the typewriter, and you were considered well equipped if you could do shorthand into a notebook. Harry could type and do a bit of shorthand but he always thought that style was the essence of good writing. Books on grammar and punctuation and literary composition he found of great help. He was a respected member of the NUJ, and on friendly terms with fellow Glasgwegian scribes such as Jack House, John Hossack and Cliff Hanley.[71]

---

[71] Cliff Hanley was once refused a job by BBC Scotland on the grounds that his accent was too Glaswegian.

As a public speaker he had no flashy rhetoric, he was not an orator in the mould of Nye Bevan, Harry Pollitt or Arthur Horner but with a street corner he was a vintage soap-box man, at Glasgow Green, Speakers' Corner, Hyde Park, almost always speaking without notes. Question time was his forte and few could match him in debate. After leaving the Communist Party he spoke regularly at open air meetings at Drury Street in the heart of Glasgow.

He did not require the Hungarian tragedy before resigning but when it happened he supported it immediately. In reply to the Soviet allegations about Fascists and the involvement of the CIA he said, 'When do you ever see Fascists setting up workers' councils?'

Harry had turned to Marxist-Humanism long before Dubçek called for Communism with a human face. While he remained in the CP for over thirty years his influence was not all that significant, particularly with the new leaders who had attended the Lenin School in Moscow. Many who left the Party following the Hungarian revolution of 1956 sought solace by joining the Labour Party. Some disappeared into the limbo of trade union officialdom. Others just stopped doing anything political at all. Harry McShane was made of sterner stuff. He donned his thinking cap and went back to reading all over again the early writings of Karl Marx when he was a young humanist, and then the older Marx who wrote *Capital* volumes 1 to 3.

Despite what happened in Russia after 1917 he never expressed regret at supporting the revolution in its infancy. Like his colleague of that time, John Maclean, he saw it as a great uprising from below. Before he threw in his lot with the new emergent Communist Party of Great Britain he was already a confirmed Marxist, a revolutionary Socialist. Long before he left the Party he realised things had gone all wrong. The hopes engendered by the Russian Revolution were dashed and cruelly betrayed. How this came to pass he set about finding out, reading the lives and opinions of some of the early revolutionaries who had been there. They had been sending out warning signals laced with predictions as to what was likely to happen inside the Soviet Union if the rot was not stopped.

As well as being a thinker Harry was a practical man and along with the late Eric Heffer and other kindred spirits who had left the CP they formed an organisation called the Socialist Workers Federation, while launching a newspaper called *Socialist Revolt*.

The Socialist Workers Federation was not a political party. Those connected with it had no grandiose ambitions except spreading Socialist propaganda by word of mouth. For a while Harry was a regular contributor to *Forward*, the Socialist weekly, writing a series of articles. All his political life he relished the challenge of debate which for him was the water of life. Opponents he never feared, taking the view that the bigger they are the harder they fall, and they do not come higher than Archbishop Winning, or Lord Boyle.

The memory of Adam Smith will survive quite well without any help from the Institute named after him by the far right. Their knowledge of the Kirkcaldy sage seems very slim and sometimes verges on the pathetic. At the Bi-centenary Conference organised by the Adam Smith Institute, among others on the platform were Lord Boyle, Education Minister for the Tory Government, and J.K. Galbraith from the USA. Speaking from the body of the hall Harry pulled no punches and his verbal blows sent his opponents reeling. He quoted a letter from Adam Smith to Sir John Sinclair, 'I dislike all taxes that may effect the necessary expenses of the poor. They according to circumstances either oppress the people immediately, subject them, or are repaid with great interest by the rich.' Then he cited Smith's attitude to labour and labourers and commented 'that if working men they would be put down by the authorities.' This was a fervent plea for the memory of the real Adam Smith to jump out of its Tory straitjacket. It was a *tour de force* and Lord Boyle was hanging on the ropes. When he did reply he concentrated only on Harry McShane and revealed that here was the educator deficient in his knowledge of the famous philosopher. A professor from Japan referred to Harry's contribution 'It takes a Scotsman to know a Scotsman.'[72]

---

[72] In a letter to Raya Dunayevskaya dated June 4th 1973 McShane writes of the event as follows: 'Lord Boyle set out to debunk Marx by attacking the labour theory of value. He talked the old rubbish about skilled workers producing more value than unskilled labour. He thought he was boosting Smith. I made the only speech from the floor. I said that to dispose of the labour theory of value was to reject Smith as well as Marx, so where does that leave you? I was astounded by the effect. J.K. Galbraith said he agreed fully with me and added, 'it takes a Scotsman to expound Marxism.' In his essay 'Harry McShane and the Scottish Roots of Marxist-

In his lifetime he shared the platform with some of the greats of the Socialist Movement. He toured Scotland with John Maclean and other members of 'the Tramp Trust', and also spoke with the legendary Tom Mann at the market town of Mansfield. In his later years he did solo spots all over the country. His friend, the late Bill McCulloch, before he died, could still recall vividly an evening in a pub at Kilburn listening to Harry on the Irish question. On one occasion Sheila Rowbotham, the socialist and feminist, was so moved after hearing him speak that she wrote a poem as a tribute to him. He was much sought after with invitations to speak to a variety of public gatherings and I remember him addressing the Glasgow Bar Association on the question of Marxism and Law, and he also spoke at the German-Goethe institute in Glasgow, and he took part in talks and debates at many universities in Scotland and England. When he spoke with Bernadette McAliskey (nee Devlin) at the Woodside Halls in Glasgow the place was surrounded by hundreds of jeering Orangemen, with hundreds of police to escort the audience in and out.

All this activity he relished with enthusiasm. When Old Father Time started to catch up with him he was in his 90s and his public appearances had to be severely curtailed. The last time he spoke in public was at a May Day celebration at Glasgow Green when tribute was being paid the Calton Weaver martyrs on the bicentenary of their murder. The main speaker on the May Day platform that day was Ron Todd of the TGWU who said it was an honour to speak on the same platform as Harry McShane. Elspeth King of the People's Palace presented him with a special medal that she had had produced in commemoration of the Calton Weavers.

He was a historian without a PhD but he had an essential know-ledge of various periods in Scottish history. Like so many other Socialist pioneers he was self-educated. Glasgow's Mitchell Library was one of his favourite haunts. Michael Donnelly, former curator of the People's Palace, can recall seeing him surrounded by books of a historical nature. The Reformation and the impact of John Knox had a fascination over him. In company and in conversation he could cite facts and quotes from his life and times. He did not

Humanism' Peter Hudis confirms that the event 'caused a sensation' so much so 'that it was reported by several newspapers, including *The Times*.'

see Knox as just a follower of Calvin or a firebrand breathing flames of anti-Catholicism but rather as an intelligent Scot making justifiable sermons in the context of the sixteenth century Reformation. He had read the dialogues between Knox and Mary Queen of Scots many times and his considered verdict was that perhaps through an excessive streak of stubborness and clinging too much to dogma Knox threw away a lifeline of accommodation offered by Mary.

An enthusiast of working class history he was the first to revive memories of the striking Calton Weavers of 1787. The Glasgow Trades Council commissioned him to write a booklet depicting this struggle. A stone commemorating the six martyrs killed by the military on the instructions of the then Lord Provost and town council was erected by public subscription in 1836. To their credit, in 1931, Glasgow Trades Council renewed the stone and prompted by Harry the council agreed to erect an adjacent stone dedicated to the Calton Weavers. This stone was put in place in the Abercrombie Street burial ground and Harry spoke at the commemoration ceremony in 1951.

Although he never sought any honours he did accept the Freedom of the City of Glasgow award, after some persuasion. After this was presented to him by the Lord Provost in company with the Glasgow Cathedral minister the band struck up *I belong to Glasgow* instead of the National Anthem, much to the annoyance of the minister.

When one looks at the Labour Lords and at those people who have used the Movement for personal advancement I think about Harry McShane. A few days before he died I asked him how he was fixed for money. He said. 'I'm fine, I've got over forty pounds.' Let that be his epitaph after eighty years a Marxist.

McSHANE

.. a real

fighter

to

the

end

HARRY McSHANE
Opposed injustice.

When ex Communist Party member Harry McShane died in 1988, even popular papers like the Daily Record recorded the fact – presumably because they considered that politics and political history were of interest to their readers

THE reddest of the red Clydesiders died yesterday. Harry McShane was just three weeks short of his 97th birthday.

A lifelong Marxist, Harry was the epitome of the Labour movement in Scotland. He continued to fight against what he saw as injustice right up until his death.

He spent the last few years of his life in a Church of Scotland eventide home, busily writing to friends and trade union colleagues all over the world.

He regularly sent letters to Downing Street, pointing out to Mrs Thatcher the error of her ways.

MARCHES

McShane began his political career in the old Independent Labour Party in 1908 while he was an engineer in the Clydeside shipyards.

He later came under the influence of that other great Red Clydesider John Maclean.

He broke with the ILP and joined the fledgling British Socialist Party but later followed Maclean into the Communist Party, where he stayed until 1953.

McShane finally found their centralisation and bureaucratic control too stifling.

During his long life he took part in the workers' revolt that saw tanks in George Square and was

By DAVE KING

jailed three times for organising protests and rent strikes.

He was also prominent in the hunger marches of the Thirties and was a formidable scholar, orator and political thinker.

McShane was always proud of his skills as an engineer and worked for a time in the Yukon goldfields.

Ten years ago he published his memoirs, appropriately entitled No Mean Fighter.

Three years ago McShane was honoured by his native city when he was given the Freedom of Glasgow.

Last year, at the age of 96, Harry was on the platform at the annual May Day rally in Glasgow to be awarded a special badge commemorating the bi-centenary of the Calton Weavers.

They were among the first Scots trade union martyrs – shot by troops while taking part in a strike over wage cuts.

The old battler

TWO years ago, after he had moved into a Church of Scotland home in Glasgow, McShane staged a hunger strike in support of the staff's battle with the Kirk over union recognition.

And a few months ago actor Russell Hunter received much acclaim for his part in the BBC Scotland TV play, The Dunroamin' Rising, about a former Red Clydesider who stages a hunger strike in an old folk's home. Many observers believed the play was based on the life of Harry McShane.

225

Harry McShane (centre) achieving
Freedom of the City of Glasgow

NO MEAN FIGHTER

McShane: the last of Red Clydesiders

By **WILLIAM HUNTER**

HARRY McSHANE, who died yesterday, was a worker. For people who saw the world as he did — and for many who did not — he fulfilled many other roles. He was a scholar, philosopher, orator, journalist, pamphleteer, protest marcher, rebel. He was the most dapper of revolutionaries.

Above all he was a worker.

His first brilliant achievement was to become an engineer. Not many poor Irish Catholic boys in his apprentice days struggled manfully enough to become journeymen. He kept at his heavy trade until he was 69.

"I loved work," he said when he retired. "That's why I never went to secondary school to complete my poor education." He seemed to see no contradiction that his way with work was the antithesis of Marxist methodology to destroy, then rebuild. His greatest pleasure was to renew machines.

"When things came into the works which had broken down, I loved to get into them," he said. Search for work in 1928 took him to the Yukon to build and keep going two big American-made shovels for a mining company. He loved to recall that his boss was called A.N.C. Treadgold.

Until his late 80s he remained chairman of his trade union branch. And, yes, he did sometimes enjoy stopping work.

"Oh, yes," he would conceded, "I did sometimes lead men out for trivial reasons. I had a strike once because the works clock wasn't big enough and the hooter wasn't loud enough. We won that one. They gave us a clock you couldn't help seeing, and a hooter that blew you out the gate."

His body was built for work. His bantam height carried readily the shoulders of a heavyweight. Everything was always neat. His morning shave was surgical. His shirt collar appeared to have been moulded to his neck. That, too, showed the pride of a former tradesman.

"I'm an engineer. Engineers always used to put on their blue suits and their bowler hats to go to the Kirk on Sundays."

He had a great good knack of sounding happy and irascible at the same time. His joyously gritty way with the world showed most at those few times when he was slowed down by less than total good health. He took illness as a personal affront. He described a bout of pneumonia as "a series of chills." A limp in one leg became "an attack from the Left."

The pneumonia caught up with him when on the stump making speeches through the Highlands. He had to be taken to hospital in a hurry. In a two-bed ward a young woman doctor stripped the other bed to pile on him extra blankets.

She left him briefly to return with the biggest glass of whisky he had ever seen. Harry McShane recalled: "I though to myself, *oh ho*, what's next?" He was only 78 when he told that story. He had decided he wouldn't become old until he reached 90.

In all his life he made only one boast that his friends can recall. He liked to brag: "I am the worst chess player in the world."

About how he saw his place in world communism he once conceded when he came back from a big meeting in Moscow: "Well, yes, all right, I did see Stalin, but I don't think he saw me."

As the last of the Red Clydesiders he sometimes found himself made both angry and sad by what he considered the pay-packet aridity of much working-class discussion.

"Whenever trade unionists gather there is any amount of militancy about wages, but no politics. They take the life out of the thing, whereas man is capable of developing to heights that are not dreamed of."

One of the smaller losses of his death will be to miss his vigilant letters to the Editor. He hated to go a day without his Herald.

Hugh with his parents at the beach around 1925

Hugh and Liz with sons Scott and Jim, Rothesay 1949

Hugh with Liz and
daughter Laureen

Hugh with sons
Scott and Jim, 1950

Hugh (left) with son Scott around 1955

(opposite and overleaf)
A note of condolence from Raya Dunayevskaya on the occasion of the death of
Hugh and Liz's son Brian in 1965. Raya Dunayevskaya, as well as being an
international activist in her own right who had stayed at the Savage household
on her visits to Glasgow, had been Leon Trotsky's secretary

Hugh —

Words are quite impotent
things when such tragedy strikes
the death of a son who had
everything to live for but suddenly
was there no longer. Believe me,
as one who has experienced past
such tragedies, that this is no
"condolence" note in any ordinary sense.

However, I am a Marxist not only politically but "personally" and when Marx's only son died and the family did not even have enough money to get a casket for the child, the only truth that sustained Karl and Jenny was the knowledge that no one really dies, not because of religion's fake heaven but because life, though, is continuous and lives on in the who wove to fashion a world to youth would have been proud to add their human dimension to. And I feel certain that you, so, though so young, did know his dad was working for a better world and wants you to see him only alive working alongside of you for that real human world. I embrace you —

232

Calton Weavers Memorial
3rd September 1787

It should not be forgotten that 205 years ago, in response to a vicious wage cut imposed by the weaving employers, weavers in Glasgow and the West of Scotland took strike action. During a large protest demonstration a confrontation took place at the Drygate Bridge over the Molindinar Burn when the military who had been called out at the request of the Lord Provost of Glasgow were ordered to fire on a peaceful demonstration crossing the bridge. Six weavers were killed and a large number wounded.

It is to the undying shame of the magistrates, most of whom were merchants, that the Lord Provost gave the colonel in charge of the military the Freedom of the City of Glasgow. He also presented to each soldier a present of shoes and stockings from the city funds.

At a period when the working class has been under attack for many years, anti-union legislation has become acceptable amongst our so-called leaders. The Friends of the Peoples Palace feel we should reaffirm our solidarity for martyrs prepared to die for these principles.

We hope that all the people of Glasgow with an interest in retaining the real and proud history of our city will congregate at the

Calton Burial Ground, Abercromby Street
1 p.m. Saturday 5th September 92

where Elspeth King will unveil the new memorial stones dedicated to the immortal Calton Weavers of 1787.

Norman Bissell of the E.I.S. Lanarkshire Area will address the congregation as will Jim Freil of the printers union G.P.M.U.

Come along. Bring your trade union banners.

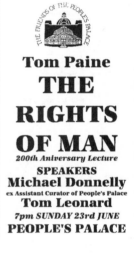

Tom Paine
THE
RIGHTS
OF MAN
200th Aniversary Lecture
SPEAKERS
Michael Donnelly
ex Assistant Curator of People's Palace
Tom Leonard
7pm SUNDAY 23rd JUNE
PEOPLE'S PALACE

Hugh Savage at the restored graves of the Calton Weavers

233

SOCIALIST REVOLT

ORGAN OF THE SOCIALIST WORKERS' FEDERATION

Vol. 1, No. 8   Price 6d.   Jan.-Mar., 1957

CONTENTS

EDITORIAL

LABOUR CONSTITUTIONALISTS

We cheered the courageous Hungarian workers who, with great cost to themselves, took strike action for political purposes. Even the Labour leaders showed signs of enthusiasm.

The same Labour leaders advised us not to use industrial action as a means of stopping the war on Egypt. They would fight it, they said, by every means " within the constitution."

This obsession about the constitution makes the working class movement look ridiculous. Rules and procedure laid down by our class enemies before the movement existed are to be observed. The methods adopted for the appointment of a Tory Prime Minister have caused members of the Parliamentary Labour Party to worry about the departure from constitutional procedure.

Serious economic issues are coming to the front. We must not concern ourselves about the constitution when our living standards are attacked.

Vigilance Needed

The desperate drive of the British ruling class to face up to rivals in the struggle for markets must, very soon, involve attacks on the living standards of the workers.

The attempt to take control of the Suez Canal by force is followed by a decision to support the idea of a European Free Trade Area. This latest move is supported by Lord Aldenham, Chairman of the Westminster Bank. He sees it as necessary to meet competition from West Germany.

Sir Percy Mills will use the nationalised gas, electricity and coal to cheapen production. The next move will be an intensified drive to lower costs in the export industries.

This effort will, undoubtedly, have a bearing on wages and hours of labour. The fight will sharpen, but we will be victorious only if we are determined to overcome the present weaknesses in the Labour movement.

Leadership Needed

No struggle " within the constitution " will meet the needs of the working class in this new situation. The trade unions must be made to perform the functions for which they were brought into being. Instead of co-operating the drive against foreign competition, they must mobilise the workers for struggle against the employers.

The unions belong to the workers, but they are, in the main, controlled by officials. The leaders are more concerned about helping the State than helping the workers to raise wages and reduce working hours.

The struggle cannot be avoided. It will continue until it develops into a political struggle; a struggle for political power.

The Socialist Workers' Federation holds the belief that to give guidance in this situation a new Revolutionary Socialist Party is needed. All sincere Socialists should help to achieve this aim.

SOCIALIST REVOLT

can be had by writing to
HUGH SAVAGE, 57 Carmyle Avenue, Glasgow
Editorial material should be sent to
HARRY McSHANE, 151 Weir Street, Glasgow, C.5

Appendices

SOME CAMPAIGN WRITINGS BY HUGH SAVAGE

The Defence Committee for Elspeth King

To all the friends and supporters of the above committee we wish to say that despite reports to the contrary the issue that led to the setting up of the committee has not been resolved and will not be until the injustice against Elspeth King is rectified.

We are heartened by the tremendous support from the thousands of people who signed the petition, to the many artists, writers and musicians, also the many MPs and councillors who sent messages of support. They stand in sharp contrast to the paid officials who toed the Party line and supported their leader.

Never has such support been seen before for any official never mind a museum curator. The people of Glasgow always respond to anyone who speaks their language and represents their point of view. In other words they can smell a phony a mile away and they recognise a set-up when they see one. That is why they support Elspeth King.

Glasgow has always been a city of protest against injustices and is justifiably proud of its past history in this regard. The treatment of Elspeth King is a stain on this record and the Maxtons, Macleans and Wheatleys would turn in their graves if they knew what foul deeds were being carried out in the name of a socialist council.

It is so important that we remember the outstanding collection that Elspeth and Michael Donnelly have built up with the help of thousands of ordinary working class people in Glasgow in the last sixteen years. This could be under threat not only from potential asset-strippers but from the hiving off or the lending out of items indiscrimately. It is our belief that what happened to the very valuable Barra collection in Govan could very well be repeated with the larger People's Palace collection if the 'Friends' are not extremely vigilant.

Long after memories of Pavarotti

and the Bolshoi Ballet have left the scene of Culture Year 1990 the integrity of Elspeth King will shine like a pearl and the guilty people in positions of power in Glasgow will long be remembered, because the truth will come out.

So keep the support coming and to all the hundreds of people who were unsuccessful in getting the letters they sent to the press printed please send them on to us and we will print them in some way as we feel the people are entitled to know. Our next meeting will be in August, watch for the leaflets.

NEED NOT GREED

They complain about the lack of use of football pitches in public parks like Glasgow Green, Alexandra Park, Tollcross Park, yet even during the Year of Culture not one sporting event was sponsored never mind a football tournament like the Empire Exhibition Cup that Celtic won in 1938. Surely some of the millions they spent on the Glasgow's Glasgow event could have been used in this direction. At one time, even way back in the hungry 30s, there were football leagues of all types, from schools to several leagues of churches' football, juvenile leagues and secondary, junior leagues and central leagues, and there were works' teams. It was difficult to get a pitch unless you booked in advance. All of that even when there was mass unemployment.

When you look at how it was then in Scottish football, does that not have some relationship to the very low standard of our current 'national game'? It is no coincidence that there were some political figures with vision and particularly in the east end; men like Maxton and Wheatley, people who could see a better world, who knew there was a better way, whose driving force was need, not greed.

CULTURE CITY AND THE PEOPLE'S PALACE SCANDAL

The Issue

After 16 years in which they have transformed the People's Palace from a rundown moribund institution into one of the top visitor attractions in Britain, Elspeth King and her deputy Michael Donnelly, instead of receiving long-promised promotion have been victimised, humiliated and downgraded in post.

The background

In 1975 King and Donnelly began their custodianship by scrapping the jaded title 'Old Glasgow Museum' and reinstating the original name of The People's Palace. Starved of funds to augment a threadbare and woefully inadequate collection in which the people were conspicuous by their absence, King and Donnelly resolved to take the maximum advantage of the mass demolition programme then underway to build new collections.

In order to avoid needless duplication of effort and encroachment on the interests of other departments or museums they drafted and published a collecting policy, the first and, as yet, only such policy in Glasgow museums. In spite of lack of transport and adequate storage facilities they embarked upon a programme of fieldwork, involving object retrieval and photographic recording in all parts of the city. This programme eventually led to the formation of new collections on a wide range of subjects hitherto ignored, including 'women's suffrage', 'temperance', the trades union movement, the co-operative movement, political and religious history, popular entertainment, stained glass and contemporary art. They have now assembled what Mark O'Neil has called 'the finest urban collection in Britain'.

In the process of acquiring these collections King and Donnelly with their small staff mounted a series of major exhibitions, winning awards in both British and European categories and conferring upon the Palace an international reputation. Kenneth Hudson, the highly respected authority on museum standards has called the People's Palace 'one of the six best museums in Britain' and Elspeth King 'one of the three best social history curators in the world.'

In spite of this hard-won acclaim King and Donnelly had to fight against an antagonistically negative attitude from successive directors and politicians who did not share their enthusiasm for social history, the People's Palace nor its location on Glasgow Green.

New Images versus Reality

Matters came to a head with Glasgow's winning bid for the title of European City of Culture 1990. Those given the task of creating a new image to match the city's cultural accolade were embarassed by the 'warts and all' approach of

237

the People's Palace displays, and its record-breaking attendances.

After being promised by the Directors of the Festival Unit that the Palace would play a central part in the 1990 programme, its two curators instead found that its role was being deliberately marginalised. As revealed by Festivals Unit Depute Director Neil Wallace, the Director of Museums deliberately set out to sabotage new 1990 displays at the Palace by attempting to send Museums Council money back. In any case the programme was eventually cancelled at the halfway stage, leaving the 18th century room dismantled and bare, and as Wallace confirms, the Palace remains 'desperately understaffed and underfinanced'.

When even this failed to undermine the growing popularity of the Palace, and the 'Early Glasgow' displays received rave reviews in professional journals, drastic action was taken.

Elspeth King, so recently shortleeted for the post of Director, was compelled by the successful candidate, Julian Spalding, to apply for an allegedly 'new post' which was in fact her own. The wording of the advertisement was designed to insult and demoralise her – 'An enthusiastic and forward looking Keeper is required to undertake the management of collections at a number of museums including the very popular People's Palace.'

The inclusion of the management of the Palace collections was a deliberate catch-all so that if Elspeth King failed to get the post, her current position and that of her deputy would be undermined. The resulting interviews, in spite of the Council's Equal Opportunities Officer, were a mere formality. Elspeth King was judged to be 'unsuitable Keeper material' and the 'new post' was awarded to Mark O'Neil of Springburn Community Museum, regardless of his relative inexperience and inferior academic qualifications. Mr O'Neil, who had been given his first job in museums by Elspeth King (and who was known to be the chosen candidate months before) is now empowered to tear-up her collecting policy which Director Julian Spalding (who has publicly confessed his ignorance of social history) does not support.

No amount of window-dressing can conceal the fact that this action by a small and unrepresentative group of councillors and officials is a crudely executed attempt to dismiss King and Donnelly by making their working conditions intolerable.

If you agree with us that this action is malicious and destructive, support us in our campaign to secure justice for Elspeth King and Michael Donnelly by writing to or lobbying your Councillors on their behalf.

It is not too late, this injustice can still be reversed. To do otherwise is to bring both Glasgow District Labour Party and Glasgow's reputation as a Cultural Capital into disrepute.

RAVENSCRAIG, ANOTHER SELL-OUT?
[PUBLISHED IN THE *GLASGOW KEELIE* ISSUE 3 JULY 1990]

Once again we are back to the drawing board in the fight to retain the Ravenscraig complex. This despite all the production records and all the phony praise. Surely the workers at this steel works and elsewhere will have learned something in the last decade as they have watched the Scottish industrial base be decimated by the multi-national companies ably assisted by both Tory and Labour governments. After Linwood, Scotland's first and last car plant, closed there followed the shipyards Alexander Stephen's then John Brown's which led to the UCS work-in, but other yards with household names like Barclay Curle, plus many others disappeared without even a whimper. Do any workers really believe that an all-party and joint trades union campaign will succeed where others have failed? Do they really believe that Thatcher was not told of his plans by Scholey? After all, did she not appoint him to the job? Can you imagine Rifkind and Forsyth on the picket line?

In the above closures – and it is only a handful, there were hundreds more – in the overwhelming majority the firm or its work was transferred down south to England or abroad. Surely this should direct the workers' attention to the whole question of how big a cog they really are in the big monopoly wheel. Significantly the industrial struggle that came nearest to

victory was the miners' strike. Despite the whole might of the state from the police to the courts along with Her Majesty's shadow cabinet led by Kinnock to the Trades Union Congress, the one thing that defeated them was disunity. If the miners had not been divided by the Thatcherite stooges in Nottingham and else-where they were very near to victory as admitted by McGregor, the ex-Coal Board chairman, in his memoirs.

So the one thing rank and file steel workers should not forget is the need for united action at the shopfloor level and in every section of the steel industry up to and including international solidarity with steel workers world wide because you have more in common with a steel worker in South Africa than you have with Scholey. You were maybe bought off with generous redundancy payments, although even these are declining as Thatcher tries to solve her economic problems at the workers' expense. Stop being reasonable, start being awkward. It's your job that is on the line, it's your family that will suffer. Above all do not let any politician, Tory or Labour or even Scot Nat, use your fight for survival as a stepping stone to a political career. Do not forget former shop stewards like Airlie and Reid who built a reputation then a career while the workers went down the road to the 'broo'.

There is quite a debate going on about Scotland being part of Europe. We remember that we have the lowest pensions and lowest social security benefits. No doubt that is one reason why Thatcher does not want the Social Charter to be part of her price for joining the EEC. In and out of Europe we have got to stop accepting crumbs from the monopoly capitalist table, start raising some of the demands of past socialist pioneers, 'Full employment or Full maintenance'. Why should the workers pick up the tab for the failure of the bosses to invest in new plant? Why should the workers be responsible for the incompetence of the employers and above all why should decisions taken about your future be decided by that bingo hall they call the stock exchange?

SCOTLAND'S FUTURE
[PART-PUBLISHED IN THE GLASGOW KEELIE ISSUE APRIL 1992]

The coming general election not only poses constitutional problems for the working class in Scotland, even the more fundamental question of the relevance of the existence of parliament itself. It is now seen by more and more ordinary people as a vehicle for the establishment, from the judiciary and the monarchy, to cloak the brutal oppression and robbery by the ruling class in legality.

This has been intensified in the last thirteen years under Thatcher till the Tories themselves got rid of her. In this period we have seen all the minor reforms that the workers have gained by struggle swept away, all the trade union rights that had been placed on the statute book by the six Labour Governments superceded by Tory laws.

It was no surprise that the extreme lady from Grantham would use her massive majority in parliament to do so, but what is unbelievable was the behaviour of Her Majesty's loyal opposition. Not once in the whole of the thirteen years did they depart from playing the parliamentary game. Not once was the charade of pairing ever challenged, not once was the cosy relationship between the government and the opposition ever under threat. Even in Japan the opposition walked out in protest when the government had gone too far.

The extent of Labour's betrayal reached its depth during the twelve months of the miners' strike. How could Kinnock, representing a miners' constituencey, see miners battered to the ground, mining communities overrun by mounted police, the law continually broken by the authorities and hundreds of roads sealed off and yet still reserve his hatred and venom for the miners, particularly Arthur Scargill? What kind of so-called workers' representatives participate in an evil bill like the poll-tax becoming law? Even its eventual withdrawal means years of warrant sales and poverty for the poorer sections of society. Surely a walk-out by Labour MPs would have been in order but no, they made sure their pals in the local councils sent in the Sheriff Officers and jailed certain non-payers.

THE SILENCE OF THE LAMBS

There has never been a time in working class history when the working class has been so vulnerable and so leaderless. In a period when there is massive unemployment, 5 million in fact, if we ignore the crooked figures churned out by the Tories, when at least a million are homeless with thousands sleeping rough, many of them former inmates in institutions. Last week, one of these unfortunates had his legs amputated due to frost-bite. We now have tuberculosis back on the agenda. Where are our leaders?

Where is this mighty trades union movement? Look at them all, from that useless piece of flab Norman Willis of the TUC, more concerned about losing his seat on NEDDY, a phony Tory talking shop that Lamont abolished, than the fact that the TUC has lost over 3 million members in the last two years. Surely the biggest indictment of all is that he has remained silent along with the Lairds and the Airlies, even when the most basic wages and conditions are being undermined. They also stand by when they know that child labour is being used in many factories and women have to accept slave-wages, and then the Tories make it legal and abolish the Low Pay Unit and Wage Councils.

Is it not sickening that the so-called socialist Trades Union leaders can sign sweetheart deals with no-strike clauses and turn a blind eye to overtime being the order of the day in a period of mass unemployment? Is that stupid opportunist lot of garbage not aware that the legislation that the Tories have abolished was gained not by pathetic parliamentarians but through the struggle of the rank and file pioneers who built the Labour Movement?

As for her 'Her Majesty's Loyal Opposition', would not the George Lansburys and even the Nye Bevans turn in their grave to see the kind of place-seekers that now grace the Labour benches? We have the leader of the Opposition himself, John Smith QC who defines Socialism as 'defending individualism' in a recent speech. Then we have Gordon Brown, Shadow Chancellor, who really believes he can run Capitalism better than the Tories – not that it would be difficult with the present

241

bunch – but has he never heard of Ramsay MacDonald, Harold Wilson and James Callaghan? Look what happened to them. Is it not a fact that the purpose of creating the Labour Party was to abolish capitalism not to save it? One thing is for sure, it was never intended that the workers should make sacrifices to defend a system that robs them from the cradle to the grave. Has that time not long gone? Now the Tories, having sold the country's 'family silver' to their friends in the City of London at throwaway prices with hundreds of millions of pounds given as inducements, are turning their greedy eyes to the huge pension funds held by the railway unions and the National Union of Mineworkers. They have allowed British Telecom to use the pensions funds to pad out redundancy payments made to thousands of workers that they dismissed after it was privatised. It is not good enough for Labour MPs to say 'Well we voted against these bills.' In the opinion of the ordinary worker what we are talking about is legalised theft and they are giving it the cloak of respectability by playing the parliamentary game.

All the mass street demonstrations, all the protest marches against the pit closures, all the mass opposition seen in Scotland against any attempt by Laing, the Tory Quisling who, as a Loyd's name, is really a representative of vested interests in Scotland, to foist the privatisation of water onto the people will be to no avail if it is left to Her Majesty's loyal opposition to lead the way. There has never been a period when the calibre and ability of MPs has been so pathetic, although it is not their fault alone as the method of selection of a candidate is so corrupt that only a safe or simple person has a chance of being nominated.

It was back on January 14th 1893 a conference was called to form the Independent Labour Party. It was chaired by Keir Hardie. Also in attendance was the ageing Frederick Engels, close associate of Karl Marx. The historian Edward P. Thompson called it 'the first political party that came from the bottom up and had a distinctly socialist message.'

If it was good enough for William McIllvaney to call for a boycott of Parliament on the question of Scottish Independence then surely the Labour Party has the duty and the right to walk out when a Tory government allows millions to be unemployed, millions to be homeless and sleeping on the streets, and then puts a Bill on the agenda not only justifying their actions but at the same time eliminating laws that civilised governments have accepted. Time is not on the workers' side. They cannot wait four or five years for the next election and they will not leave it to the Labour Party.

When the newly elected Clydeside MPs led by Jimmy Maxton and John Wheatley and eight other MPs left from St. Enoch's Station on Sunday the 10th November 1922 thousands of workers cheered them off. Today very few workers could name their MP and the majority could not care less. When thousands gathered in George Square after the disappointment of the last general election there was no sign of Donald Dewar and his Scottish Convention. Instead speakers led by George Galloway and other MPs promised to start a campaign to disrupt Parliament. They called themselves Scotland United – it should have been Manchester United or some other football team – and after one small skirmish they died without a trace.

As soon as it was pointed out that the only way forward for Scotland to be taken seriously in its fight for independence was for all MPs who had been elected as supporters of Home Rule to resign their seats, turn their backs on the Unionist House of Commons, forgoe their parliamentary salary and expenses, and set up shop in Edinburgh, that was the end of any serious attempt to take the fight any further. We are told that we have to wait another five years until the next general election. As usual it's always tomorrow for the workers. If all the MPs who shed crocodile tears about the unjust Act of Union 1707 wish to look for some precedent they have to look no further than the former English Colonies of the Empire, starting with Ireland and America.

The Scandal of the Burrell Collection

For many years behind the scenes the famous collection has been threatened by serious water leaks from the unique stainless steel roof which is a feature of the widely-acclaimed building. Now Chris Burlow the city architect and one time director of the infamous Glasgow's Glasgow exhibition of the 1990 Year of Culture has broken his silence and admitted that for some years they have been trying to contact Barry Gasson, the Burrell building's original architect. Already they have had to remove most of the sculptures from the vicinity of the damage but not before a famous artwork by Rodin was affected. The curator staff are concerned in case corrosion is found in others. £100,000 has been set aside by the architect's department to meet the cost but this may well be short of the final figure. The problem has been around since 1988 and Messrs Taylor Woodrow, the main contractors, and generous donators to the Tory Party cause, have denied responsibility.

However, have no fear. That outstanding defender of the interests of the Glasgow proletariat, Councillor Tommy Dingwall is Convenor of the Arts and Culture committee. When questioned on the subject by a journalist Councillor Dingwall threatened him 'with dire consequences' and also that whoever was supplying the journalist with this information would answer for it, and then he told the journalist not to call here again. In the words of his boozing pal Councillor Mutter, 'I'll do it my way.'

WE WERE THE FIRST

Glasgow's Glasgow

The Workers City group were the first working class representatives to take to the streets to make a stand for the defence of the real culture of Glasgow. At the opening day, when we demonstrated outside the Words and the Stones exhibition, eventually called Glasgow's Glasgow, our loudest derisory cheers were reserved for Pat Lally and the rest of the Labour Party leaders. How fitting and how correct. Little did Lally know that before the Year of Culture ended his very political future would be under threat.

When a group of thirty or so workers held aloft the banners saying 'There's a Lot of Con Going on in 1990' the truth of the slogan could not have been imagined, nor what would be the sorry end of this exhibition. How could we possibly know that we were at the gate of a multi-million pound scam and the biggest and most expensive flop in Glasgow's history. There was no way we could know that by the end of the year all the directors would stand accused of financial mismanagement, all the councillors who flaunted themselves at the opening would be distancing themselves from it and blaming the accountants, Touche, Ross and Co. who in turn were threatening to sue the council. What a sordid situation. It is to be hoped that the real truth will emerge and the high priced exhibition carpet-baggers will be dealt with along with all the elected officials who forgot whose interests they were protecting.

Pavarotti's concert

When the Workers City group demonstrated outside the Scottish Exhibition Centre on the night of the Pavarotti concert, we were the first group ever to hand over an open letter addressed to Pavarotti himself, written in Italian, denouncing the exclusion of the poorer people in Glasgow to the beauty of the great man's voice.

We were susequently harangued by Ruth Wishart the journalist in one of her many columns. How could this snobby little shit possibly know that the idea to appeal to Pavarotti came from an unassuming worker called Bobby Clark who, with his husky voice and with tears in his eyes, asked for something to be done about the injustice of Pavarotti being heard by only those who could afford to pay what to Bobby was three weeks social money for the privilege of hearing the great man.

Bobby Clark wrote the letter himself, in Italian. He was a popular and well-kent guy around the Scotia Bar, an ex-off shore oilworker, steel-erector to trade, but by then diagnosed with cancer (I believe asbestos-related) and on DSS supplementary benefit.

From Chicago to Glasgow 1890 to 1990 May Day

When the official labour movement has turned its back on the very principles that led to its birth we were the first and only workers in Scotland to celebrate a hundred years of May Day on the 1st May 1990. We marched through the streets of the Calton behind the Marauders pipe band after our arranged meeting in the Winter Gardens had to be cancelled due to the Labour-controlled Glasgow District Council Parks Department shutting us out of the People's Palace.

Nearly two hundred workers marched behind the Marauders with a red banner in front saying 'From Chicago to Glasgow 1890 to 1990', marching to the local Community Hall where the children of the Calton greeted us. There we heard the first reading of a play by Ann Kerr, a woman who had worked in Hollins of Boden Street, Brigton – Glasgow's last cotton mill – and was made redundant when it closed down. Her play was called *The Last Thread* and was based on the plight of workers who are paid off.

After the traditional May Day march to Glasgow Green we set up an independent socialist platform without permission from the District Council and re-established our right of free speech in Glasgow Green. It was an open platform where all groups could express their point of view. Apart from the Workers City group at least eleven people spoke who were from various left wing groups, including anti-poll tax protestors. This was the first time in over fifty years that this type of platform had appeared on Glasgow Green. We had an audience of over a hundred and fifty people, including the police.

The defence of Elspeth King

One of the nastiest and most despicable acts of any administration, either Tory or Labour, was when Pat Lally's Glasgow District Council deliberately passed over Elspeth King for the post of Director of Glasgow Museums and appointed the asset-stripper Julian Spalding. He had excellent qualifications, having seen off curators like Elspeth King who stood in his way when he was the Director in Manchester. Then to add insult to injury they appointed a nonentity called Mark O'Neil to the post of Keeper of Social History despite his lack of ability and experience, not to mention qualifications.

The Workers City group was first to Elspeth's defence, we had one of the biggest demonstrations outside the City Chambers where over a thousand people turned up to protest. We got over five thousand signatures on a petition and had several packed meetings with speakers from all sides condemning Lally. Over five hundred letters arrived at the *Glasgow Herald's* desk, more than for anything since Billy Graham, and letters reached the *Scotsman*, the *Independent, Scotland on Sunday*, the Observer, the *Spectator* and the *New Statesman*. We picketed the National Conference of Curators which took place in Glasgow at the Theatre Royal. It so impressed the delegates, and one of them said to us that he had been attending conferences for more than ten years and never ever seen a demonstration of support for any curator. Elspeth spoke at the conference and got a tremendous reception, despite the sleazy attempts of Spalding, O'Neil and Councillor Davidson, the so-called Convenor of Museums, to intimidate her by changing their seats.

Save the Glasgow Green campaign

This was one of the most sustained campaigns that was fought for many years. Most citizens know that the District Council, led by Lally, has been promoting plans to lease nearly a third of Glasgow Green to private developers for the next 125 years. They have no mandate for this policy and according to their election manifesto they are pledged to retaining public ownership and improve and develop the 'Green.

Our campaign was unique in Glasgow's political history, we are not a political party looking for votes, we are not selling literature, we are not pushing any political philosophy down anyone's throat. We have distributed somewhere in the region of forty to fifty thousand leaflets as well as many many copies of *The Glasgow Keelie* over the last nine months. But maybe our real secret weapon was the wee loud speaker van we had. It covered the whole of Glasgow from Gorbals to Govanhill, Parkhead to Byres Road, Bridgeton to Dennistoun and out to Shettleseton, not electioneering, just telling the citizens of Glasgow that the Green was not Lally's to sell, it belongs to the people for all time and they, the District Council, are merely the custodians for future generations.

In the course of these campaigns we encouraged people to demonstrate outside the City Chambers. This they did in growing numbers and you have to go back to the 1930s to get the numbers who gathered outside the City Chambers every month when the Labour group or Council itself was meeting. We always exceeded two hundred but on the day we took over the Chambers itself the crowd was nearer five hundred. It was on the day the East End management committee had to decide on the plans for the development of the Green. No room could be found large enough to hold the crowd so the full chambers where the Council met was decided upon. The councillors did not know how to handle it and for this one day the City Chambers really belonged to the people and the East End management committee rejected the development plans. One of the most refreshing incidents came when the chairman asked how many spokespersons we wanted. Most of us were thinking in terms of five or six, when one wee woman called 'Forty five'. There was confidence for you.

It must be recorded that the last two attempts by Messrs Lally and Co. to defeat the growing protests were the actions of desperation. Firstly, on the instructions of his council, he had to convene public meetings to guage opinion and explain the plans. So the super-democrat Lally arranged four meetings in different parts of Glasgow on a Sunday at 2 pm. Once again he underestimated the people. Despite the presence of himself, Jean McFadden (City Treasurer), Councillor Crawford and Bailie Brown, they were trounced; disregarding the instructions from the Chair – that each of the above individuals occupied at each of the meetings – all the meetings threw out the plans and called for no privatisation of the Glasgow Green.

The second attempt they made was really beyond belief and unprecedented, never before undertaken by any local authority. It took the form of a poll through the *Evening Times* newspaper with coupons to be filled in and returned to the Town Clerk, boxes made available on council premises for the purpose. However, it was a private poll because Mister Lally decided on the action without consulting anybody and not having the authority, making the Glasgow District Council look like a bunch of fools.

What we hope will be the final act took place on the 21st November 1990 when 350 citizens turned up to lobby the Labour group meeting at the City Chambers. All the media were there including the BBC and ITV television cameras. We did not know till later on that evening, when a journalist phoned us, that they had decided to shelve the plans for private development of the Glasgow Green. While this is welcome we must be vigilant and encourage ordinary workers to assert themselves. Do not let career politicians of any party use you as voting fodder, remember we are many, they are few.

JAMES McLAREN[1]

James (Jimmy) McLaren's early death from tuberculosis was a great loss to his friends and comrades. He came from Muslin Street, Brigton and members of his family were quite well-known in the district, perhaps not always for the best of reasons. Ned Donaldson described him as the 'white sheep of the family'. Jimmy was a hard-working activist, also a great reader and scholar. After he had contracted tuberculosis he began studying the subject and impressed upon people that they should understand its social implications, the direct connection with bad housing, under-nourishment and so on. He had a fine collection of books which he bequeathed to Hugh. Among them were studies on tuberculosis and pulmonary disease, and he died in the knowledge of what was happening to him, correctly predicting that a cure would exist within two years of his death.

It was McLaren's wish that he be cremated, also that Bill Lauchlan officiate at the ceremony. He authorised Hugh to go through his papers and do what he thought fit, expressing the wish that his *Daily Worker* shares should go to the Glasgow City Committee of the Communist Party. Other instructions were that Hugh should tell Bill Lauchlan that he was glad to have worked under such a capable fellow, and to tell Sam Aaronovitch that he had learned much from him. McLaren

also instructed Hugh to tell all the comrades in the office and on the Ward Committee that he was proud to have worked with them.

At a CP meeting in September of 1947 some acrimony seems to have taken place where at one point Jimmy had proposed Hugh and others for the Committee, and was opposed by the hierarchy. It is hypothetical to argue that he would have taken the same route out of the Party as his friends Hugh Savage and Les Forster, Bill McCulloch, Matt McGinn and Ned Donaldson, but it is surely more likely than otherwise. It is relevant that his tragic death occurred before these young communists made personal acquaintance with Harry McShane. Ironically, four years after his death McLaren's former comrade Bill Lauchlan was Scottish Secretary of the CP when he made the 'keynote speech. . . at a Scottish Congress of the CP held in Glasgow. When he finished his peroration, delegates stood up clapping again and again in praise of the Messiah. During this display of adoration Ned Donaldson and Hugh Savage remained seated.'[2]

This was one of the crucial moments in their journey out from the party. Of Sam Aaronovitch, the other comrade referred to by McLaren, Les Forster writes that when himself 'and others were having doubts about party policy, Aaronovitch remained an out and out diehard. Even when I left the

CP he was still an unrepentant Stalinist.'[3]

But as far as those who knew him were concerned the death of James McLaren 'was a tremendous loss to the working class movement because he would have reached high.'[4] Among Hugh's papers were McLaren's notes for his public lectures. He was a promising speaker and he gave classes to the Bridgeton YCL and spoke also at other branches, eg, Maryhill in 1944 where he lectured on aspects of the situation in India as it then pertained three years before Partition. His How to Win the Peace lectures were 'outstanding' according to his friends. There were also notes for his lectures on 'A Party of a New Type'. After the diagnosis of his tuberculosis he organised a Social and Welfare committee at the hospital he was attending.

Of his friend's personal points Hugh noted 'intelligence and political insight on the issues he seized eg, squatters' rights, and his complete optimism in eventual working class victory.' Hugh also noted that Jimmy 'was annoyed at having to die so young.' He attended to his friend's burial and among his own personal effects were the notes he made for the funeral service, as were his notes for a memorial service that took place in April 1949. James McLaren left the following message for his friends:

Ever since I joined the party (I) have had complete confidence in the working class. And despite the pessimists the working class will be victorious. I feel awfully contented because the party gives one a different approach not only to life but also to death. The proudest nine months of my life was when I was thought fit enough to work in the party office. When one felt that the end was near it seemed only natural to think of Lenin's quotation. I am not afraid to die, only slightly annoyed one has to do so young. And at a time when every one is required to play their part for peace and progress. I would also like to say that I have no regrets and would do exactly all the things I have done all over again. I only wish that I had met the Party sooner. Never lose faith in the Party or the working class as victory will ultimately belong to us.

---

[1] This commentary on James McLaren was compiled from the notes used by Hugh Savage for his friend's memorial.

[2] See Forster's memoir *Rocking the Boat*.

[3] *ibid.*

[4] This and subsequent information from Hugh Savage's notes for McLaren's memorial.

The Glasgow Keelie

Get the strength of the anti-poll tax groups around you

No.1 FREE ★ ★ ★ APRIL 1990

CULTURE CLASH

• *Kicked out for culture?*
Homeless in George Square

THEY CALL THEM the Bisto Kids. All the frauds, hucksters, comic singers and chancers who have jumped on the culture city gravy train.

The whole sorry saga has been dubbed 'a jamboree for the bourgeoisie'. And one thing's for sure: these characters wouldn't recognise genuine Glasgow culture if it came up and challenged them to a square go.

The hidden agenda of Culture Year is of course to make the city safe for yuppies and investors, and keep the workers safely out of sight.

They've already started by trying to kick the homeless and their soup kitchens out of George Square in case they offend the genteel tourists.

WE SAY THAT ANY CULTURE THAT IS NOT DRIVEN BY SOCIAL JUSTICE IS A SICK, SHALLOW AND WORTHLESS CULTURE.

But thankfully there is a force in Glasgow that does not share the values of war profiteer William Burrell, or the cynical manipulators of George Square and Strathclyde Region. That force is the working class.

This year has seen all that's positive in our culture come to the fore in the shape of the Pay No Poll Tax campaign – the traditions of direct democracy and mass refusal. The tradition that says 'Stuff the law, we want justice'.

IT IS THIS CITY OF DEFIANCE THAT IS THE TRUE FACE OF GLASGOW 1990.

Remembering Hugh Savage and Workers City

by William Clark

IN 1990 I was involved in running an art gallery in Glasgow. As a spin-off project from that I organised a one-off exhibition in a disused furniture warehouse in Saltoun Street. When that came to an end I had some notion of extending the project slightly, but could not drum up support amongst other artists. At a meeting of the Free University I suggested that we organise a series of quite large scale meetings in the Saltoun Street space and this was quickly organised by a few of the group. It was here I first saw Hugh Savage. He had been invited to speak on 'Workers City' by James Kelman. I remember him speak afterwards in the cafe of the space next to the bookshop. I have no intention here of romanticising my initial impression. I did not particularly take to him. Now I am astonished to think of him, and his age then. In my memory he was a much younger man. What I took to be arrogance was something deeper.

The overlapping of organisations alluded to above was typical of the times. Workers City had been operating for some months before I came along. I had been told by Kelman that they met in the Scotia Bar every Monday, and although I had very little idea of what would actually take place, I found myself being hurriedly introduced to one or two of the people while an argumentative debate was taking place over the table of what is now known as Fingal's Nook. I have no real memories of the first meeting, my mind was strained to absorb all the information. When the meetings moved to Transmission Gallery I got to know people better – having risen to the august level of making the tea and putting out the chairs. It was the small magazine which we produced, *The Keelie*, which interested me most. I gradually came to have a major input into it. My first story came about as the result of Hugh giving me a clipping from the *Glasgow Herald*. This related to the sale of the Scottish Exhibition and

Conference Centre (SECC). Together we worked out the bare bones of a story and I went digging for more information in what would become my usual haunt – the Mitchell Library – and wrote the story.

Workers City initially operated to protest about the activities of Glasgow District Council during the Year of Culture, but we continued into the early 90s, exposing the corrupt activities of one of the most criminal administrations the city had seen. The activities surrounding the SECC story are a good example of how we worked. The facts of the deal need not concern us save to say the public purse was being rifled for the benefit of a small group of councillors and their business associates. We planned to distribute *The Keelie* outside the SECC itself – the cover story simply stated 'SECC SCANDAL'. The TUC had decided to hold their annual general meeting there that year so everyone from the left was gathered outside as the group dished out *The Keelie*, which we printed in thousands. The security staff approached us and tried to stop us, only to meet defiance, particularly from Hugh, who would have said something like, 'Call the police if you want, son, we're not moving.'

The police duly came and after talking to Hugh could see no reason why we could not be allowed to do what – obviously – everyone else was doing. Luckily they did not look inside *The Keelie* which ran a story about the 'physical argument' we had had with the police in George Square during an Anti Poll Tax demonstration. Here the police arrested Gary Lewis, an actor – who was performing a short play by Kelman – under the pretext that he (dressed as Napoleon, leader of Glasgow Labour Council) had said the word 'fuck' twice and they wouldn't allow him a third, thus had *The Keelie* headline read: POLICE CHIEF DOESN'T GIVE THREE FUCKS.

At the SECC, by this time, what with all the fuss, everyone wanted one of whatever it was we were giving out. The security people walked away in a huff only to get madder when people from the Firemen's Union and the Oilworkers' Union volunteered to take bundles of *The Keelie* inside and put them on their stalls. Over the weekend the head of the SECC resigned.

The Glasgow Keelie

No. 3   The Salt of the Earth   July 1990

SINATRA

Me? In the Mafia? I've never been a Glasgow District Councillor...

— Defend Elspeth King —

DEFEND THE PEOPLE'S CULTURE

THE
Spal
Cur
her
sh

The Glasgow Keelie

Number 7

March 1991

After the Gulf war...

BACK TO REALITY

Councillor Pat Lally must be thanking his lucky stars that Saddam Hussein has pushed him off the front pages as Public Enemy No. 1. We have news for Lally, however, if he intends to force through his Tory-inspired plans for the privatisation of Glasgow Green while media attention is focussed elsewhere. The Keelie has its eye on him and his ragbag crew in the council and we'll be ready to confront and expose whatever manoeuvre he may try to pull.

On the following linked issues the Glasgow public has made its voice heard:

● Flesher's Haugh and Glasgow Green: THERE MUST BE NO SELL-OFF TO PRIVATE DEVELOPERS NOW OR IN THE FUTURE.

● The People's Palace and Elspeth King: THE MUSEUM

SPOT THE BASTARD

Pat Lally, District Councillor and Yuppies pal; John Mullin, Strathclyde Region Finance Convenor and wage snatcher; Jack McLean, Journalist and fearless attacker of single parent families. Hope you choke on it, ratbags!

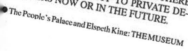

LET GLASGOW FLOURISH.

Glasgow European City of Culture 1990- Visitors to the European City of Culture during recent months have found more going on than either themselves or the city fathers have anticipated. They have landed in the midst of pitched battles, such as the Elspeth King/ Michael Donnelly affair, the save the Glasgow Green Campaign and the growing public demand to know the full cost of Culture year.

SAVE OUR GREEN FROM PRIVATISATION.

Glasgow Green, one of the oldest common greens in Europe, may soon be handed over to private developers. The Labour administration is finalising plans for a giant up-market leisure complex, to be built on part of the Green known as Flesher's Haugh, run for profit by commercial operators.

The current Labour administration gave no indication within their election manifesto of any intentions to lease this public land for a peppercorn rent for 125 years to private companies.

The privatisation proposals have outraged a large number of Glaswegians who have voiced their anger at public meetings, council chamber lobbies, by writing letters and articles to all types of newspapers, but in spite of public opposition the council have continued to ride roughshod over the wishes of the electorate.

STORM IN THE PALACE: CULTURE CITY AND THE PEOPLE'S PALACE SCANDAL.

After 16 years, in which Curator Elspeth King, and her deputy Michael Donnelly have transformed the People's Palace, with the help of thousands of ordinary working people of Glasgow, into the most popular museum in Glasgow with it's outstanding collections illustrating the historial and radical past of the Glasgow people.

Instead of receiving long promised promotions they ha been victimised, humiliated and downgraded in post, sulting in the summary dismissal of Michael Donnel But in spite of the ever growing popularity of the Pal and it's Curators Elspeth and Michael remain out favour with the present Labour administration, who steadily abandoning their historic commitment to soc ism and who are increasingly embarassed by the inc venient facts of Glasgow's radical past. The present bour administrations Saatchi and Saatchi view of so history has resulted in the under-funding of the Pa and the witch-hunting of Elspeth King and Michael I nelly. After many months of intolerable treatment by Labour-controlled Council, Michael Donnelly spoke ou defence of Elspeth King, himself and their life times v and was immediatly sacked without notice by the Lal Group Leader Cllr Pat Lally and Julian Spalding, Dire of Museums.

POPULAR OPPOSITION.

The people of Glasgow and Glasgow District Labour P have opposed this administrations policies with little effect . We are therefore asking that the National La Party initiate a public inquiry into this affair. P accountability is the essence of effective and democ municipal government

- I wish to add my name to the protest

....

....

Send to: Hugh Savage
204 Hamilton Road
Glasgow G41
Tel (041) 778 3154

It turned out that he used to 'organise trade fairs in Iraq'. This was the point when we were arming Saddam just prior to the first Gulf War. The man in question, David Sale, now runs the Secret Intelligence Museum in Bletchley Park which has all the old enigma code breaking equipment.

Hugh's contribution to the Workers City group was of course his great experience of political activism, this demonstrated itself most ably in direct actions. Yet he never lived in the past, never reminisced as such. He also had a great sense of sexual equality and seemed perfectly at home speaking to people much younger than himself. His political mind was advanced.

Workers City was also a cultural group. Transmission Gallery was at that time not only our meeting place but also the venue for very 'avant-garde' exhibitions. While waiting for people to assemble we would all occasionally walk round the exhibits. I remember him particularly taken with the work of Jo Spence.

His notions of the past and our culture would mesh (without even touching on his work for the People's Palace) in projects he would undertake under the auspices of the group. One of these was the commemorative stone for the Calton Weavers which he more or less funded out of his own pocket. Their burial plot was well on the way to becoming forgotten (and of course with it, the memory of what they stood for) by a Council who would rather prostitute anything municipally owned. Hugh understood that the cultural history of Glasgow was a political one, and that its history was in the process of being censored, particularly in projects such as the Year of Culture.

When the 'celebrations' came to an end I happened to be listening to the World Service very late at night. The Year of Culture 'accolade' had passed on from Glasgow, and as the reporter summed up he mentioned Workers City (in that refined dulcet tone) as a group criticising the Council's activities. Although I was glad that what we did had been broadcast to the World, what happened then has more or

less been covered up or wilfully ignored by cultural administrators and the press. A mini rerun of it took place in 1999:
the Year of Architecture.

Perhaps it is/was the scale of the corruption which people
cannot/will not comprehend; or the constant barrage of
publicity material declaring how wonderful our councillors
are. We had no illusions about this. Hugh had followed the
careers of these people and knew that many had built
themselves up on the back of undetected crime. At one point
I gained a list of the councillors on the Arts & Culture
Committee. When I consulted Hugh he looked at it and said,
'Well, he's done about five years for murder, that guy is semi-
literate, this one as you know is Lally's yes-man. . .' It was
just mind-blowing to think the city's culture had been put
into these people's care.

What for some might seem like a lack of respect for me
was both pertinent analysis and usually quite funny. When
we were handing out *The Keelie* we got talking about the then
Lord Provost, Susan Baird. She had been appointed by her
friends to fundraise for the Museum of Religion but had 'lost'
money rather than make any of it. I asked him what he
thought of her and he told me: 'She's just a wee hairy pie.'

Hugh's encouragement to me focused on my writing.
'Name names, publish photographs of the bastards – shame
them.' Perhaps the force of it is lost on the written page, but
it was very direct, he passed on an energy. At one
demonstration outside the old Regional Council we gave out
The Keelie and waited for the councillors to emerge and run
the gauntlet of protesters. He came up to me – I seem to
remember him pointing at them for me and saying these
words as if they were an instruction, as if I had to complete
some task of perception: 'Just look at them, just look at them,'
he repeated as I watched a single file of characters emerge
who seemed to have fallen out of a Bruegel painting. They
even looked corrupt, but were so pathetic, shambling,
hopeless, ugly, the years of mendacity had poisoned their
souls. But I kept looking.

It was a fiery anger Hugh encouraged in people, and he could talk to anyone and they would naturally and willingly pay attention. He was very much in the common sense tradition, but when he spoke of the people who had betrayed the people he cursed them with all his anger, and our anger we translated into our activities. When, as part of the political reconstruction of arts administration during 1990, Elspeth King was removed from her position, it was Hugh who led by example. This probably gave a greater impetus to his activities with Workers City, in that a personal friend had directly suffered, and the work of the People's Palace with which he had a close association. This too was under threat and he could witness millions being spent on an inept futile project known as 'Glasgow's Glasgow'.

He had first hand experience of the political drives built into, not only that massive failure, but the overarching game that the Council were playing. One of the first batch of cuttings he gave me were from the mid-1970s on the 'Cantley Affair' which had seen the '90s leader of the Council, Pat Lally and the '90s Lord Provost caught out by a 'scandal' which eventually caused the Labour Administration to be removed from office.

Hugh had no illusions about the character of these two people or the act they played out in public. Anyone even vaguely familiar with the procedures of local Labour Clubs in Glasgow knew very well what was going on. One could go so far as to say that most people with common sense have an instinct or intuition that politics is corrupted by money and power. But the fact is that Hugh would go out on the streets and loudly proclaim it, find and present evidence.

The support generated for Elspeth King was enormous. There were more letters sent into the *Glasgow Herald* about this issue than the Poll Tax. It was essentially the role of Julian Spalding which was thrown up by King's removal, he and the administrative layers beneath him – Robert Palmer, Neil Wallace – proved too weak to resist the political moves to the right. No doubt with the funding of 1990 came certain conditions, but these could have been easily dispensed with:

ultimately the city probably had a large measure of autonomy in actual spending allocations. This makes it all the more atrocious what they actually did. Within Workers City we could see that the City officials thought of culture as something to be brought into the City. They could not countenance the fact that culture *already* existed, was indeed indigenous.

We could also see that the City Council (who had charge of the funds) were prone to corruption and manipulation by the non-parliamentary right. Several public assets were being sold off by means of a system whereby (a) the Council would underwrite the debts which had been let accumulate (by the Council's own mismanagement), (b) the assets would be sold off at a token sum to a company made up of Councillors and businessmen who ran the scam, and (c) the whole thing would be presented under the rubric of cultural development.

And that network was publicly ratified in 1990 with the creation of Glasgow Development Agency. Lord Macfarlane, its first chairman, even joked that they should have called it the Glasgow Corporation. With Glasgow Cultural Enterprises we saw Sir Ray Johnstone and Pat Lally join in many Council/ Business developments including 'ownership' of the refurbished Concert Hall. By the time of the Elspeth King affair it was essentially the agenda of Workers City which was adopted in any of the stories which the press ran with. By the end of the year things were falling apart so fast the Council had become a laughing stock.

Hugh, with his connections to the People's Palace and knowledge of the history of the city, was possibly more personally incensed by the attempted sell-off of Glasgow Green, the history of which had been consigned into the dustbin category of local history (as if history only happens elsewhere). This particular campaign obstructed the Council's plans. They had ignored local opposition to the development – obviously because of personal incentives – and had been caught perpetrating a fraud on the people of the city: the pretence was that competitive tendering was in operation but both companies proved to be one in the same. I came on the scene a little late to speak first hand of the tactics – but I felt it was here the group came into its own and developed its potential. It was also in these direct confrontations that the Council and their cronies came to know and hate the Workers City group. It felt like a success to have stopped the plans and this would have heartened the group but so much was happening the momentum kept them going.

Workers City functioned on weekly planning meetings, those of us who would socialise afterwards obviously had further discussions, actual events or activities would take place during the week and usually involve a physical presence at some sort of demonstration. Obviously people had other things to do – so the schedule was pretty full. I found the commitment tough and I was still in my twenties

I have no memory of Hugh as some older sage – he contributed one-to-one and was extraordinarily modest. An aspect of Workers City I would find hard to talk about would be the difficulty (my difficulty) with some of the attitudes of the other members of the group. They showed no sense of treating the sexes with equality and respect. Hugh was somehow much more advanced than people his own age with the same upbringing. I now realise it was because of this sheer involvement – the extent that he learned and acquainted himself with progressive knowledge and radical politics and activism – that had shaped his identity, but there was something more: an innate generosity and honesty of spirit. At the time I took it as a part of his spirit or personality, as one does a friend, but it is hard to define what drove him. I think for us all he was some kind of solid foundation, as if he would always be. He was very natural, one would never feel inclined to analyse Hugh. He had a low almost gravelly voice which would build up in momentum when talking in groups but be quite whispery when talking alone.

After the Workers City Group split up and drifted away I saw Hugh only infrequently. Towards the end of the group we (from my viewpoint) had begun to focus on the production of *The Keelie*. I began to be interested in a type of writing that I felt I was devising for myself – in the midst of conversation with people I trusted who had valuable things to say. Walking across the carpark to the Scotia after a meeting, I remember Brendan McLaughlin say that at least we had provided some record of opposition, some other history.

Hugh would praise and encourage my writing and although I have always winced at praise, knowing full well how limited my knowledge was, I did take some pleasure in that my work interested people that I respected. This was something new to me, something that people do not experience who go to college or university. I have always felt that one should experiment in the raw. Just improvise. Probably my deepest conversation with him was sparked off by something I'd written about a Scottish banking consortium who had old money connections with the opium wars which I had discovered was on the take with the old Council culture shuck. What was new-found knowledge for me was history for him but it felt like we were both exploring it together.

It was the conversation that circled round us all that generated our thought on particular issues. There were things which I felt I could only talk about with each of these people. I can say with Euan Sutherland it was the art scene things, or with Brendan it was music, or with Jim it was parapolitics; but with each person I developed a keen relationship: I listened to them. I talked to them. Our thoughts propelled us. Interchangeably we worked together; some combinations were better than others. Most of us were blundering into potentially violent situations and we quickly had to get to know who was reliable. It should also be said that bad feeling existed within the group which predated my arrival. I remember spending hours wasting time trying to solve old problems which were nothing to do with me. Eventually some people just left dissatisfied, and others joined.

I felt my role was as a writer and then an editor of sorts. I had no experience of editing but just arrogantly assumed the role as if I had. Hugh grunted and groaned and would say, 'All right son.' But that was at the end of you talking to him, and him making murmuring sounds. God knows what went though his brain when I started on about some story I had got in my head.

But Hugh's sharpest knife blows were to the Labour Party. He believed that they never should have sought parliamentary status. He talked of the first two Scottish Labour members voted to the House of Commons for the new Labour Party. Everyone went down to cheer them off from Central Station. 'That was the last anyone ever heard of them.' They sold out for probably not very much and that was in the glory days. Hugh believed that had been much the same story ever since and he felt he had good evidence for it. The fact that the much revered John Smith became the leader of the Labour Party appalled him. In George Square he told me, 'if the people who started the Labour movement could somehow be told that their movement would in the future be run by a QC they would have all not bothered and gone home.'

I was on my guard when I talked to Hugh, I didn't want to say something stupid. I suppose most times I did, but he has had a strange influence on me. His words have stuck.

The reality of any political struggle and campaign is ugly. Workers City were an incongruous bunch, but we were left with quite a solid core at the end. We ended up feeling that we reflected issues rather than created them. But the members of the group felt it time to move onto other things. Workers City had acted as a support group for a variety of political struggles, eg. Govan Labour Party scamming, Rutherglen & Carmyle against pollution, the fight to save Glasgow Green, Action on Asbestos. After the demonstrations I would always look back at the scattering of 'lefty' leaflets that people had given out and the recipients chucked away – I did this because you would never see any of *The Keelie* lying there: people kept them.

I should add that we were hated by practically every left-wing group we came into contact with. But ordinary people seemed to respond to what we were doing.

No Summer Soldier or Sunshine Patriot
Hugh Savage 1918-1996:
Socialist & Militant Trade Unionist

by Tommy Gorman

HUGH SAVAGE is remembered by those who had the good fortune to know him for many things; being a man of principle all of his 76 years, to many of us for the comradeship he gave of freely. I admired him for his stubbornness and the intransigence he demonstrated from time to time. Despite his personal toughness there was a softer side to his nature which Mags Coyle and I experienced when our daughter Patsy was born and not expected to survive. The kindness of Hugh Savage and Leslie Forster helped us through that bleak time in our lives. So if this essay is nothing else it is my acknowledgement of their comradeship which helped Mags and I through troubled times. Patsy, by the way, is now a cheeky teenager.

Hugh became chairman of his trade union branch, an executive member of Glasgow Trades Council and a member of the District Committee of the Plumbers Trade Union. All of this was affected when he came into conflict with the leadership of the Communist Party in Scotland.

Hugh Savage is better known in recent times as a member of Workers City (a group which emerged during Glasgow's year of culture in 1990), for his fight to save Glasgow Green from being sold for private development and his champion-ing of the People's Palace museum. However, in my view, the support that he showed in the campaign in defence of Elspeth King and Michael Donnelly, former curators of the People's Palace, sums up Savage's *raison d'être*. The revulsion he felt at the treatment meted out to his two good friends by a Labour administration brought out all that was in his character; indignation at victimisation, commitment to those in struggle and an organisational approach to the problem. Many would say that Elspeth and Michael were unsuccessful in that confrontation but history will judge. Who were the real losers? In all he did and everything he tried to do, the admiration that Hugh felt for Thomas Paine shines through and Paine's influence is evident in his perspective on humanity. Hugh Savage considered the 'rights of man' – and women – to have contemporary as well as historical importance.

My most vivid memories of Hugh centre around his encyclopaedic knowledge of all things Glasgow; politics, strikers and protesters, culture (high and low), football, boxing and athletics; the city's buildings, parks, museums and their history. He was an expert on most matters concerning the city and proud of his roots in the east end.

However, what Hughie knew most about was the people of Glasgow, the famous and the not so well-known; from Matt McGinn, Maggie McIvor and the eccentric millionaire AE Pickard to the famous anarchist Guy Aldred who was based in Glasgow for many years. He knew of their history, their achievements and why they were important within this great city's rich vein of history.

One of my favourite memories of actually spending time with Hughie is being taken by him to a small cemetery just outside Rothesay when he was living on the Isle of Bute. This pilgrimage was to the grave of Bartholomew Dick, better known as Glen Daly, Mr Glasgow. A lifelong friend of Hughie's, Glen was a well-known singer and entertainer. He had a long association with Glasgow Celtic Football Club and recorded one of the oldest and best-known football anthems, *The Celtic Song*. I remember hearing it for the first time as a young boy in the 1960s at Parkhead. The song is still played at every Celtic home game.

The Celtic Supporters' Club on the island is based in the Galatea Bar, Rothesay and is named after Glen Daly not only because of his bond with Celtic fans everywhere but also due to the fact that he retired to the town and had played the Winter Gardens there on many occasions. The name Glen Daly is synonymous with the best days of the Ashfield Club. He is also famous for his appearances at this well-known venue in Possilpark in the north west of Glasgow. A number of his performances at this club were recorded as live LPs. My mother, father, Auntie Agnes and my Uncle Hector, like many of their generation took every opportunity they could to see Glen Daly in the Ashfield or at the Pavilion Theatre in Renfield Street.

Hugh Savage knew him long before he became known by his stage name, prior to his breakthrough into show business, and they remained lifelong friends. It was as fellow shipyard workers that they met as young men when they both toiled in the John Brown's yard in Clydebank. It remains a mystery to me why currently there is no available biography of Glen Daly.

As a shop steward in 'Broons', Hugh Savage raised health and safety issues on behalf of his workmates. He knew how poor the working conditions were and it came as no surprise to him that many of his former mates suffered severe health problems in later life. Nobody could fail to be shocked at the thousands of workers who have suffered premature deaths due to asbestos exposure in the shipbuilding industry. Hugh would talk about this on his visits to the old Clydeside Action on Asbestos offices in St Margaret's Place down at the Briggait, near Glasgow Cross. He was very supportive of the work carried out by this group.

Hugh Savage and Leslie Forster met in 1940 and they both joined the Communist Party about the same time, as did an outstanding young comrade, James McLaren who died of tuberculosis while still only in his twenties. They were the angry young men of their generation. All who knew McLaren agree that he was an extremely able and well-read young man and a great loss to the socialist cause. With Hugh and Harry McShane, in 1953, Les Forster resigned from the party and has never ceased to be politically aware despite, as I write, being in his eighty-fifth year. As a communist Les was prominent in the postwar squatters' movement and led the famous occupation of the Grand Hotel in Glasgow in support of homeless families.

Around this time, in the postwar period, there were also significant squatter's protests and occupations in other parts of the UK, organised by the Communist Party. Probably the most famous being the events which took place at the Ivanhoe Hotel in the centre of London. This was seen by millions of cinema-goers on the newsreels of the day. When he was a shop steward employed by the old Glasgow Corporation as a builder's labourer, Les was a prominent leader of the successful strike which prevented the sale of council houses at Merrylee in Glasgow. In this fight he worked very closely with another great socialist Ned Donaldson from Springburn who was also active until his death just a few years ago.

Despite the setbacks and problems that life threw at them Savage, Forster and Donaldson never lost sight of their youthful goals. An active trade unionist in the railway industry Leslie published an account of his life appropriately titled *Rocking the Boat*. He and Hugh were involved in the the publication of an excellent history of the famous 1911 strike at the Singer sewing machine facory in Clydebank. They later co-authored the biography of an outstanding socialist pioneer – *All For The Cause: Willie Nairn 1856-1902: Stonebreaker, Philosopher, Marxist*. Harry McShane admired Nairn as the first Scot who really understood Marx. It is worthy of note that, on publication, in the early nineties, Peter Fryer who was the *Daily Worker* correspondent in Hungary in 1956 wrote a warm review of *All for the Cause* in the *Workers Press*. In January 1992 this book was also reviewed in the *Glasgow Herald* by one of Scotland's finest journalists, William Hunter, who had a great affection and respect for Hugh and his comrades. Hunter also wrote an informed obituary in the same newspaper following the death of Hugh Savage in April 1996, with an excellent photograph of Hughie taken outside the People's Palace. Included were the following observations which are well worth repeating:

> By trade he was a plumber. His nature was to remain
> an old-fashioned craftsman. He was a perfectionist.
> Throughout a politically rebellious career as a shop

steward he believed in doing a fair day's work for the bosses, following his trade from shipbuilding to house building and then gas fitting he was an expert welder.

He first came to public notice during the Clydeside apprentices' strike during the Hitler war. Although by then a journeyman, he helped out the lads. It was a particularly bitter dispute. Cabinet Ministers threatened all the apprentices with war service if they would not yield. Shop stewards responded by threatening to shut down every yard on the Clyde. Hughie, then at John Brown's yard, was one of the more experienced campaigners and he helped the young workers to a famous victory.

It was one of the few triumphs he enjoyed. Being a bit of a boxer, however, he never failed to relish a fight. Always nattily dressed, he looked a douce agitator. He had the wry smile of a street battler who expected to lose more contests than he won. But he was a wild-catter. Whoever went on strike he was for.

I first met Hughie and Les through political events and demonstrations. The pair attended socialist meetings in Glasgow for decades and very often they would make informed contributions, if they considered the level of debate worthy of their input. Sometimes they did not think it was. Like many socialists they would especially attend meetings if Harry McShane was on the platform which he was until well into his eighth decade. As many Glaswegians are aware McShane was a major political figure despite the fact that he had not been a member of a political party since the early 1950s. McShane was involved in political work with the great Scottish socialist legend John Maclean as a member of the 'Tramps Trust' before Maclean was victimised and imprisoned by the state. He was also a renowned leader of the National Unemployed Workers Movement which organised the unemployed in the 1930s to fight against the 'means test' and for the right to work.

No Mean Fighter, the biography of Harry McShane

produced by my comrade and friend, Joan Smith, has been acknowledged as an important source of information on Glasgow, its labour movement, the struggle against the first world war and other aspects of McShane's active life. I was fortunate to be included in some of the discussions with Joan and Harry in her house in Priory Road in London's Crouch End. Harry had great respect and affection for Joan and her husband Steve Jeffreys who, at that time, was a leading member of the Socialist Workers Party.

Intellectually, Harry was a giant in the socialist movement and a great influence on the thinking of all of us who were privileged to work with him at close quarters. An outstanding working class activist all of his life, he was a Marxist who actually understood Marx and an authority on a whole range of subjects the most complicated aspects of which he had an ability to explain to workers in terms that they could understand. All of those associated with him speak warmly of the debt we owe to his legacy. Hughie and I discussed this often and he told me a story about the anarchist street meeting in the city centre where the speaker, trying to drum up support for the meeting, delivered the following slogan:

> *Workers of the world unite*
> *You have nothing to lose but your Harry McShanes*

When I reminded Harry of this he claimed not to have heard the story. However, he had a fine sense of humour and had a good laugh at it.

McShane being that bit older than Hughie, Les and the others was regarded as the leader of the small group who stood firm against the leadership of the Communist Party in Scotland. It is worthy of note that many members left the Communist Party in the mid 1950s and there were more than a few opportunists among them. After the Hungarian Revolution in 1956 some went to the Labour Party, others moved to the right within the trade unions and others left serious political activity altogether. McShane, Savage, Forster and their comrades stuck firmly to Marxist principles and decided to try to link with other like-minded socialists in the UK, and as we shall see, in Europe and the United States.

Included among these 'like-minded socialists' at that time was Eric Heffer who later became a Labour MP and a leading figure on the left of the Labour Party. But in 1948 he was expelled by the Communist Party after a membership of nearly ten years and never ceased to contend that the charges against him were political. Heffer was a joiner and a leading shop steward in Liverpool, working on building sites and in ship repair, and highly respected for his militant approach to industrial relations. When Heffer learned the exciting news that the Glasgow militant leader Harry McShane had left the CP along with a number of other comrades he invited them to Liverpool.

Following talks between the Glasgow group and a few Mersey socialists, a conference was organised in Liverpool in May 1954. Out of the discussions that followed the conference it was agreed to form the Federation of Marxist Groups which then became the Socialist Workers Federation. Another associate in the Federation was the veteran dockworkers' shop steward I.P. Hughes, also from Merseyside, who had an impressive record as a shop floor militant. He had left the CP around the same time. Subsequently they published a number of issues of a professionally produced newspaper *Socialist Revolt – Organ of the Socialist Workers Federation*. The paper's articles were all written by group members and edited by McShane, an experienced journalist who had spent many years employed by the *Daily Worker*. Each issue of the paper included the following information:

> *Socialist Revolt* can be had by writing to Hugh Savage, 57 Carmyle Avenue, Glasgow and editorial material should be sent to Harry McShane, 151 Weir Street, Glasgow.

> This paper was brought out under great difficulties. We are not strong in numbers and must dig deep into our pockets to pay for the paper. We want to extend the paper and bring it out more frequently

SOCIALIST REVOLT

ORGAN OF THE SOCIALIST WORKERS' FEDERATION

Vol. 1, No. 9   Price 6d.   April–June, 1957

CONTENTS

EDITORIAL

WAR BETWEEN THE CLASSES

Now that the floodgate of discontent is open, will our "leaders" continue to collaborate with our employers? For years the workers and employers were represented as partners in industry."

Our "partners," while appealing for greater productivity, put profits before wages, and as a result provoked the greatest industrial conflict in Britain since 1926. The inherent conflict of interests between workers and employers, bedded in the present system, found expression among the engineering and shipbuilding workers. The struggle came sooner than many of us expected.

Now that the picture is changed, new thoughts come to mind. Will our "leaders" again meet the employers in productivity committees, or will they strike at them left and right? That question must arise in the minds of any workers.

The Labour Party

The recent strike started when the Communist and Labour Parties were calling out for a General Election. Even during the strike, speakers demanded the defeat of the Tories and the return of a Labour Government.

This prompts two questions. First, would the employers have granted the wage demands of the workers had the Labour Party been in power? Second, did the Parliamentary Labour Party give any indication of support for the workers on strike? Our readers know the answers to these questions. The whole question of the relations between the trade unions and the Party they pay for is being discussed widely in the factories and shipyards.

All sections of the Labour Movement are, in theory, serving a common cause. Some of us have hoped that parliamentary action would go hand in hand with

industrial action in a struggle against the class enemy. The ambitious statesmen of the Labour Movement think otherwise, and up to now, they have carried the day. That rising flood of discontent will drive them into retreat.

Comrades Overseas

While attention is directed to trade rivals abroad, little notice is taken of our working class allies overseas. In Germany, where postal, railway, shipyard and textile workers have wrung concessions from the ruling class, the decision of the shipyard workers during the recent strike to regard ships going there for repairs as "black" gladdened our hearts.

It brings back memories of the days when the slogan "International Solidarity" was to the forefront in our May Day demonstrations.

Our international duty is not completed by simply recalling the Russian Revolution, important as that is. The greatest strides towards Socialism have yet to be taken, and they will be taken by the workers in the highly industrialised capitalist countries.

Recently an excellent book on Jim Larkin appeared. The importance he attached to unity between workers of all countries comes out clearly. Let us learn from it.

The workers of Western Europe can speed up the march to Socialism. On that we must concentrate our efforts. The recent strike brings the British workers near to the front line. We must remain there.

The Socialist Workers' Federation has, since its inception, stressed the importance of strike action. We repeat one of our earliest slogans: "*The Strike Is Mightier Than The Vote.*"

Hugh Savage was crucially involved in the production of *Revolt*, *Socialist Revolt* and the *New Commune*. He also contributed articles alongside – among others – Harry McShane, Eric Heffer, Leslie Forster and I.P. Hughes.

SOCIALIST REVOLT

(INCORPORATING REVOLT)

ORGAN OF THE SOCIALIST WORKERS' FEDERATION

Vol. 1, No. 7　　　　　　　　　Price 6d.　　　　　　　　　Oct.-Dec., 1956

CONTENTS

EDITORIAL

SIX MILLION OF US

Six million workers have applied for wage increases. Will they unite or take the risk of being defeated one at a time ? Will they support leaders who will place their faith in negotiations and pray that the employers will make a small concession and ease the situation for another year.

We have seen the Standard Motor workers at Coventry driven back to work in order to settle the matter by negotiations. We have seen the Clydeside shipyard workers driven into retreat. We can now visualise the national unions struggling separately against employers who, working in harmony with the Government, intend to resist the wage demands put forward by the workers. Must this always be so ? Can it not be changed ?

The General Council of the T.U.C. was set up with the purpose of giving leadership to the workers in all industries. It was to be a unified command. What does it lead ?

Betrayal

The General Council called the General Strike in 1926. The leaders of the General Council capitulated before the Government.

Since then it has flirted with class collaboration, wage freeze and increased production. It has failed to lead the workers against their class enemies. It has become a propagandist body for a Labour Government, but it is not prepared to lead the workers against the Government and the class it represents.

The General Council members don't seem to know the purpose for which a General Council was formed.

Redundancy

The boom is coming to an end. As we go to press we learn that 800 men at the Stanton Iron Works, Derby-shire, are going on to short time. More men have been dismissed in Birmingham. There will be more of this.

Will it gladden the hearts of the " more production " fanatics to learn that at the Stanton Iron Works new orders are not keeping pace with production ? That is why workers employed there will work only nine shifts a fortnight instead of ten.

This situation will develop despite the rosy predictions of those who think the capitalist system has changed. It makes it imperative that the fight for higher wages should be accompanied by a struggle for a shorter working week.

The Political Aspect

The political implications will soon become clear if the workers decide to strike in support of their wage demands. Wages questions are discussed in Parliament only when the workers decide to withhold their labour power. The Emergency Powers Act was introduced to meet such a situation, and has been made use of on a number of occasions. Once the Act is operated, the State serves its purpose of protecting vested interests. This will happen if six million workers go on strike. It is for this reason everything will be done to prevent such a strike.

The union leaders lack the vision of Eugene V. Debs. They have a narrow, limited outlook. They fear the political consequences of such a strike. They have never recovered from the shock of the General Strike.

It will not happen—yet. The rank and file must fight for the wage increases in every way possible. At the same time they should consider how unconquerable they would be if six million of them struck together.

than once per quarter. We ask all our readers to consider sending a donation to the Secretary of the Socialist Workers Federation. He is Eric Heffer, 54 Avondale Road, Liverpool 15.

Articles in issues still available to us include 'Marxism and Internationalism' by Hugh Savage; 'Marxists and the Labour Party' by Tom Cowan; 'The Socialist Road for Britain' by Eric S Heffer; 'Revolutionary Socialism' by Harry McShane; 'The Tragedy of Ireland' by Leslie Forster; Hughie also penned an article 'Don't Blame Marx'. There were discussions about the class nature of the Soviet Union and whether or not Russia was a state capitalist society as put forward by Tony Cliff, then of the Socialist Review Group, later to become leader of the International Socialists, and then, in 1997, the Socialist Workers Party.

The Glasgow members involved with the Socialist Workers Federation were never affiliated to Cliff's organisations but attended meetings and other events over many years. In 1961 Paul Foot came to Glasgow to work as a young reporter on the *Daily Record* and Hugh, Les and Harry remained in contact with him. He often spoke with great affection of his time in Glasgow and the influence that McShane and his comrades had on his political development. Socialist meetings at that time were held in the Horseshoe Bar in Drury Street. Foot's recent death was a great loss to the socialist movement and many despots will feel safer now that he is no longer with us. Hugh Savage always retained an extremely high opinion of Paul Foot despite political disagreements between them from time to time.

There was also an opportunity for readers to write letters to the paper, *Socialist Revolt*, which they did. One was in reply to an article by Heffer on What Kind of Party, which really intrigued me when I read it recently. It was from a J. Britz who wrote to the paper agreeing that Comrade Heffer had made some valid points in his article in an earlier edition but he could not agree with his ideas on Democratic Centralism. He continues his letter in reference to the article:

He says that Democratic Centralism can be put in four principles, but he leaves out one of the most important ingredients, without which the 'Democratic' part is missing. I refer to the right of minorities to express their point of view within the revolutionary organisation. This will allow the minority point of view to be both expressed and discussed, to allow minorities the right of becoming the majority.

I don't know what happened to this correspondent but personal experience informs me that if a minority point of view seriously challenges the position of the leadership then the minority soon become, not the majority, but ex-members of the organisation. Like many others I have found an abundance of centralism, it's the democratic bit that has always escaped me; just like it eluded Hugh Savage and his comrades on their exit from the Communist Party.

Eric Heffer was a principled socialist when he met the group from Glasgow and, in my opinion, he and his wife Doris remained so all of their lives. Hughie always retained an affection and respect for him. When Harry died Dave Sherry and myself were the main organisers of a Socialist Workers Party commemoration meeting in his honour. Paul Foot spoke exceptionally well and with great passion that night. The event was indeed a memorable evening and a fitting tribute to McShane.

One of my tasks was to contact Heffer and invite him to speak at the meeting. He was unable to attend and was very sorry as he liked McShane very much. Harry had stayed at his house in Liverpool a number of times and got on famously with Eric and Doris. In order to help make the event a success he sent a warm tribute in respect of his old comrade. I will repeat the full text of his tribute sent to me on 17th May 1988 and read out at the meeting which took place in the Winter Gardens, Glasgow Green on Sunday 22nd May 1998 with an audience of over 300 in attendance.

I hope your meeting tonight in memory of my old

friend and comrade Harry McShane is a great
success.

Harry was a wonderful comrade and never at any
time betrayed the interests of the class from which he
came and which he represented, the working class.

There were those who, once he had gone, were only
too happy to praise him but who at no time
supported him or his revolutionary socialist ideas
when he was alive. Hughie, Les and his friends were
well aware of that. McShane believed in the class
struggle and all his life was a class fighter. Because
of personal and political experiences his attitude
changed on some issues but although repudiating
the bureaucratic regime in the Soviet Union, at no
stage did he repudiate the Russian Revolution. Like
Rosa Luxemburg, whilst critical of the way things
developed, he understood that the Russian
Revolution, for the working class, was the greatest
event of this century.

He kept his socialist faith to the end and was a great
inspiration to us all. The ideas he put forward are in
fact the only ones which can build a new classless
world in the future. Unless capitalism is ended the
future of man and womankind is bleak indeed.

In saluting the memory of McShane, Hugh Savage
and their comrades, let us also pledge ourselves to
carry on the fight. Despite all the setbacks this is not
a time to despair, but a time to press on with the
fight, no matter the odds. For in the end, Socialism
will be triumphant.

As mentioned earlier, the Socialist Workers Federation
made some interesting international links. André Marty was
one, ex-secretary of the French Communist Party who was
expelled from the French CP in circumstances similar to
comrades in Britain leaving the CPGB. In a report to the
party in 1952 Marty alleged that the leadership of the party
were involved in a policy of class collaboration. This did

not go down too well with the leading comrades. Eric Heffer and other members of the Socialist Workers Federation went to Marty's home in France for discussions with him. Extracts from his book, which explains why he was ostracised by his party, were printed in Socialist Revolt under a heading, 'Why world famous leader was expelled from the French Communist Party'. It included excerpts from Marty's book:

> When the members of the CP ruling group understood that I had thus called on the Central Committee to break with their parliamentary policy, in order to return to a class policy with revolutionary perspectives which alone are capable of effectively defending the workers' interests, they should at least have asked me for an explanation. That was not done.

> André Marty was in a long line of Marxists who failed to find the Holy Grail of democracy and centralism in the same place at the same time.

> The Communist Party includes in its ranks workers who are ardently revolutionary; it is supported by proletarians who wish with all their strength the end of the capitalist regime. To put before them any ideas of class struggle and class action, ideas which were well known to the workers and approved by them, was impossible; the leadership would have been beaten.

But the treatment he received from his former comrades in the French Communist party was astonishing. And even more so when his history in the communist movement and lifelong dedication to the international class struggle is subject to scrutiny.

The great French socialist was born in 1886; his father was exiled from France for ten years because of the part he played in the 1871 Paris Commune. Marty himself joined the Communist Party in 1923 and became a member of the Central Committee in 1925 serving on the Political Bureau. He held several posts in the Communist International and

REVOLT

THE ORGAN OF THE SOCIALIST WORKERS FEDERATION

No. 6   3d.

MARTY'S STORY

Why world famous leader was expelled from the French Communist Party

Andre Marty, the 69-year-old revolutionary leader who played a leading part in the Black Sea mutiny at the end of the first world war, was organiser of the International Brigade during the Spanish Civil War, and has been a member of the French Parliament for a number of years, is now outside the Party he served since 1923. He has written a book on why he was expelled. The book has not been translated into English, but we are in the position of being able to print extracts which indicate the reasons for his expulsion.

Alleging that the C.P. leadership carried through a policy of class collaboration, Marty says, " Such a policy has always been denounced by the revolutionary working class movement and the Communist International as sacrificing the workers' interests ". Starting out on this basis Marty soon found himself in trouble with the leaders of the Communist Party.

Marty's Report

Making a report to the Central Committee on February 18th, 1952, he criticised the weak policy of the Party in regard to the war in Indo-China and demanded a complete transformation. He alleged that the Party was carrying out a Social democratic policy.

Marty says, " when the members of the C.P. ruling group understood that I had thus called the Central Committee to break with their parliamentary policy, in order to return to a class policy with revolutionary perspectives which one are capable of effectively defending the workers' interests, they should at least have asked me for an explanation. That was not done."

ANDRE MARTY—

Marty was born in Perpigan on November 6th, 1886. His father was exiled for ten years because of the part he played in the Paris Commune in 1871.

Andre Marty joined the Communist Party in 1923 and became a member of the Central Committee in 1925. He later served on the Political Bureau of the French Communist Party. He held several posts in the Communist International and was a member of the Political Secretariat of that body when it was dissolved in 1943.

He was sentenced to 20 years imprisonment for his part in the Black Sea mutiny in 1919. He was pardoned in 1923. He was charged with treason and with inciting troops in Morocco. He was charged on several occasions following that.

BUILDING WORKERS - FIGHT NOW

Butler's Bombshell.

Butler has dropped his mask, the true face of the Tory capitalist has been shown, and the worker must suffer the full consequences of the crisis. The working-class can only offset the effects of the budget by fighting back, and they can only do this by using their organised strength. The building worker must as part of the whole working class movement, begin now to get put into operation what is long overdue, a Building Workers' Charter.

Security—Never Under Capitalism.

Security can never be achieved under the Capitalist system. This all Socialists know, but concessions can be gained by struggle, and it's time Building Trade Workers got certain conditions which are accepted facts in most other industries. In 1945, with the advent of the Labour Government, whole sections of the movement were diverted into accepting policies which were short-sighted to say the least. In Building, despite the fact that the Essential Works Order, guaranteed a 44 hour week, the N.F.B. accepted a 32 hour guaranteed week, with a clause that it was effective for one week only. The Holiday scheme is really a farce. The pay for holidays is related to a stamp system, which means that an operative who suffers illness or unemployment, gets less cash when the holiday arrives. This applies also to the Bank Holidays, etc. In any case, even with a full card the worker does not receive full payment, he is always short of the normal weekly wage.

Bonus.

In 1947, as a result of the employers demanding that an increase in wages be coupled with the acceptance of "incentive Bonus," plus vigorous campaigning by right-wing leaders and the Communist Party, "bonus" was foisted on the

---

was a member of the Political Secretariat until 1943 when Stalin dissolved the International. His record as a communist and a militant is extremely impressive. He was sentenced to twenty years imprisonment in 1919 for leading the famous Black Sea mutiny. Pardoned in 1923 he was then charged with treason and with inciting troops in Morocco and was charged with other political offences at great risk to personal safety. Marty was organiser of the International Brigade in the Spanish Civil War and served as a communist in the French Parliament for a number of years. It is consistent that Hugh Savage and the other comrades made contact with such a prominent international socialist.

Another prominent figure in close contact with the group

was Raya Dunayevskaya who was, for a time, secretary to Leon Trotsky in Mexico. She also worked closely with C.L.R. James during his time in USA. She became associated with *News & Letters*, a publication closely associated with the Black Power movement and militant autoworkers in Detroit, Michigan. For many years this group included the outstanding black activist and writer, Charles Denby, whose biography *Indignant Heart, Testimony Of A Black American Worker*, first published in 1952, remains a classic read for anyone wishing to understand the militant trade unions organised by black workers in the Detroit auto factories. Once again, we owe a debt to Pluto Press for making this book available in the UK. Interestingly, in the foreword to the 1979 'Pluto' edition Denby makes an interesting comment on political developments in nineteen fifties America:

> In Part 1, the original *Indignant Heart* published in 1952, I wrote that I was born and raised in Tennessee, and used the name Matthew Ward. The names of other people were also changed. The reason for this was to protect individuals from the vicious McCarthyite witch hunt then sweeping the country, which resulted in the persecution and literal destruction of many people. Few who did not go through that experience of national repression of ideas can fully understand the truly totalitarian nature of McCarthyism and the terror it produced. It is interesting to me that McCarthyism was destroyed at the same time that the Montgomery Bus Boycott developed – 1955-56.

It is fascinating that Charles Denby made the shift from being a militant factory worker to become editor of the radical newspaper *News & Letters*. Elsewhere in his book he makes reference to his 30 year political partnership with Dunayevskaya.

Dunayevskaya maintained a correspondence with Harry McShane over a long period. When she came to the UK for a speaking tour in the 1970s while in Scotland she received the hospitality of the Savage family home and became a friend. Two of her books *Marxism & Freedom* and *Philosophy & Revolution* are well known and her pronouncements have been debated by those concerned with the more difficult aspects of Marxist theory since the 1950s. Herbert Marcuse the French philosopher and McShane each wrote a preface for editions of *Marxism & Freedom*, originally published in 1958, two years after the Hungarian workers uprising, and reprinted several times, latterly by Pluto Press in the UK. On *Marxism & Freedom* McShane commented:

> This book, by its theoretical approach, performs a service in the present situation. It raises the banner of theory without letting us forget that the working-class struggle is the source of all theory. 'Marxism,' says the author, 'is a theory of liberation or it is nothing.'

> This book, by its theoretical approach, performs a service in the present situation. It raises the banner of theory without letting us forget that the working-class struggle is the source of all theory.

A reading of Dunayevskaya's work gives an insight into the difficulties faced in the 1950s by socialists within communist parties worldwide. It attempts to clarify theoretical questions, including that of workers' democracy and the role of the rank and file. These questions were intensely debated among UK socialists in the 1970s and 1980s. The crucial question for the Socialist Workers Federation people and other Marxists in the nineteen-fifties was the class nature of the Soviet Union and the attitude taken to resistance from workers in the satellite states which were a part of Stalin's empire. Referring to the resistance of workers in these states McShane commented:

> The necessity of work under conditions of capitalism has been stamped on the minds of workers over many generations, but those who have never rebelled against these conditions, at one time or another, are comparatively few. The urge for action has always come from below; from those who work

with, and are dominated by the means of production outside their control. The worker as a human being has feelings, desires and passions that are thwarted by present conditions. This leads to thought, actions and then more thought. Therein lies the danger for the rulers of the world in the days ahead.

Hugh Savage and the others had the greatest of respect for Dunayevskaya and her influence encouraged an interest in the philosophical aspects of Marx. McShane's observations on her work are an indication of the faith they shared in Marxism and the spontaneous resistance of oppressed peoples.

Susan Jacoby in her outstanding book, *Freethinkers*, on the history and origins of rational thought and secularism in America, gives a great insight into the contribution Thomas Paine made to the American Revolution. She tells how he was vilified not only during his life but also after death. American President, Theodore Roosevelt referred to him as a 'filthy little atheist'. In 1797, before he became 'The Great Reformer' and actually read Paine's work, William Cobbett, published a scurrilous biography of him:

> How Tom gets a living now, or what brothel he inhabits, I know not, nor does it much signify. He has done all the mischief he can do in this world; and whether his carcass is at last to be suffered to rot on the earth, or to be dried in the air is of very little consequence . . . Like Judas, he will be remembered by posterity; men will learn to express all that is base, malignant, treacherous, unnatural, and blasphemous by the single monosyllable of Paine.

At the funeral of Hugh Savage, Leslie Forster, Elspeth King and I were privileged to be asked to speak by the family. I owe Les a debt of gratitude for the final words of my own contribution which he delivered on 10th April 1996 at the funeral of his old friend and comrade:

Hugh had his favourites in the world of politics and literature, ranging from the radical republican Thomas Paine and the playwrights Sean O'Casey and Oscar Wilde. For him none came bigger than Tom Paine. During the American Revolution, when it seemed that the revolution would go down to defeat, by campfire light, Paine wrote on a drumhead:

These are the times that try men's souls
the summer soldier and the sunshine patriot
will in this crisis
shrink from the service of his country.

What would the American revolutionaries of 1776, the comrades of Thomas Paine, think of the imperialist butchers who are the present day custodians of their legacy? Would they have hoped that by their efforts and sacrifices today's world would be a better place now than it was three centuries past? Would they baulk in dismay at the carnage in Iraq?

Many will argue that talk of Marxist theory, workers' democracy and class politics is the language of the past. If they are right we have no future. But at the very least, the anti-globalisation movement provides hope that there can be international resistance to the world of Bush, Blair and Berlusconi.

In my view, Hugh Savage's philosophy was a combination of ideas. He believed in internationalism, democracy and workers' control of society. Until his dying day he was convinced that the working class could bring about a better society by developing its best traditions of democratic self-organisation. This was 'socialism from below' as opposed to the method of socialism still prescribed by advocates of a vanguard party. Hughie was never a 'summer soldier', never a 'sunshine patriot'. He was a class fighter and he fought for the socialist cause in all seasons. Hugh Savage is an example to all who wish to embrace change.

Bibliography and some Further Reading

Aldred, Guy *No Traitor's Gate! The Autobiography of Guy Aldred*, in twelve monthly numbers [Strickland Press 1956]

Aldred, Guy, editor and compiler *Rex v. Aldred: London Trial 1909, Indian Sedition. Glasgow Sedition Trial 1921* [Strickland Press 1948]

Ashley, Maurice *John Wildman, Plotter and Postmaster: A Study of the Republican Movement in the Seventeenth Century* [Jonathan Cape 1947]

Bell, Tom *Pioneering Days* [Lawrence & Wishart 1941]

Boyd, Andrew *The Rise of the Irish Trade Unions* [Anvil Books 1972]

Burrows, Edwin G. and Wallace, Mike *Gotham: A History of New York City to 1998* [Oxford University Press]

Caldwell, John Taylor *Come Dungeons Dark – the life and times of Guy Aldred, Glasgow Anarchist* [Luath Press Ltd, Ayrshire 1988]

Caldwell, John Taylor *Severely Dealt With* [Northern Herald Books, Bradford 1993]

Carlile, Richard *Jail Journal and Other Writings* edited and arranged by Guy Aldred [Strickland Press 1942]

Challinor, Ray *John S.Clarke: Parliamentarian, Poet, Lion-Tamer*

Christie, Stuart *My Grannie Made Me An Anarchist: The Christie File: Part 1, 1946-1964* [Christie Books 2002]

Christie, Stuart *The Albert Memorial: The Anarchist Life and Times of Albert Meltzer 7 January 1920–7 May 1996* [The Meltzer Press 1997]

Cole, G.D.H. *The British working-class Movement 1787-1947* [Allen & Unwin 2nd edition 1927]

Connolly, James *Labour Nationality and Religion* [Irish Transport and General Workers' Union 1935]

Connolly, James *Labour in Irish History* [New Books Publications 1983]

Connolly, James *Selected Writings* edited by P.Berresford Ellis [Pluto Press 1973]

Connolly, James *Labour and Easter Week 1916; a Selection from the Writings of James Connolly* edited by Desmond Ryan, Introduction by William O'Brien [published in Fleet Street, Dublin, At The Sign of the Three Candles 1949]

Daly, Glen *My Glasgow* [published mid-1960s in Glasgow]

Dunayevskaya, Raya *Philosophy and Revolution; From Hegel to Sartre, and from Marx to Mao* [Delacorte Press, 1973]

Duncan, Robert and McIvor, Arthur *Militant Workers: Labour and Class Conflict on the Clyde 1900-1950; Essays in Honour of Harry McShane [1891-1988]* [John Donald 1992]

Ellis, Peter Berresford and MacAGhobhaain, Seaumas *The Scottish Insurrection of 1820* [Pluto Press 1971]

Ellis, Peter Berresford *A History of the Irish Working Class* [Braziller Inc. NY 1973]

Forster, Leslie and Savage Hugh *All for the Cause: Willie Nairn 1856-1902, Stonebreaker, Philosopher, Marxist* [published by themselves 1991, assisted by Margaret McQuade McAuslan and Clydeside Press]

Forster, Leslie *Rocking the Boat, Memoirs of a Glasgow socialist and whistleblower* [Clydeside Press 1995]

Forster, Leslie, and Donaldson, Edward *Sell and be Damned, The Glasgow Merrylee Housing Scandal of 1951* [Clydeside Press 1992]

Fulford, Roger *Votes for Women; the Story of a Struggle* [Faber & Faber 1958]

Gallacher, Willie *Revolt on the Clyde* [Lawrence & Wishart 1936]

Gammage, R C. *History of the Chartist Movement 1837-1854* [facsimile edition, Merlin Press 1969]

Glasgow Labour History Workshop *The Singer Strike Clydebank, 1911* [Clydebank District Library 1989, prepared by Ishbel Ballantine, Chik Collins, Leslie Forster, Hugh Maguiness, Arthur McIvor, Hugh Savage, Liz Tuach]

Guerin, Daniel, *Fascism and Big Business* [Monad Press 1973]

Haddow, William Martin, *My Seventy Years* [Wm. McLellan 1943]

Hannan, John *The Life of John Wheatley* [Spokesman 1988]

Hannington, Wal *Unemployed Struggles 1919-1936* [Gollancz Ltd. 1936]

Hannington, Wal *The Problem of the Distressed Areas* [Gollancz Ltd. 1937]

Howell, David, *A Lost Left: Three Studies in Socialism and Nationalism* –

on James Connolly, John Maclean and John Wheatley [University of Chicago Press 1986]

Hudis, Peter *Harry McShane and the Scottish Roots of Marxist-Humanism* [John Maclean Society 1993]

Johnston, Thomas *Our Scots Noble Families* [Argyll Publishing 1999]

Johnston, Thomas *History of the Working Classes in Scotland* [Forward Publishing 1920]

Johnston, Thomas *Memories* [Collins 1952]

Kibblewhite, Liz and RigbyAndy *Fascism in Aberdeen: Street politics in the 1930s* [1978 APP]

King, Elspeth *The People's Palace and Glasgow Green* [Richard Drew Publishing 1985]

King, Elspeth *The Scottish Women's Suffrage Movement* [People's Palace Museum 1978]

Kelman, James *Some Recent Attacks, Essays Cultural and Political* [AK Press 1992]

Kelman, James *'And the Judges Said. . .', essays* [Secker & Warburg 2002]

Kenefick, William and McIvor Arthur (editors) *Roots of Red Clydeside 1910-1914*

Knox, William *Scottish Labour Leaders 1918-39, A Biographical Dictionary* [Mainstream 1984]

Larkin, Jim *In the Footsteps of Big Jim: a Family Biography* [Blackwater Press 1995]

Lenin, V. I. *'Left-Wing' Communism, an Infantile Disorder* [Progress Publishers, Moscow 1970]

Leonard, Tom *Radical Renfrew* [Polygon 1990]

Leonard, Tom *Places of the Mind: The Life and Work of James Thomson ('B.V.')* [Jonathan Cape1993]

Lowe, David *Souvenirs of Scottish Labour* [W & R Holmes 1919]

McCabe, Joseph *Twelve Years in a Monastery* [Thinkers Library 1912]

MacDougall, Ian (compiler) *Voices from the Hunger Marches Volume 1* [Polygon 1990]

MacDougall, Ian (compiler) *Voices from the Spanish Civil War* [Polygon]

MacDougall, Ian (editor) *Militant Miners – recollections of John McArthur and letters of David Proudfoot* [Polygon 1981]

MacFarlane, Margaret and Alastair *The Scottish Radicals: Tried and Transported to Australia for Treason in 1820* [Spa Books 1981]

McGinn, Janette *McGinn of the Calton: the life and works of Matt McGinn 1928-1977* Introduction [Glasgow City Libraries 1987]

McGovern, John *Neither Fear Nor Favour* [Blandford Press 1960]

MacLachlan, Kenny *One Great Vision; Memoirs of a Glasgow Worker . . .* [self published 1995]

McLay, Farquhar (editor) *Workers City* [Clydeside Press 1988]

McLay, Farquhar (editor) *The Reckoning* [Clydeside Press 1990]

Maclean, John *In the Rapids of Revolution* edited by Nan Milton [Allison & Busby, 1978]

McShane, Harry and Smith Joan *No Mean Fighter* [Pluto Press 1975]

McShane, Harry *Three Days that Shook Edinburgh* [1933, reprinted AK Press 1994, with an introduction and biographical details by Les Forster and Hugh Savage]

McShane, Harry compiled the Glasgow District Trades Council's *Centenary Brochure 1858 – 1958: A Hundred Years of Progress*, with a foreword by Emmanuel Shinwell

McShane, Harry *Calton Weavers Memorial 1787* [1931 pamphlet]

Meikle, Henry W. *Scotland and the French Revolution* [Maclehose, Glasgow 1912, reprinted Kelley, New York 1969]

Melling, Joseph *Rent Strikes: People's Struggle for Housing in West Scotland 1890-1916* [Polygon1983]

Melzer, Milton *Bread and Roses*: *The Struggle of American Labor* 1865-1915 [Living History Library 1967]

Middlemas, Robert Keith *The Clydesiders:A left wing struggle for Parliamentary power* [reprint by August Kelley, New York 1968]

Milton, Nan *John Maclea*n [Pluto Press 1970]

Newsinger, John *Rebel City: Larkin, Connolly and the Dublin Labour Movement* [The Merlin Press 2004]

Paton, John *Proletarian Piligrimage* [Routledge 1935]

Pelling, Henry *The British Communist Party: A Historical Profile* [A & C Black Ltd. 1958]

Pollitt, Harry *Serving My Time* [Lawrence & Wishart 1940]

Ryan, Meda *Tom Barry: IRA Freedom Fighter* [Mercier Press 2005]

Shinwell, Emmanuel *Conflict Without Malice* [Odham's Press Ltd. 1953]

Shinwell, Emmanuel *The Labour Story* [McDonald 1963]

Stewart, William *Keir Hardie: A Biography* [I.L.P. publication dept 1921]

Thomson, Willie (editor) *Fighting the Good Fight? Socialist History 7* [Pluto Press 1995]

Tracey, Herbert (editor) *The Book of the Labour Party* in 3 volumes
[1921]

Tribe, David *President Charles Bradlaugh MP* [Elek Books 1971]

Webb, Sydney and Beatrice *The History of Trade Unionism 1620–1920*

Wood, Ian S. *John Wheatley* [Manchester University Press 1990] part
of the Lives of the Left series

Young, James D. *John Maclean, Clydeside Socialist* [Clydeside Press
1992]

others

'Anarchist-Communism in Britain, – its history and development' –
an anonymous article downloaded from the site of the journal
ORGANISE! for class struggle anarchism special edition Issue 42

Meek, Ronald L. essay 'The Scottish Contribution to Marxist
Sociology' reprinted as a pamphlet from *Democracy and the
Labour Movement* [Lawrence & Wishart 1955]

McShane, Harry (editor) *The Scottish Marxist-Humanist* from 1962-
1976 [some issues in 'The Harry McShane Collection,
1959-1988: Scottish Marxist-Humanism's development in
dialogue with Raya Dunayevskaya.']

Index